BOYS INTO MEN

Raising Our African American Teenage Sons

Nancy Boyd-Franklin, Ph.D.
and A. J. Franklin, Ph.D.
with Pamela A. Toussaint

A PLUME BOOK

PLUME
Published by the Penguin Group
Penguin Putnam Inc., 375 Hudson Street, New York, New York 10014, U.S.A.
Penguin Books Ltd, 27 Wrights Lane, London W8 5TZ, England
Penguin Books Australia Ltd, Ringwood, Victoria, Australia
Penguin Books Canada Ltd, 10 Alcorn Avenue, Toronto, Ontario, Canada M4V 3B2
Penguin Books (N.Z.) Ltd, 182–190 Wairau Road, Auckland 10, New Zealand

Penguin Books Ltd, Registered Offices:
Harmondsworth, Middlesex, England

Published by Plume, a member of Penguin Putnam Inc.
Previously published in a Dutton edition.

First Plume Printing, May 2001
10 9 8 7 6 5 4 3 2 1

Selections from *Acts of Faith* by Iyanla Vanzant, Copyright © Iyanla Vanzant, 1993.
Reprinted with the permission of Simon & Schuster.

Selection adapted from *Black Man Emerging* by Joseph L. White and James H. Coñes III,
Copyright © Joseph L. White and James H. Coñes III, 1999. Reproduced
by permission of Routledge, Inc.

℗ REGISTERED TRADEMARK—MARCA REGISTRADA

The Library of Congress has catalogued the Dutton edition as follows:
Boyd-Franklin, Nancy.
Boys into men : raising our African American teenage sons / by Nancy Boyd-Franklin,
A. J. Franklin, with Pamela A. Toussaint.
p.   cm.
ISBN 0-525-94496-6 (hc.)
ISBN 0-452-28085-0 (pbk.)
1. Afro-American teenage boys. 2. Afro-American teenage boys—Conduct of life. 3. Child
rearing—United States. 4. Parent and teenager—United States. I. Franklin, A. J.
(Anderson James) II. Toussaint, Pamela. III. Title.
E185.86 .B6494 2000
649'.132'08996073—dc21
99-057187

Printed in the United States of America
Original hardcover design by Leonard Telesca

Praise for *Boys into Men*

"*Boys into Men* addresses the joys and challenges of raising healthy African American teenage boys and shows us the way. If you really care about the future of our children, you will read this important book."
—Gail Elizabeth Wyatt, Ph.D., professor, UCLA School of Medicine, author of *Stolen Women: Reclaiming Our Sexuality, Taking Back Our Lives*

"The remarkably well written stories provide us with real examples of the issues that our youth and their families have to deal with. Nancy Boyd-Franklin and A. J. Franklin tackle the tough issues with hope and a sense of caring that is reflected on every page . . . Parents—and all those charged with promoting the development of our children—will benefit from reading *Boys into Men*."
—Dr. James P. Comer, Maurice Falk Professor of Child Psychiatry, Yale Child Study Center, and associate dean, Yale School of Medicine

"This is the book parents have been waiting for. This insightful resource is a must-have on the shelves of anyone concerned about the welfare of millions of black boys across the country."
—*Black Issues Book Review*

NANCY BOYD-FRANKLIN is a family therapist and psychologist, and a professor in the Graduate School of Applied and Professional Psychology at Rutgers University.
A. J. FRANKLIN is a professor in the doctoral program at the City University of New York and a psychotherapist in private practice who specializes in the treatment of adolescent males.
PAMELA A. TOUSSAINT is the coauthor of *Mama's Little Baby* and *I Call You Friend*.

"Plainspoken and inspiring."
—*The Washington Post Book World*

"Sensitive and timely."
—*Publishers Weekly*

"A heartfelt true-to-life account that inspires with its
honesty and compassion."
—*Library Journal*

"A survival guide that gives hope and inspiration to parents,
teachers, counselors, and community members by drawing on
strong family values and cultural and spiritual strengths . . .
Offers realistic situations, practical advice, and positive
messages . . . This important new book addresses every
parent's concerns . . . African American parents now have a
resource to turn to for guidance as well as encouragement."
—*The Savannah Herald*

"Provides useful, specific information . . . The authors are
sensitive to the particular pressures on young black
men . . . They offer parents encouragement and a wealth
of further resources."
—*Booklist*

"The Franklins' parenting advice emphasizes positive
attitudes and role models laced with strong spiritual values."
—*The Roanoke Times*

To our children who have inspired us
and
To our parents who have guided us

Contents

Acknowledgments

We give thanks to God for giving us the opportunity to write this important book and for guiding us through the process.

We thank and appreciate Hazel Staloff's editing and coordination of the central word processing responsibilities. Her flexibility and extraordinary availability during the writing and assembling of this work contributed greatly to its completion. Appreciation is also extended to our agent, Agnes Birnbaum, for leading us through the early stages of this project and for her support throughout the entire process. To Deb Brody and Cindy Achar, our editors at Dutton, we are grateful for their being very responsive to our needs and helpful guides through the publication of this book. We are also thankful for the contribution of Pam Toussaint.

We are indebted to our children, Deidre, Tunde, Remi, and Jay, for their willingness to read and provide comments on our stories about them and our own parenting challenges. Without particular friends supporting us by reading, commenting, and providing suggestions on all or parts of several versions of the manuscript, this work would not be as rich in suggestions and insights. We especially want to thank our good friends Rosemary Allwood and Dr. Vernon Allwood, Dr. Paulette Hines, Ray and Sid Ivey, Edna Wells Handy, Dr. Brenna Bry, Dr. Shalonda Kelly, and Nancy's sister, Audrey Boyd. Our appreciation is extended to our colleagues Jo Ann Tatum, Dr. Corinne Linquist, Dr. Evelyn Orozco, and Brian Jacobson for their thoughtful comments. Special thanks and blessings go to Mom, Regina Boyd, whose indefatigable energy and willingness to read in detail the many versions of the manuscript helped us to convey our message in this book. We greatly appreciated her help with family responsibilities, which allowed us periodically to dedicate our time to writing. We are also very grateful to Rev. DeForest B. Soaries Jr. and Rev. Larry Williams for their support and advice.

—Nancy Boyd-Franklin and A. J. Franklin

All honor and praise to my Lord Jesus Christ, who always causes me to triumph. Much love to my girls Melinda Weekes and Brenda Reid, also to Darren Hicks and Sherman Givens, who have been charged with the awesome task of training up our Nubian princes in the way they should go. God bless you!

—Pamela Toussaint

Boys into Men

INTRODUCTION

Where you will sit when you are old
shows where you stood in youth.
—YORUBA PROVERB

We are African American parents of four children, two of whom are sons. We are a blended family. Our three older children were born during A.J.'s first marriage, and we have shared the joys, responsibilities, and challenges of coparenting with their mom. Our children are now thirty-five, thirty, twenty-nine, and sixteen. Our oldest son and daughter-in-law have recently made us grandparents of a beautiful little girl. Although we love and have worried about the safety of all of our children, a great deal of our concern as parents has focused on the safety of our sons.

Both of us are psychologists and family therapists, and we have each spent more than twenty-five years helping African American parents and their children to get through the minefield of the teenage years. We call it a minefield because the challenge as black parents is to get our sons through this period in life without a mine, such as drugs, alcohol, violence, gangs, or school failure, blowing up in their faces. Our goal in writing this book has been to give you a guide that you can use to help your son become a proud, healthy African American man.

Teenage years are a tough time for everyone. The bad news is that everyone goes through it. The challenges of these years are starting even earlier, as young as eleven, and ending even later, into the twenties, for many kids today. The good news is that teenagers become human again at around twenty-five. The challenge is surviving the years in between.

In addition to parents, we also want this book to help other community members and groups—churches, ministers, schools, teachers, counselors, other professionals—and all of you who are genuinely concerned about the challenges facing African American young men and would like to help. We hope that this book empowers you to also make a difference in their lives.

There is tremendous diversity in the black community in America today. Persons of African descent include African Americans whose ancestors were brought here originally as slaves from Africa, families whose roots are in the Caribbean or Latin America, and persons who were born in Africa. There is also an increasing number of biracial and multiracial children. Families and their children also have different experiences based upon socioeconomic level, geographical area, educational background, skin color, religion, and spiritual beliefs. All of these diverse issues can impact how they view the black experience and the process of child rearing.

Given this level of diversity, a discussion of the variety of unique issues for all parents is beyond the scope of this book. We feel, however, that irrespective of where you come from, your son—by virtue of his skin color, appearance, and the way in which he carries himself—may be confronted with many of the issues discussed in this book. It will help you to cope with the parenting challenges you will face.

We have assembled resources from numerous areas in one place so that they can guide you in helping your sons through the difficult passage of the teenage years. With this in mind, we have cited experts in the field throughout and have included many of these books in the Resources sections at the end of each chapter.

In Chapter 1, we will discuss the challenges that our sons face, including building a strong racial identity in a world that may try to make them "invisible." The challenges of racism, violence, drugs, alcohol, and gangs are real. They can be overwhelming for you as parents. This book will give you many ideas on how to avoid the pitfalls.

We believe strongly in "family." It has been an important force in both of our lives. As black people, our families have always been an important strength and part of our survival. In Chapter 2, we will give you many ideas as to how you can strengthen your family and help everyone to work together to raise your "man-child."

Another strength that has helped us personally and as African Americans to survive has been our spirituality. Even if you are not religious, we hope to help you use your own spiritual beliefs to effectively raise your sons (and all of your children). Chapter 3 is one of our favorite chapters in the book because it can help you to learn how to draw on your own spirituality to get through the challenges of raising African American kids today.

The world has changed a lot since we were kids. Your sons will have many more things "in their face" than you ever had. Our chapter on parenting can help you combine strong love with strong discipline and consequences in parenting your sons. As you read this book, try to keep an open mind and be willing to try something different. Many African American parents find themselves repeating old patterns not because they work but because they have become habits.

We believe strongly in education for African American kids. We come by this belief honestly; our families drilled it into us. Never is the minefield more evident than in the schooling of African American male children. Chapter 5 is full of ideas to help you to help your son thrive in the learning process. Many African American families today are raising their kids in predominantly white schools and communities. If this is your reality, Chapter 6 will help you to understand your son's experience and help him to deal effectively with this situation.

The middle chapters (7–11) were written to help prepare you for the minefield. We address the challenges that put fear in the hearts of so many black parents: peer pressure (Chapter 7); rap, media, and hoop dreams (Chapter 8); sex and sexuality (Chapter 9); drugs and alcohol (Chapter 10); and violence and gangs (Chapter 11). Each of these chapters is full of advice that will help make you a smarter parent by helping you to know what to look for and even more important what to do if your son is being pulled by one of these challenges.

Bureau of Justice statistics (1997) indicate that an alarming number of young black men are under some form of "justice control," either in prison, on probation or parole, out on bond, or being sought on a warrant by the police. Often this is a result of involvement in the drug culture or because of violence, which presents a danger to all young men, including "good kids." If you are worried that your son may be at risk, this book offers strategies that will empower you to help take him back from the streets.

Whether you are raising your son in a city and struggle daily with these realities, or if you've moved to a suburban area and are concerned about your son's racial identity, or if you thought that your zip code could protect your child and found out otherwise, this book will help you to strategize to help your sons cope with this troublesome age.

The last part of our book is one of the most important. It tells what you can do as a proactive African American parent or other concerned adult to keep your son on the right path. It also tells the inspirational stories of parents, counselors, teachers, ministers, and other concerned community members who have worked together to "take our sons back from the streets" (Chapter 12).

Too often we, as black people, have been suspicious about getting help. In many of our communities, there are myths that counseling or therapy is for sick folks, crazy folks, rich folks, or white folks. These myths have kept many of us from seeking help for ourselves and for our children. In Chapter 13, we answer parents' questions about how to recognize when your son needs help and how to find the help he needs.

Our final chapter is a special gift from us as parents to you. We know that raising kids is a tough job. So often parents need a "shot in the arm" to keep their hope and faith alive. If you are a parent opening this book with many burdens, start (and end) with this chapter. It is a parent's survival guide—a way to recharge your batteries emotionally and spiritually so that you can be an effective, loving parent. It will help you to remember to love and to take care of yourself.

If you have been given the gift and challenge of raising a black male teenager, you have taken an important step by reading this book. It will help to guide you on your journey. With careful reading and appreciation, it can empower you to make a difference in his life and that of all your children.

1

You Must Act as if It Is Impossible to Fail
—Ashanti Proverb

Challenges in Raising African American Teenage Sons

Our older son has been six foot four since he was sixteen years old. In the black community, that means we have been scared for him for a long time. We remember one day when we were living in Brooklyn. We were cooking in the kitchen and trying to stay out of the way while keeping an eye on our son and "his boys," who were lying around our living room. We were happy, as parents, that his friends felt comfortable making ours their second home (and our refrigerator, their third).

We noticed that they were tossing an object back and forth. This did not alarm us until we saw that they were about to leave the house with a very realistic-looking black water gun!

At that moment, all of our professional training as psychologists went out the window. We were instantly transformed into Scared Black Parents. Images, one more horrifying than the next, flashed through our minds of our son and his friends being gunned down by a cop, who acted first and asked questions later. We ranted and raved and preached at those boys. We did not want any of them to forget that despite their parents' love and best hopes, and despite their individual achievements, they were "endangered" in a world that responded to them through a false lens of stereotypes and racism.

We were aware once again that we may never be able to completely stop worrying about our sons. This incident made us even more determined to prepare them in every way we could to handle the challenges they face.

Raising African American sons is one of the greatest challenges on the face of the earth. Worrying goes with the territory. But if we are to make a difference for our young men we must follow the words of the Ashanti proverb above: "You must act as if it is impossible to fail." We can't afford to lose one more young black man to early death, violence, drugs, alcohol, or AIDS. Our job as parents, as a community, and for all of those concerned about black youth is to take them back from the streets, order their steps, and set them on the right path to manhood.

Challenges in Parenting Black Males

- Keeping them alive past age twenty-five, given the rate of homicide and violence among and against African American males
- Preparing them adequately for encounters with racism, prejudice, and discrimination that will affect their ability to take advantage of opportunities in life and achieve success
- Ensuring that they have a good education—helping them to see its importance and advantages as they chart their life path
- Helping them become responsible adults—persons who understand the importance of commitments, collective unity, and partnership
- Developing a positive racial identity

Keeping Them Alive

As black parents, our greatest fear for our sons is basic survival. Homicide is the primary cause of death for black males between the ages of thirteen and twenty-five. The threat of violence to our sons comes from many sources: crime within the black community, mistaken identity, drug-related incidents, gang activity, police brutality, and a host of others. As we learned from the tragic shooting of Ennis Cosby, son of the entertainer Bill

Cosby, no amount of money, education, and celebrity status can guarantee the safety of a black man in America. As African American parents, we must take a proactive role by talking to our sons early on and teaching them the strategies that will help them to avoid trouble and survive to adulthood.

Helping Them to Overcome Racism

Getting past racism has been a challenge for most black people. For generations black boys—known to be intelligent, curious, engaging, and talented—have had acts of discrimination and prejudice discourage them. We do not want it to break their spirit, snuff out their hope, or rechart their life path. Too many have drifted into dysfunctional and counterproductive behavior because they felt that their talents were not respected. Others have adjusted their goals to lower, less ambitious aims. There are also those who defy the discouragement of racism, channel their talents in ways that supersede barriers, and succeed at levels beyond all expectations. All we have to do is to look around us in our communities to see examples of black men who have made it.

Throughout this book we discuss how black male teens are seen by society. Whatever our hopes, parents have a responsibility to recognize that many of our sons' opportunities in life are affected by how they are viewed by others. These same perceptions, in various forms, persist for our sons in their school and workplace experiences. No matter what our beliefs and attitudes toward racism are, as parents we cannot afford to be naïve. It is still a potent force in the lives of African Americans. We must teach our sons the ropes for surviving without self-destruction in the midst of personal and institutional racism. They must be taught that they can be anything they want to be if they are willing to work hard for it.

Racism today is sometimes very different from what it was in the past. In many cases it is more subtle and can easily be denied. This creates a serious dilemma for many black parents. It is important for children to learn about individual responsibility and not adopt a victim mentality. We do not want them using racism as an excuse for everything negative that happens to them. On the other hand, if they internalize the negative messages that they may encounter, they may begin to doubt or even hate themselves. Whenever something negative happens, many African Americans in this country struggle with the question: is it my fault or is it racism? How do we prepare our children for this? One wise black man once said: "When you have that kind of impossible question, wonder first if it's racism—it preserves our self-esteem." Since many African Americans have numerous opportunities in life to wonder if they are at fault or if racism or prejudice are operating, this constant process of second-guessing and personalizing every insult or assault can be exhausting and self-destructive.

In our own family, we have faced this difficult dilemma many times. Our three older children went to Howard University and came home to Brooklyn often on weekends, holidays, and vacations. They spent a lot of time on highways riding in cars with friends. We were worried that our older son and his friends would be targeted for "DWB" (Driving While Black) during long stretches on the New Jersey Turnpike. This is a road well known for racial profiling, where cars driven by minority males are stopped by the highway police for no reason other than the race or ethnicity of the drivers and passengers. We had to actively prepare our son for that possibility. We told him that if he was stopped by the police not to make any fast moves; to keep his hands in view at all times; not to talk back; and to call us as soon as he could.

There is a fourteen year gap between our older son's age of thirty and our younger son. We are again raising an African American male on the edge of manhood. For us, history is repeating itself. Last year our younger son, who was then fifteen years old, and two of his friends asked us to take them to the mall. It was understood that we were to just drive them there and back, but we were to get lost in between. After making arrangements to pick them up, we felt obligated, as black parents, to review with these teenagers—none of whom had ever been in any kind of trouble—how to handle certain incidents that might arise during their simple mall visit.

We gave them a series of "what if" questions. What would they do if they saw other kids "cutting up"? They told us that they would "go the other way." When we then asked, "Suppose you were accused of something by the mall police?" one of our son's friends really surprised us. He reached in his wallet and pulled out a small green card on which his mother had written, "What to do if you're stopped by the police." This list was almost the same as the advice we had given our older son almost fifteen years earlier.

This experience started us thinking—do other black parents prepare their kids for such situations? We began asking friends, and each reported similar experiences. One mother told us that her son had been on a subway platform in New York City at 3:15, a time when subways are full of high school students dismissed for the day. On the packed platform, a girl from her son's school was being bothered by boys from another school. Her son and a group of his friends, all of whom were black, came to the defense of this girl, and a fight erupted. The police were called, and all of the teenagers were herded down to the police station and charged with assault. Because our friend had prepared her son for this possibility, he knew what to do. He became the group's spokesman, and his leadership ensured that the situation did not get out of hand while they waited for the teens' parents to arrive. His mother had also prepared him by letting him know she would be carrying an inexpensive beeper so that she could be reached immediately. The extra preparation and forethought involved in addressing these issues make parenting a black son that much more challenging. (See Chapter 11 for more guidelines.)

Some parents, praying that their children will inherit a better world, do not warn them about the racism they will encounter, fearing that such warnings may give rise to prejudiced feelings in their children. This approach often leaves children defenseless if they are confronted with discrimination. We feel that all parents have a responsibility to prepare their sons for these realities and help them turn these negatives into positive action in their lives.

As you read the challenges above, there may have been a moment when you felt overwhelmed by the minefield that our sons must pass through to reach manhood. We know that these challenges are real and that your worries are genuine, but we have written this book in order to give you the tools to empower you to do what you can do to inoculate your son as he faces these challenges. Just as his shots protected him from disease as a young child, your love, cultural and racial pride, strong African American family values, faith in God, spiritual beliefs, and the determination of your community can make a difference in his life.

Getting Them a Good Education

We, as a people, have used education as a way of moving up out of difficult life circumstances to something better. For many African American parents, the struggle of ensuring that our sons get the education they deserve becomes more trying in adolescence. It is not just the growth of adult interests, or being independent, or hanging out with friends, or girls, but it is the array of pressures that seem to come with being a teenager. The change often starts when they move from a smaller primary school to a larger middle or junior high school and high school, with a more diverse mix of students.

Here is an example of a mother's frustration about what was happening with her fifteen-year-old son:

"I don't know what's gotten into Billy these days. He was such a good student before, but now he's cutting school and his grades are failing."

"What's wrong with you, boy?" she asked.

What was troubling for Billy was feeling lost in moving from a middle school of about six hundred students to a high school with two thousand. The teacher support he had relied on in his former school was replaced by what seemed to be a multitude of teachers during the course of the day, none of whom took any interest in him. He was overwhelmed by the size of the classes. He felt little confidence in his ability to handle the academic work. Few of his friends from middle school had enrolled in this high school. Without the support of his friends, he feared for his safety. He thought his mother understood little about his feelings and thoughts about making new friends and understanding the different groups at school—which ones to ally himself with and which ones to stay away from—so that he could ensure his safety.

Sometimes the size of our sons' high schools and the large number of teachers, counselors, and administrators can be difficult for us to understand and deal with. These institutions are not likely to be as responsive to our needs as parents as our children's smaller elementary schools. Sometimes our sons give us a clear signal that they don't want us meddling in their school affairs. Often our energy is diverted at this age to the educational needs and advocacy for our younger children because we feel that our older children are better able to take care of themselves. This is a serious mistake.

Staying involved in your son's high school education is critical to ensuring his academic achievement. And it has never been as important in the African American legacy of education as it is today. A high school education is no longer sufficient for most of the jobs that exist, much less for the careers we may wish for our children. Successful completion of high school is directly related to your son's future jobs, college opportunities, or entry into a technical school. A high school diploma or GED is also necessary for entry into the armed forces.

Raising Our Sons to Be Responsible Adults

Much of our expectations and efforts as parents are directed toward this goal. The teenage years put a strain on our efforts. What makes this even more difficult is when we look back to our own teenage years and the influence our parents had on us.

Peers and the media have replaced the family as major influences on the lives of our sons. The following summary of a University of Michigan study shows the dramatic shift from the 1950s to the 1990s.

Order of Importance in Teenagers' Lives

1950s	*1990s*
Family/Home	Peers
School	TV/Videos/Internet
Church	Family/Home
Peers	Celebrities
TV	School

In the 1950s the family (home), school, and church were major influences on our kids' lives. In the 1990s peers have replaced the home and the family, followed by TV, videos, and the Internet. The family comes in a weak third place. Church

nake the list of the top five. These results have far-
plications.

are often confused as to how to handle their teenage
etimes it can be extremely frustrating for parents when
their sons appear to ignore parental guidance. Some parents feel
their attempts are futile and desperate. Others tell us that their
sons pay lip service to them on "the small stuff" but then resist on
the big issues that can make a difference for their future.
Nevertheless, the challenge for you as a parent of teens is to stay
involved in your sons' lives—even more so at this age. (See
Chapter 4 for more ideas on staying involved.)

The bottom line is, your "manchild" is becoming a man. Scary,
isn't it? You aren't alone. This book was written especially for you.
The stories of other triumphant-but-ordinary parents will help
provide the inspiration you need to make it through.

Realities Our Sons Face

Our kids are growing up in a time that is more dangerous
than our early years. Historically, black men and boys have been
at risk since they were brought here from the shores of Africa.
During slavery, assertiveness was punished, their manhood was
threatened at every turn, black couples could not marry, and
most black families were forbidden to live under the same roof.
As author Toni Morrison once said, "It's an absolute wonder that
we're even alive." But despite making remarkable strides since
slavery, many of us are still struggling daily with unemployment,
lack of opportunities, poverty, homelessness, disease, AIDS, and
other societal ills. The sad fact is that even black parents who
have achieved material success have to contend with some of the
same challenges and fears for their black male children as those
living in poverty.

A.J. has written about the "Invisibility Syndrome," which
describes how society turns a blind eye to the worth, potential,
and ability in young black men. Instead of viewing them as individuals, many people respond to stereotypes. They confuse TV
images of young black men in handcuffs with every black male
with whom they come into contact. These images continue to
fuel racism, discrimination, and stereotypes that are born of fear.

Our sons learn at a young age that they will be followed in stores, that women will clutch their purses as they approach or will refuse to get on an elevator if they are inside.

Keep Hope Alive

In order to successfully overcome these odds, we must work to keep our own hope alive by focusing on the positives in our sons and developing all of their talents. Often this requires finding the strength within ourselves, our families, and our spirituality so we can continue to believe in our sons and be able to convey that belief to them effectively. We have talked to many parents who have learned to keep believing in their sons no matter what. We want our sons to grow up to be positive African American men with a strong racial identity and high self-esteem, able to make their positive, unique contributions to our society, and to walk in the surety that, as Jesse Jackson often has young people repeat, "I am somebody."

Developing a Positive Racial Identity in Our Teenage Sons

It is essential that you develop in your son a positive racial identity and high self-esteem. Knowing that he is special will be a powerful force in his life. Your son must know first that he is loved by you and that his family believes in him.

Many parents tell us that they feel they have talked until they are blue in the face, but their teenagers are not listening. To those of you who are despairing in this way, we say, keep talking. Family messages are extremely important. Teenagers have the capacity to look interested and be miles away; they are also capable of looking totally bored but absorbing every word you say.

Recently at dinner our youngest son was mouthing off about something. Our older son shocked us all by saying, "You should listen to the folks on this one—they said the same thing to me and now I know it's true." This was a wake-up call for us. We had been convinced that most of what we had said to him had gone in one ear and out the other. As his sisters chimed in with examples of similar experiences, we realized that our older children had all learned many of the lessons we had tried to teach them and would pass them on to their own children.

Fostering a strong racial identity can take many forms. Here are ten starters:

1. Many magazines such as *Ebony, Essence, Emerge,* and *Black Enterprise* are focused on the African American community. Look for bookstores where you will find books, pictures, and posters of prominent Africans and African Americans. Display these articles proudly in your home and talk about them with your kids.

2. Tell them about the legacy and history of Africa and the role of African Americans in United States history.

3. Read books like the ones cited at the end of this chapter to help you in what to say.

4. Take your kids to black cultural events, such as plays, concerts, celebrations, and community activities.

5. Celebrate Kwanzaa (see description at the end of Chapter 2) or incorporate it into your Christmas tradition, if that is a holiday your family observes.

6. Work on your own racial identity:

   • Do you say negative things about black people in front of your children?
   • Do you believe that black people are equal to white people in ability?
   • Do you convey a pride in your cultural history?
   • Do you convey pride in your family to your children?

7. Encourage your children to do book reports or other school assignments on famous African Americans.

8. Collect your family tree or family history to help your kids understand their own "roots." Tell your children of the pride you have in your family.

9. Counter negative media images with positive ones.

10. Talk to your children about the need to have pride in their heritage and to give something back to their community.

You should also teach your sons African American history and your family history. We cannot count on schools or the media to convey positive messages to our children. Black pride in the accomplishments of other Africans and African Americans must be taught. Tell your son about the contributions African Americans have made to this country. Tell him about Sojourner Truth, Frederick Douglass, Marcus Garvey, Martin Luther King Jr., and Malcolm X. Tell him your family stories. He can take pride in those who came before him and who survived.

Here are some things that will help build your son's self-esteem:

- Tell your son (and all of your children) daily that you love him (them).
- Tell him that you pray every day for his safety and protection.
- Tell your son often that he is somebody special.
- Tell him that he is growing into a strong African American man.
- Tell him how proud you are of him.

Our younger son read our book and added a few suggestions of his own for building self-esteem and teaching responsibility:

- Teach your son that hard work pays off.
- Tell him, "Don't give up at what you are doing."
- Encourage him by saying, "All good things come to those who wait."

RESOURCES

Bennett Jr., Lerone. *Before the Mayflower: A History of Black America.* Chicago: Johnson Publishing, 1993.

———. *The Shaping of Black America.* Chicago: Johnson Publishing, 1993.

Boyd, Herb, and Robert Allen (eds.). *Brotherman: The Odyssey of Black Men in America.* New York: Fawcett, 1996.

Franklin, John Hope, and Alfred A. Moss, Jr. *From Slavery to Freedom,* 7th ed. New York: Knopf, 1994.

2

IF WE STAND TALL, IT IS BECAUSE WE STAND ON THE BACKS OF THOSE WHO CAME BEFORE US.

—YORUBA PROVERB

African American Families and the Manchild

I grew up in a big family with lots of relatives around. My family was always "taking in folks." My parents wouldn't let us call their friends by their first names. I had more "aunts," "uncles," and "mommas" than I could count. I must have been in first grade before I figured out who was a real aunt and uncle and who wasn't. (Malik, age fifteen)

One of our greatest strengths and resources as African Americans has been the love of family members. Many of our families are extended families, and it is not unusual in the black community for mothers, fathers, grandmothers, grandfathers, aunts, uncles, cousins, older brothers and sisters, and relatives of all kinds to all be involved in rearing a child. This is a very important inheritance of our African legacy. Even during slavery African Americans struggled to maintain family ties. For some of us, our church family has provided a safe place for our kids, and an opportunity for them to be around nurturing adults and role models such as the minister, minister's wife, deacons, deaconesses, church mothers, fathers, brothers and sisters, Sunday school teachers, and youth group leaders.

Still other African American families have "adopted" family members. Often this involves taking in children in times of need. African American children may be raised by extended family members for many reasons. Historically, if African American parents fell on hard times and were unable to care for their children, it was very common to send them to grandma, grandpa, or their aunt or uncle. For some of our families that has meant "sending him down South" where he can get away from the streets or "his boys" and have the benefit of the wisdom of other family members.

Sometimes, wanting better educational opportunities for their children has led parents to move them in with relatives in another state. Single parents or parents with many children often reach out to extended family for help in raising a child, especially when the child's behavior is causing problems. If a parent is hospitalized, abusing alcohol or drugs, is in a long-term residential treatment program, is incarcerated, or is a youngster herself, extended family members are the ones who are asked, and sometimes offer, to lend a hand. Sometimes African Americans have sent children to stay with or be raised by extended family temporarily in order to allow parents to get a better job, work extra hours, finish or advance their education, or to expose their children to the active presence of positive role models.

Well-functioning African American families have always adopted people into the family who were not blood related. These may have been friends, neighbors, and often godparents. Many of us grew up with "play" mamas, papas, brothers, sisters, or cousins who were a part of our extended family. Often these adults filled the gap while our parents were working or acted as role models for us when we were growing up.

These special people have served an important role in our communities and families, and have helped to provide protection or a village to care for, nurture, and raise our children. In today's world, as African American families prepare our sons for the often threatening world they will face, these individuals can become an integral part of their survival.

African American Mothers and Sons: Special Bond, Special Challenges

If you are an African American mother who is actively involved in your children's lives, we would like to acknowledge you for all of the attention, effort, and love it takes to bring a black son into this world and raise him to manhood. Mothers are so often blamed for the problems of sons that it is rare for them to be commended for all that they do. It is your devotion to your family and determination that have kept you going even when things are hard.

We would also like to applaud those of you who advocate on your children's behalf. We know that you have often been mislabeled by schools, and other groups working with your children, as pushy. Don't be discouraged. Advocacy can pay off. Successful African American men and women often talk about a parent who actively advocated for them and pushed systems to respond to their needs. Many of us would not be where we are today without mothers like you.

African American mothers for over four hundred years have known that the deck was stacked against their sons from birth. By the time our boys leave the young and small stage, about nine years old, they are perceived as dangerous. These messages can be subtle yet damaging. One example, described by Jawanza Kunjufu in his book *Countering the Conspiracy to Destroy Black Boys*, is the "fourth-grade failure syndrome" in which some teachers begin to apply stereotypes to black boys and to be threatened by them. Unfortunately, this often leads to school failure and has a very negative effect. (In Chapter 5 we discuss ways in which you can make sure that this does not happen to your son.)

Mothers love their sons and daughters so much that their protective instincts are immediately mobilized when they think their children are being treated unfairly. African American mothers, aware of the many risk factors facing our male children, have often overcompensated by trying to give them the love that society often denies them.

Raising Daughters, Loving Sons

How much loving is too much? Can there be such a thing as too much protection and not enough training? An old saying in the African American community notes that some of our families "raise our daughters and love our sons." This clearly is not true of all of our families, but if it rings a bell for you, read on. This process occurs when some families require little of their sons in terms of household responsibilities, good school performance, expected church attendance, contributions to the family, and, for older sons, getting a job, moving out of the home, taking care of any children they father, etc. In contrast, daughters are often expected, from a young age, to go to church, excel in school, take care of younger kids (particularly if a parent is working), cook, clean, be in by a certain hour, and so on.

Parents are sometimes not aware how their everyday treatment of children conveys certain unintended messages. Unwittingly, we may be training our children to become the opposite of our expectations.

Sara told her fifteen-year-old daughter Ann to watch the younger children while she ran some errands. On the way out of the door she shouted at Bill, her seventeen-year-old son, to get off the phone and not to get in Ann's way while she was gone. When Sara was asked why she didn't put Bill in charge of the younger children instead, she laughed and said, "Oh, Bill won't know how to handle those kids." When Sara was asked why not, she responded, "You know how boys are." It was clear Sara never expected—or taught—Bill how to take care of the younger children. It was easier for Sara to instruct Ann in this way. It felt more "natural," and it was something Ann needed to know how to do if she was going to be prepared for future motherhood. The sad part of this was that Bill lost out on this equally important preparation for fatherhood.

The Special Role of African American Fathers

If you are an African American father who is actively involved in your children's lives (whether you live with them or not), we want you to be assured of how important your relationship with your children is, and how much of a difference it is making in their lives. You know that your children reflect your values, so you invest yourself in them. All too often the media focuses attention on African American fathers who are not involved in the way that you are. If you often feel invisible when African American families are discussed, you are not alone.

A.J. has talked and written about the feelings experienced by many African American men who are active, involved fathers but who seem to be ignored when the statistics for "father-absence" in our communities are quoted.

I have always made a point of having some dad/son (or daughter) time with each of our children on a regular basis. I try to plan activities with all of my children as well as one-on-one with each child. This is not every day or every week, but over time my children experience a variety of ways of being together, staying in touch, and sharing life experiences with me. I don't keep a scorecard of contacts, but I do try to keep a sense of its success by my feel for the quality of our relationship through talking, sharing, feeling good, and being close.

Finding some activity that creates a level of shared interest and participation is one way to do it. I started taking the children at an early age on fishing trips, taught them "the ropes," and planned many fishing vacations. It became an activity we all engaged in and came to enjoy. Later on some of their favorite activities became another opportunity for me to bond with them.

Like many adolescents and young adults, as they became more independent they spent less time with their parents than they had in the past. This is normal as children become teenagers. But the previous activities still served as a foundation for our relationship. We found ourselves wanting to find the time to do some of the same things we enjoyed more often when they were younger.

If you are a stepfather, grandfather, or an adoptive father who is giving your love to and raising children who may not be your blood relatives, we acknowledge your contribution also. As a community, we need to hold up examples of fathers and other male figures who are functioning well and trying to give their sons positive fathering. We applaud those African American males who grew up with excellent role models and father figures, and are now giving something back to our communities by becoming mentors and role models for boys who have not been as fortunate. As we discuss the challenges facing our families, we must not lose sight of those among us who are struggling and doing a great job in spite of tremendous odds.

My stepson was not sure of himself at basketball. He would get upset when the other guys "trash-talked" at him. I started going to his games. I would sit right up front with the team. After a while I became almost an unofficial coach. I figured if I was giving Brian a pep talk, I might as well give it to all the guys. (Warren, stepfather of Brian, age fourteen)

Overworked Fathers: Physically Present/Emotionally Absent

Many men, even those who are technically living in the home, are not really there for their sons. In these families the substantial part of daily child rearing is done by women. As therapists, we have noticed that this is often true even in situations where both mother and father share household tasks. Often, fathers who have long commutes to work or are frequently traveling on business spend little time with their sons. Other fathers, though in the home physically, are not emotionally accessible. To allow these scenarios to continue may leave a devastating hole in a boy's life. Every father has something unique to offer his son, and he should make a special effort to contribute to his child's growth.

One tragically ironic scenario in black (and many other) communities concerns fathers who have a great deal to offer their sons, and who are involved in jobs where they serve as role models for others, but are unavailable to spend quality time with their own sons. Some fathers erroneously believe that their sons need them less as they grow older. In reality, particularly for black male adolescents, *just the opposite is true.* With so many distorted images of manhood, persistent racism, and the street influences of drugs, crime, and gangs, the need for clear instruction from male role models about how to develop a positive identity is that much greater. They need their father's active involvement in their lives!

The value of a father's (and other males') input and love cannot be overestimated. Young men must be taught how to be responsible men, how to treat women properly, how to serve one's community, how to be excellent fathers, how to have integrity; and how to develop positive self-esteem and strong racial identity. We encourage fathers to explore the following questions to determine how they are approaching their relationship with their sons:

- How much (quantity) and quality time do I really spend with my son each week?
- Do I give more time to other priorities, such as my job, my friends, or my activities, than I give to my son and family?
- Do I bad-mouth my son's mother or other black women?
- When was the last time I talked with my son about what's going on in his life?
- What messages do I give my son about how to be a man by my words and by my example?
- When was the last time I shared some of my own childhood and life experiences with my son?

If your honest answers to these questions were less than you would have liked, it is never too late to reverse this process and increase the quantity and quality of the time that you spend with your son. Do it today!

Divorce or Separation: Challenges for Half of Our Families

More than 50 percent of the children in the United States are not living with both of their biological parents. This may mean that a father or mother is apart from his or her children because of divorce, separation, or remarriage. If at all possible, the parent who does not have everyday contact with the child should be involved in his life. The ideal situation is one in which the parents talk regularly about the needs of the kids, even though they are not living in the same household. A number of experts in the field have recommended co-parenting in which parents living apart share custody of their children. The effects of losing a parent to divorce or separation are also experienced when a parent's boyfriend or girlfriend, who may play a significant role in a child's life, leaves the relationship. When the romantic relationship between the adults ends, the child is often cut off from a person to whom he has grown very close.

The situations described above are common. The problem is that people are human. The challenge, as hard as it is for ex-partners, is to rise above their differences with their ex-spouses and address the best interest of their children.

Mary slammed the phone down, and her thirteen-year-old son looked up startled by the loud noise. He had been pretending to watch TV as his mother angrily argued over the phone with his father, from whom she had been divorced for two years. At the end of the conversation his mother rushed by him on the way to the kitchen and said, "Promise me you will never be anything like your father. Don't let him teach you any of his ways when you see him this weekend."

If you are finding the process of life after divorce or separation a difficult challenge, consider the following questions. Take your time, search your soul, and examine your conscience before you answer:

- Have you allowed differences with your ex to get in the way of effective co-parenting of your children?
- Are you and your ex working together to effectively co-parent your children?
- Have you contributed to the best of your ability to the financial support of your children?
- Have you bad-mouthed your ex in front of your children or allowed others to do so?
- Have you and your ex sat down and explained to your children the reasons why you are or have separated or divorced? (Many children assume that it is their fault.)
- Have you allowed issues of child support to interfere with issues of visitation?
- Have you put your children in a difficult loyalty conflict by in effect forcing them to choose between you and your ex?
- Have you allowed your anger at your ex's new relationship to get in the way of his or her contact with your children?

If your answer to any of these questions is yes, we strongly recommend taking some of the following steps:

- Sit down and talk to your son and other children. Ask them the above questions and *listen* and *be open* to their feedback.

- Remember that even if it is not your intention, you can put your kids in a double bind, or loyalty conflict by giving them the message that they have to choose between their parents.
- Have an honest discussion with your ex about the children and their needs.
- Avoid blaming.
- Seek help from a counselor to explore your own behavior and motivations and to get help and support for yourself.
- Seek family therapy or counseling to help you, your children, and your ex sort out these difficult issues. Ask the therapist or counselor to meet with you and your ex to discuss ways in which you could work together effectively for the sake of the children. (See Chapter 13 for help with finding a counselor or therapist.)
- Seek the help and intervention of concerned individuals that you both respect. These may be family members, a minister, a friend, a school counselor, or a pastoral counselor.
- Do not be alone. There are many support groups such as Parents Without Partners (see Resource List) that are available and can help you to get help and feel less isolated.
- Join a support group for parents or have your children join a group for children of divorce sponsored by a school, church, or community center.
- Read some of the books at the end of this chapter.

Maintaining Family Ties after Divorce/Separation

There is a saying in the black community that you can divorce parents but not grandparents. This may be true, but one unfortunate outcome of separation and/or divorce is that children often lose the support of the other parent's extended family. Many of these folks can be a great help in times of need or can give an overburdened single parent the time to take a much needed break. Bad feelings on both sides, however, can lead to an emotional cutoff.

The grandmother's and grandfather's relationship with a child is cherished in our communities. For many African American children growing up with separated parents, grandparents often serve as a link to the father (or mother). Even if a father is not involved, children who visit, see, or talk to their paternal grandparents regularly may have more of a feeling of connection to their fathers than those who do not. Regular phone calls to grandparents or special cards for birthdays and holidays are ways to help maintain the ties.

Absent Fathers

A 1994 report from the Center for the Study of Social Policy and Philadelphia Children's Network estimates that 50 percent of African American children grow up without fathers in the home because of the high divorce rate discussed above. The consequences have been significant. When African American fathers are not present to teach their sons how to be responsible men or manage the stress of being black and male in the United States, gangs may offer them the only male guidance they can find during their transition to manhood. Many young gang recruits are boys from fatherless homes who are hungry for male role models. Seventy percent of the black men in jail grew up in fatherless homes, according to Joe White and James Coñes, authors of *Black Man Emerging*. If you are a father who has been absent or less involved in your son's life, know that it is never too late to reach out.

Many single mothers have sought other male role models for their sons among their extended families and communities. With the help of these willing men, many single mothers have been able to provide strength, structure, love, guidance, and strong family bonds for their sons, in spite of the odds.

In and Out Dads

Both our sons and daughters desperately need male role models and crave a father figure. Many of our men have not been responsible and have not taken an active part in raising their children. Many more drift in and out of their children's lives inconsistently and often without warning. Still others breeze in to play the "hero," periodically offering money, trips, expensive clothes and sneakers, video games and trips to McDonald's, and then aren't heard from again for months. They are not available to be partners in the business of raising their own sons. This is an infuriating pattern that makes many mothers want to "end the pain of the roller coaster," as one parent put it. Unfortunately, if this results in a cutoff from the father, your children are deprived of an important person in their lives.

In teenage years, many kids express a desire to reach out to and search for fathers or mothers whom they have not known. This is often hard for the parent or guardian who has been raising them alone. Try to get past your own feelings and encourage your kids if they ask to contact an absent father (or other parent). Wait for them to express the desire to do it.

Dads: The Invisible Single Parents

I feel like I'm invisible. Everyone talks about single mothers. No one even thinks to mention single fathers. I paid a whole lot of dues to raise my kids alone. (John, single father of three)

John is right! Single fathers are often treated as if they are invisible. Many African American fathers are raising their kids alone or with the help of extended family. It takes a special father to do this job. In this book we want to make you visible and offer you some support. You are doing a very important job. Your kids will someday understand how hard it is to be a single parent and the sacrifices you've made for them. We encourage you to get support also.

I went to see my son's guidance counselor. It's hard because I'm a single father trying to raise my son on my own. His counselor told me about a father's group at a community center. It's been a big help. (Tommy, single father of a thirteen-year-old son)

If you are looking for help and support, don't forget to check with your kids' guidance counselors and teachers at school. They can be a big help and often hear about resources in the community.

If you do not find what you need, ask your son's guidance counselor if there are other single parent fathers in your son's school. Reach out to them and start your own group or just play ball together once a week and give yourselves time off from fatherhood.

Special Messages for Single Moms

If you are a mother raising your sons and daughters alone, you may find that there are times when the burden becomes great. Take heart from the many generations of African American mothers who have successfully raised their children as single parents. Seek out their wisdom; ask those in your community whose children are now grown for their advice and help.

As we have talked to single parents like you, a number of messages keep coming through:

- Do not doubt your ability to parent your children. You can do the job. Take heart from the many generations who have gone before.
- Do not be alone. Reach out to family and extended family members, other single moms, and concerned individuals in your community.
- Find a support group for single parents.
- If none is available, start one in your community, in your child's school, or in your church.
- Seek out and find positive male role models for your sons and daughters.
- Remember the African proverb "It takes a whole village to raise a child." (See Chapter 12.) Look for and find that village.
- Take care of and give to yourself. (See Chapter 14.)

We know that you love your sons, and it is that love that will get you through the joy of the good times as well as the rough moments.

I felt like I had nobody. Here I was raising these kids alone. I didn't plan it this way, it just happened. I needed help, but I didn't know where to turn. I would go up to my kids' schools and meet other parents like me. A couple of us got to talking. We started out meeting at my kitchen table. We didn't have all the answers, but we started a support group for ourselves. It really helped me survive. (Kisha, single mom with three children)

If you find yourself alone like Kisha, start talking to other parents in your community. Reach out to others.

"Mother" Gibson was like the mother of our church. She had raised tons of kids. One day I was talking to her after church. I told her that I

was trying to raise my kids right, but it was so hard. I told her that I'd love to find a support group. She told me she was getting ready to start a group at church for other parents like me. I can't wait to get started. (JoAnn, single parent of two teenage sons)

Seek out the advice of the elders in your community. Ask one of these wise folks to start a group for parents. All they can say is no, and they may be honored to be asked.

◆ ◆ ◆

Do not look where you fell, but where you slipped.
—*African proverb*

◆ ◆ ◆

Many African American parents find themselves alone because they have the mistaken notion that if they ask for help that means that they have been bad parents. They forget that raising a black son is a difficult job for anyone. Many of our families have taught their children that problems at home are "nobody's business but our own" and cautioned us not to "air our dirty laundry in public." For some, this was a survival mechanism designed to protect our families. For others, however, it has kept us from seeking help and advice when we desperately need it. If this is your own response, it is likely that this position is further isolating you. We think you'll find that it limits your success as a parent and makes the job harder. As the proverb above implies, we need to stop looking at our failures as parents and start addressing the root causes of our "slips." Often this can be helped by sharing the burden. The following suggestions may be helpful:

- Seek the advice of a counselor or a friend whose parenting style you admire.
- Ask your son's guidance counselor (or if he has been in serious trouble his probation officer) to call a family meeting. Get the courage to ask at least one extended family member or close friend to attend.
- Don't wait until your son is in big trouble to reach out to family members and seek professional help.

The "Manchild"

Some mothers, especially those who are raising a son alone, may find that they gradually depend on their son to be their right-hand man, or the man of the house. Many say this directly to them with pride. They might even describe a son as their "best friend," confidant, or "only joy." Without realizing it, some mothers may substitute the love and connection they had with a husband or boyfriend to their son.

As soon as Joanne walked into the house, she called her fifteen-year-old son Ade's name. She would share the details of her day with him, fix his favorite meals, and plan all of her leisure time activities, such as going to the movies, in the company of her son. For years their evenings and weekends together were a ritual. She found herself upset when he began to want some independence. Joanne was hurt and resentful that her son/best friend was spending his time going out to the movies and other activities without her. She found herself irritated with his preoccupation with talking to girls on the phone, wanting to hang out with the boys, and he was less interested in doing the things he and his mother used to enjoy together in the past.

Joanne had always done things for her son. This was fine when he was younger, but he was now fifteen and she was still waiting on him hand and foot. He was not required to do anything in their home.

One of the challenges for black mothers is to look honestly at our own behavior. Our sons are at risk. But we cannot use this as an excuse for giving them less responsibility. In doing so, we are doing them a grave disservice. The danger in these behaviors is subtle. Two-parent families are not exempt from this behavior. Mothers and fathers can both fall into the trap of demanding less from their sons.

We all want what is best for our sons, yet it is so easy to confuse our efforts to help and be supportive with overprotectiveness. We have to resist the temptation to do too much as part of our commitment to raising them to be responsible adults. Even as we write this, we recall the many times that we have reminded our sons to do something when they needed to take responsibility for themselves.

Training for Responsibility Quiz

If you are in doubt whether this applies to you, ask yourself the following questions:

- Has your son ever worked and earned money (even a summer job)?
- Has your son ever done volunteer work in a community organization?
- Are you consistently doing things for your son that he can do for himself? Does your son:
  - wash his own clothes
  - clean his own room
  - clean other parts of the house
  - iron his clothes
  - know how to cook
  - take responsibility for planning and preparing some meals for the family?
- Does your son have assigned chores in the household? Do you make sure that he does them?
- Do you have a son over the age of eighteen living in your home who is not working or going to school?
- Do you still contribute to the support of a son who is over twenty-five?
- Do you see housework as women's work?
- Do you wake your son up every morning?
- Do you remind him every day (more than once) of the many things he needs to do?

A Manchild in the One-Parent Home

In the pain of separation or divorce, many fathers and mothers, boyfriends and girlfriends, make negative comments about each other to their children, often without considering whether the information is appropriate to share with a child or whether it is in the child's best interest to have a negative view of his parent. You need to consider the consequences of the comments that you make to your children throughout their lives, especially as they enter adolescence. It is very hard for a boy (particularly one without a father in the home) to develop a positive self-image or view of manhood if he constantly hears negative comments about his father. Mixed or negative messages can be very confusing and harmful to children, particularly coming from persons they love or are attached to. The following are a few soul searching questions that have been helpful to other African American parents:

- Do you bad-mouth your son's father (or mother) in his presence more often than you speak positively of them?
- Have you encouraged your son's visits to see his father (or mother) on a regular basis? Even when the parent may be in a new relationship or when he or she isn't meeting child-support obligations?
- Have you included your son's paternal or maternal grandparents and other relatives in his life?

Carefully consider your answers to these questions. Take inventory and ask yourself if this behavior is in your child's best interest in the long term. Bad-mouthing another parent can hurt a child deeply and damage his own self-esteem.

The Importance of Grandparents and Other Extended Family Members

John and Debbie's mother died when they were four and three years old. They had never known their father. "Nana" and "Grandpa" took them into their home and raised them with lots of love and good strong values. To this day, some of their best memories are of the wonderful family meals Nana would cook and the way in which Grandpa taught them how to read and required them to read a newspaper each day. John and Debbie, both successful adults with their own families, say they owe their lives to these two special people.

The involvement of extended family members has often been the glue that has kept our communities strong. If you are an African American grandparent, aunt, uncle, cousin, older sister, or brother who is raising or helping to raise a child or adolescent, you are doing an invaluable service for our community. Traditionally, these family members have often made the key difference in a young person's life.

John and Debbie's experiences are not unique. African American grandparents have been rising to the challenge of raising grand- and even great-grandchildren for generations. For some, however, taking in grandchildren can be very difficult. Often these grandparents, having spent many years raising their own children and working long hours, are looking forward to retirement and an easier life. They are faced with the impossible decision of leaving their grandchildren in an unhealthy situation or taking them in and raising a very different generation. Here's one grandmother's story:

I thought I was done. I raised five children of my own, and they are all grown now. Most of them are doing fine, but my youngest daughter, Hakia, has always had a tough time. I didn't know at first that she had gotten involved with drugs. I didn't know how bad things had gotten until I visited her and my grandson. He was only three. I found him dirty and uncared for. Hakia would often leave him alone in the house with no supervision. I begged her to get help for herself, but she wouldn't. What could I do? I took my grandson in and I am raising him.

That was three years ago. He's a good boy and I love him a lot, but I was hoping to do some things for myself now. I had gotten my GED and was planning on going to college. I work all day. I feel that he needs me in the evenings. He is six now and only in first grade. We have a long way to go. I guess my dreams will just have to wait.

If you are a grandparent (aunt or uncle, or older brother or sister) in this position, seek the help and support of others in your community who are struggling with similar issues.

- Don't go it alone; isolation is deadly. Raise your grandchild around other families.
- Get help or counseling. It can be a great comfort and help to talk to a counselor about the challenges you are facing. Most counselors can offer time-proven advice that friends sometimes cannot.
- Join a support group. There's safety in numbers, especially a group of other like-minded grandparents. If there isn't anything appropriate in your neighborhood, why not start a family support group at your church, community center, or at your grandchild's school?
- Involve other family members, even those who are farther

away. Use letters, E-mail, and the telephone to keep concerned family members abreast of how you and your grandson are doing. Tell them about both the great achievements and the challenges.

- Try to arrange regular break times when the child can visit with other family members for a weekend, stay for a holiday, or spend a summer.
- Identify at least one relative or close friend who can serve in a co-parenting role, even if they live a distance away.

Ask and You Shall Receive

Parents and other family members who are raising black sons need all the help they can get. Reach out and be honest with family and extended family about your needs and those of your son. Many parents and extended family members make the mistake of assuming that other family members know what is going on with their son, and they then assume that relatives don't care or don't want to get involved when they aren't quick to offer help. In fact, these relatives may indeed know the details of an adolescent's behavior and may also be concerned about his welfare, but will not step in unless they are asked.

History Repeats Itself: Family Messages over the Generations

Norman (age fifty-five) was raised in Mississippi in a very loving black family. Because he grew up during segregation, his parents encouraged him to be passive in his dealings with authority figures, especially white folks. His parents meant well. They were trying to help and protect him. This legacy, however, has made it very difficult for Norman to be assertive when he needs to be.

Recently Adam, his thirteen-year-old son, came home from high school beaten up by other kids. He told Norman what happened. Adam hoped that his father would come with him to school and stand up for him with the school authorities and the other kids. Norman told his son that he would just have to deal with it himself.

Because of his father's messages, Adam too has learned to hide his pain and to be passive in dealing with authority figures. Norman didn't realize that there were ways to teach his son that a black man can be appropriately assertive and stand up for what he believes.

Have you ever caught yourself yelling at your kids and realized that you sounded just like your mother? Was there a day when you went to give your son a beating and realized that you had sworn never to do this to your kids because of what your folks had done to you? Have you ever found yourself preaching on and on to your kids and heard them say, "You sound just like Grandpa"?

Family messages and patterns repeat over the generations. Sometimes we don't even realize that we are repeating things that we learned from our parents and the "old folks." This can be helpful when we are repeating a positive family tradition, but it can also be destructive. Black folks often say, "Well, my parents did it and I turned out all right." Time can make us forget sometimes how hard it was for us when we were growing up.

Here are some other examples of family messages that parents are sending their children:

Carol, a thirty-four-year-old mother, said, "I couldn't believe it when the words 'Men are no good' came out of my mouth. I knew my kids were right there hearing this. My mama used to say that around me all the time."

Kinshasha, a forty-two-year-old mother, had always resented the fact that although she had three older brothers, her parents expected her to do all of the housework and cooking. One day she was shocked when her thirteen-year-old daughter screamed at her, "You never make Willis do anything and he's older than me!"

These family messages are very powerful, particularly since many parents are not aware that they keep acting them out without realizing the pattern. Sometimes our behavior gives a different message from what we are saying. Remember, actions speak louder than words.

Alex was a nineteen-year-old who was referred to Nancy by the court. During an angry argument, he had severely beaten his girlfriend. She called the police, and he was arrested. In a counseling session, he recalled this memory about his father and mother: "It was the second time that I had come home and found that man knocking my mother around. That day I just lost it and snatched him and beat him to a pulp." Alex was trying to protect his mom. He swore that he would never treat a woman the way his

*father treated his mother. But Alex had learned to settle things with his
fists. The stage was set for him to repeat this in his own relationships.*

Skin Color and Family Messages

*Mandela, a handsome fifteen-year-old dark-skinned African American
boy, had struggled his entire life to deal with his family's messages about
skin color. His mother and other family members had always favored
Karim, his younger brother, who was light skinned. He dreaded family
gatherings, where he often heard comments about Karim like "He's so
fine" or "He has good hair."*

Ever since the days of slavery, when light-skinned individuals
were given special privileges because they were the slave master's
children, the African American community has struggled with
messages about skin color. The "Black Is Beautiful" movement of
the 1960s and 1970s attempted to reverse the negative and
painful messages many African American families had given to
children about skin color in previous generations. To this day,
African Americans still struggle with this issue.

George Wolfe, a famous African American playwright, has
commented, "We are putting people on the moon, and some
black folks are still talking about 'light skin' and 'good hair.'" We
must make sure that we (or other family members) are not giving
these negative messages to our children.

Some light-skinned African American males can also face
challenges:

*Paul is a very light-skinned twelve-year-old African American boy. He
had just moved to a new school, and a group of other black kids had
harassed him and told him, "Get away, white boy." He came home from
school very upset.*

*When he told his parents, they talked to him honestly about his skin
color. They reminded him that African Americans come in all shades.
They showed him some ways that he could respond next time to let those
boys know that he was also African American and proud of his identity.
Next time they bothered him, he said, "I'm black just like you and proud
of it." His parents gave him positive family messages about his skin color.
They helped to instill pride in his African American heritage. These family messages can shape our kids' self-esteem and their racial identity and
influence how they feel about themselves.*

All of the generational family messages discussed above can be changed, but we must first recognize that they are there. We have found that it is very helpful to have parents ask themselves the following questions:

- What messages did your parents and other family members give you when you were growing up?
- Which ones do you want to pass on to your own kids?
- Which ones do you want to change?
- How did your folks parent you?
- What did you like about their parenting?
- What did you dislike?
- What would you like to change?
- Do you find yourself repeating your parents' behavior without even realizing it? In what ways?
- Have you tried to change and can't? Are you not sure what's going on? Seek help from a family therapist or counselor to figure it out. You can begin to change these family patterns so that they are not passed on to the next generation.
- As a child, you might not have had a choice, but you do now as an adult.
- Empower yourself to know that you can *choose* the behaviors you want to change and the ones you want to keep in parenting your own children.

All Together Now: Close Families

Many African American families are close-knit with a great deal of contact and communication among family members. Even if family members have moved away, regular phone contact is maintained and family news spreads rapidly through the grapevine. A couple of years ago, our oldest daughter was accepted into graduate school in New York. She was so excited and frustrated that she could not immediately reach any immediate family member by phone, that she called her cousin in Maryland, who called her dad (A.J.'s brother). We learned her good news when we arrived home that evening and got a message from A.J.'s brother on our answering machine telling us how wonderful it was and how happy he was about our daughter's great news.

Yet there are challenges for the close-knit family, as this example shows:

Brian's family had always been close. They ate at Grandma's house every Sunday. Brian was Grandma's "special child," and his sisters complained that he was spoiled. Whenever he wanted something, if his mom said no, he threw a tantrum and then went to Grandma.

His mom was trying hard to teach him responsibility and had insisted that he earn his next pair of Nike sneakers by doing extra work in addition to his regular chores. He went to Grandma, who bought him the sneakers, no questions asked.

The greatest challenge for the close knit African American family is making sure that everyone is giving the same messages and expectations to your son. In these black families, typically everyone has an opinion he or she wants heard. This can be very confusing for your kids. Everyone may be offering contradictory messages to your son. If this is the case, you need to pull together the adults in the family and get agreement. When teenagers are given conflicting messages, they tend to act out even more.

If your family fits this description, here are some suggestions:

- Have honest discussions with other family members in order to help them understand the situation.
- Help them understand the problem of giving mixed messages to your son.
- Remind them that adolescents sometimes play one parent or family member against the others.
- Call a family meeting of key members to discuss the issue.
- If the situation threatens to become severe, ask family members to go together for family therapy or counseling in order to learn how to best help your son. (See Chapter 13 for suggestions on getting help.)

❖ ❖ ❖

Two men in a burning house must not stop to argue.

—Ashanti proverb

❖ ❖ ❖

A part of the "job" of adolescents is to test our limits. If a father is very tough and a mother is very easy (or the other way around), a son may manipulate and play them against each other. If parents, grandparents, older brothers and sisters, and sometimes other extended family members are not in agreement, adolescents will often act out. For example, a mother may set limits for her son but work late hours. In the mother's absence, if the boy's grandmother covers for his misbehavior, his acting out will worsen. When a child has two (or more) different family members sending opposing messages about "how to be," it causes more acting out. Here's an idea of what happens when this occurs:

Kwame, sixteen, had been told repeatedly by his mother that he had to stick to his curfew and call if he was going to be late. For a Saturday night party, his mother agreed to a very unusual 1:00 A.M. curfew. Kwame was having a great time partying and had so many beers that he got drunk. He came home at 5:00 A.M., knocked on his sister's window, and she let him into the house. His mother, who had fallen asleep, was never aware of when or in what condition he came home.

This story illustrates many points. Sometimes well-meaning family members form alliances with our sons. Obviously, they are doing this out of love, but they are somewhat misguided. By protecting Kwame, his sister hid the problem of his lateness and his drinking from his mother. The next time Kwame went further. This time the consequences were more serious:

Two months later, Kwame and his boys again went to a party. He had an 11:00 P.M. curfew, but he was not worried about time because his mother was never awake when he got in. He again got drunk, stayed out past curfew, and went "joy riding" in a stolen car with his friend Nyere, who was also drunk. When it was Kwame's turn to drive, he ran a red light and hit another car. Two children were killed in the crash. Both Kwame and Nyere were charged with driving while intoxicated (DWI), and Kwame was also charged with vehicular manslaughter.

This story illustrates the way in which misbehavior can increase if adolescents are not being monitored by parents and if other family members cover up their actions. As a result, the behavior may continue until it becomes a tragedy. If Kwame's mother had stayed up until her son came home, she would have known what time he arrived—and how he got inside. Kwame's sister could have been helped to see that her behavior was hurting rather than helping him. If Kwame's mother had informed her daughter of her rules and expectations, a family understanding about curfew would have been achieved. As parents and role models, we cannot afford to "go to sleep" on the job but must continue to monitor our son's behavior continually. Many parents insist that their kids wake them up when they arrive home to be sure that curfew rules are obeyed. This is also a good method for parents to get a sense of whether alcohol or drugs were involved in the evening's event. For instance, if Kwame's mother had been awake the first time he came home past curfew, she might have become aware of his alcohol problem, and a tragedy might have been avoided.

Out There on Your Own: Cutoff Families

All families differ in how they respond to challenges. In some families the relationships are so poor that there is little exchange of information about one another. Other families may contain members who are struggling for survival themselves and are in no position to help. When relatives are embarrassed about their situation, they are often unwilling to reach out. Family secrets, old wounds, and jealousy are common reasons why families may become cut off.

Cutoff families often take a hands-off policy where no one wants to get involved. Some families are emotionally cut off and have members who don't speak to one another. Others have situations where no one is willing to offer help. If you are in a similar situation, you may need the help of a pastor or church elder, a school official, a probation officer, a therapist, or a counselor to help your family see how serious the situation has become and to help family members come together. Surprisingly, some family members that might seem cut off turn out to be the ones who contribute the most—but only if the old issues are addressed and resolved. If the above descriptions seem to fit your family, the following are suggestions to combat emotional cutoff:

- Check yourself. Have you also become cut off from your son and his day-to-day life?

- Seek the help of a good family therapist or counselor. (See Chapter 13.)
- Have you become cut off from your extended family?
- Search yourself to see if there are old family wounds or emotional cutoffs that may be preventing you from asking for help or others from offering it. Work on releasing any anger or bitterness you feel—for your sake and your son's.
- Uncover any secrets in your life, in your son's, or in your family that you are afraid will be revealed when you ask for help. Resolve to be up-front. Why not start the process before the secret explodes?
- Reject the feeling that you have failed if you ask for help from your family or share your problems.
- Make a diagram of your family tree, called a genogram. Include all family members, living close and far, and see if there is someone who can offer help or respite (i.e., a place to stay, a home, financial support, a male role model, etc.). You may be surprised at what you will find.
- Keep track of your son's schoolwork, peer group, street activities, curfew, and money supply for a month and be prepared to discuss these issues at a family meeting.
- Think about ways you can encourage other family and extended family members to be involved. Welcome their input when they show interest, even if you don't agree with their advice.

Strategies for Strengthening African American Families

Creating a Family of Choice

Andrea is a thirty-one-year-old single parent who is raising her fifteen-year-old son, Mark, alone. She works in a department store and often has to work overtime to make ends meet. Both of Andrea's parents are alcoholics. Her father was very abusive to the entire family when she was growing up, and continues to abuse her mother. Her older brother is a drug addict in another city. For many years Andrea tried to remain connected to her family. She reached out to them; they never responded. She has lived alone since she gave birth to Mark at sixteen. She is determined to keep her son and herself free from alcohol and drug abuse.

Last year she sought counseling because she was afraid that Mark was being lured into alcohol and drug use by "his boys." Andrea had gone to her family for help, but they dismissed her concerns and said that she was overreacting.

At work, she was connected with other single parents like herself who had sons Mark's age. Her best friends from childhood were very support-ive. One was married, and her husband often reached out to Mark. The most important person, however, was Andrea's "play brother" Daryl who had grown up next door to her. He was like family and was able to offer Mark an after-school job in his painting business that occupied Mark's time in something positive and kept him off the streets and away from some of his peers who were heavily involved in alcohol and drug use.

Some African American parents have told us that, in truth, they have cut off from their extended family because the family mem-bers are very dysfunctional and offer no support for their positive goals for their sons. Andrea learned to "work her network" or to create a "family of choice." Healthy, functional African American families have always done this. If they move to a new area, they adopt new nonblood family members. Many of us grew up with terms like "play mama," "play brother," or "cousin." When blacks migrated north, away from their close-knit southern neighbor-hoods, they lost those day-to-day relationships. It is essential that we rebuild them as best we can with new people in our new environ-ments for the survival and health of our families. We are "aunt" and "uncle" or "Mom" and "Dad" to many of our kids' friends.

Creating Family Time

One way to help your son (and all of your children) feel grounded and connected to family and extended family is to establish regular family rituals. It is best if these start long before the teenage years, because that is a time in life when kids often pull away from the family and seek to establish their own rituals. That is the bad news; the good news is that we found that they will cherish those rituals in the future, especially when they have their own families.

The movie *Soul Food* is a wonderful illustration of how an

African American family pulls together over the ritual of Sunday dinner. Although many of us grew up with the ritual of family dinners, involving lots of home-cooked food, it can be a struggle to continue this tradition today. With our busy schedules, it is often hard to get everyone together. Our family has tried to forget our busy schedules once a week and have everyone sit down on Sundays. Don't sacrifice this important time to nurture the family relationship.

Big holiday dinners at Thanksgiving, Christmas, Easter, Mother's Day, Father's Day, or picnics on the Fourth of July can give children a real sense of belonging. Often these are at the home of a special person such as a grandmother, mother, or an aunt. Sadly, as the members of a generation pass on, no one may step into the void, and a family can lose its anchor. Children miss that special person and the family rituals (even teenage boys, who will swear to you that they are "grown"). One way to avoid this is to rotate whose house everyone goes to for a holiday each year.

Use these events as opportunities to tell your children stories about their family members and their ancestors. African culture is an oral tradition in which our legacy as a people is passed on through storytelling. It's a great time to tell the younger ones about their family (plus it gives the adults an excuse to tell embarrassing stories about one another!). With our older children we have noticed that the stories told at these family gatherings—which are often hilarious—become treasured and repeated again and again to their friends as they get older.

Another holiday occasion is Kwanzaa, an African American celebration each year from December 26 to January 1. Created by Dr. Maulana Karenga, Kwanzaa has grown in popularity and is now celebrated by large numbers of African American families. In Maulana Karenga's book on the holiday (see Resources at the end of this chapter), he explains that the word *Kwanzaa* was derived from a Swahili word meaning "first fruits." It is a special cultural celebration based on the "Nguzu Saba (the Seven Principles). These principles call upon African Americans to commit to the values of: Umoja (Unity); Kujichagulia (Self-Determination); Ujima (Collective Work and Responsibility); Ujamaa (Cooperative Economics); Nia (Purpose); Kuymba (Creativity); and Imani (Faith)."

Dr. Karenga describes Kwanzaa as a special time for gathering together family and friends to honor spiritual values (the Creator and Creation); a commemoration of ancestors who have died; and an opportunity to commit oneself once again to the spiritual and cultural values of "life, truth, justice, sisterhood, brotherhood, respect . . . for the human person, for elders and for nature." Dr. Karenga's book describes the symbols and the ceremony.

Many African Americans who celebrate Christmas follow it with Kwanzaa, which has become a special ritual and tradition for many families.

Family reunions have always been very popular with African Americans, and in recent years even more families have embraced this tradition. If your family or extended family does not have such a ritual, consider starting one. Start small, including just people in the immediate family or in a small geographic area. We traditionally have our family reunion every Fourth of July at our house. This has been our way of keeping our adult and adolescent children close to us and to their extended family.

Family vacations together can also be important (and memorable) rituals. They have had a particularly special meaning in our family. When A.J.'s first marriage ended, he struggled to spend special time with the children in the summer. He rented a small beach house in Virginia Beach for a month each summer. Grandma (A.J.'s mom), his brother, and all of the cousins (and all of the cats) would share the house for that month each year. When Nancy entered the family, she joined in these summer vacations. This became a very important part of our family's bonding time. To this day, many years later, Virginia Beach stories are still the source of many fond memories. It also helped to create special bonds between the cousins and our godchildren who lived in Virginia Beach, and they spent many summers together.

Each of these family rituals reaffirm the belief which we inherit from our African ancestors: "I am because we are, because we are, therefore, I am." When our sons encounter the realities of racism and hardships in the world, these same rituals will inoculate them, help them preserve their identity, and will nurture their much needed sense of belonging.

RESOURCES

Gardner, Richard. *Psychotherapy with Children of Divorce*. Northvale, NJ: J. Aronson, 1991.

Karenga, Maulana. *Kwanzaa: A Celebration of Family, Community and Culture)*. Los Angeles: University of Sankore Press, 1998, 2560 West 54th Street, Los Angeles, CA 90043; (323) 295-9799.

Kunjufu, Jawanza. *Countering the Conspiracy to Destroy Black Boys*. Chicago: African American Images, 1985.

White, Joseph, James Coñes III. *Black Man Emerging: Facing the Past and Seizing a Future in America*. New York: Routledge, 1999.

3

No One Can Uproot the Tree Which God Has Planted.
—Yoruba Proverb

Spirituality and Religion in Raising Our Sons

I was heading downhill fast. I had been arrested twice for drugs. But my mom wouldn't give up, she kept praying for me and talkin' to me and getting help for me. She finally turned me around. (Jarrod, age nineteen)

Many African American men, in describing their journey to manhood, identify a strong spiritual family member—often a mother, grandmother, father, or grandfather—who prayed for them constantly and never gave up. One might have taken him to church, seen that he went to Sunday school or joined a youth group where he could be with "good kids," or instilled spiritual values in him in other ways. This effort on the part of caring, spiritually grounded adults often helps to make the difference between boys who survive the lure of the streets and those who don't. It also helps parents survive the task of raising healthy children. "I don't know what I would do as a parent if it wasn't for God in my life," says one recently divorced mother of three teenage sons.

The Importance of Spirituality
to Our Ancestors

Spirituality was a part of every aspect of life in Africa. Traditional spiritual beliefs were tied to a fundamental belief about how to be a person. Dr. John S. Mbiti, a professor of African religious studies, notes, "A person cannot detach himself from the [spirituality] of his group, for to do so is to be severed from his roots, his foundation, his context of security, his kinships and the entire group of those who make him aware of his own existence."

In traditional Africa, much time and energy was spent in prayer, worship, sacrifice, and ceremony in the belief that once the god or gods were consulted, life would go well. But in many traditional beliefs, spirituality was also a part of everyday living. It formed a part of how a person acted in the world. One of the very powerful messages of Alex Haley's book *Roots* was how African spiritual beliefs were a central focus in the survival of the many generations of his family.

It is very important to teach our children about the cultural as well as the religious roots of their spirituality. We can look to both our African origins and our African American culture to provide powerful principles for our sons and daughters to live by.

One important spiritual lesson we can take from our African ancestors is the notion of collective unity. For all African tribes, there was a spiritual link between the God of the universe, the survival of the tribe, and the individual. Therefore, unlike the American system where the individual is most important, most African belief systems have as their basis the concept described by Dr. John Mbiti as "I am because we are; and because we are, therefore, I am."

This concept of collective unity and survival extended beyond the individual and the family to the community. For many of us, the spiritual connection and sense of allegiance to our people has expressed itself in our desire to "give something back" to our community. When many of us were growing up, this message was given to us by our parents. So many of our young people today, unfortunately, have not had this value instilled in them. Our sons can learn a valuable lesson as they observe us—especially mothers and fathers—being givers of ourselves. This process begins with those in our immediate surroundings.

There is a lot of meaning behind the golden rule, "Do unto others as you would have them do unto you." Our children must come to understand that their behavior has a direct impact on their communities. What we do for and in our communities defines our communities. This strong belief in community can also "inoculate" our children, particularly our sons, against negative forces.

Countless studies have shown that being spiritually centered along with having a strong support network of extended family, friends, and peers can help to lessen the risks from temptations and influences leading to destructive behavior. By the frequent repetition and modeling of these beliefs, we become "the voice in our children's ears" and living examples for them as they grow, become more independent, venture out of the home, and are exposed to the culture of the streets.

Spirituality and Modeling Values

Many of us of African descent throughout the world share a deep and abiding sense of spirituality and a belief in God or a higher power. This spirituality has provided strength and proven to be a survival skill in times of trouble. We have all heard countless stories or testimonies of the power of faith at work in people's lives and in overcoming whatever crisis they endured. For some, this spirituality is expressed by active involvement and attendance at a church, mosque, or hall; for others, it is a more private spirituality or a personal relationship with God. Still others find that they need a balance of both the private and the public aspects of their faith in their lives.

Many of us find guidance for our values in formal religious practices, but regardless of our faith and our view of the world, respect for other people, dignity, making and keeping commitments, and fulfilling responsibilities are all an extension of our spiritual being. It is fundamental to our setting goals, believing in ourselves, having confidence in what we are doing, and getting through life.

We believe that for spirituality to be a source of power in our lives, especially as black parents, it must be relevant to our day-to-day struggles. It cannot simply be a religion we subscribe to once a week—or once a year—if it is to do us any real good. As parents, it is very important that we live out our spiritual beliefs before our sons. Only as we exhibit strong spiritual beliefs and a commitment to open communication with our sons can these beliefs become an integral part of their lives: if these spiritual beliefs are true for us, then they will bear good fruit in our lives.

The Spiritual and Religious Diversity in the Black Community

Tremendous diversity among religious and spiritual beliefs exists in the African American community. This diversity includes: Baptist, African Methodist Episcopal (AME), AME Zion, Methodist, Episcopalian, Catholic, Presbyterian, Lutheran, Church of God in Christ, Jehovah's Witnesses, and Seventh Day Adventists. African Americans are also members of the Nation of Islam, Sunni Muslim, and other Muslim groups. Still others are involved in the practice of African religions, such as Yoruba (from Nigeria) or practice the religions of ancient Egypt. Some African Americans who do not believe in formal religions may have a deep sense of spirituality and feel connected in a spiritual way to a higher power and to their culture, their family, and community. Whatever your spiritual belief system, we encourage you to share it with your sons and to encourage them to make it an active part of their lives. This is one of the most significant contributions that you can make to them, and to their future as black men. Help them to understand how the power of your spiritual beliefs strengthens you and helps you to recover from difficult times.

In this book, we share our experiences and favorite readings. We respect your religious and spiritual traditions and ask that you search for similar spiritual messages in your own belief system. We believe that many of the messages of spiritual empowerment and survival are universal and transcend our differences.

The Contribution of the Nation of Islam and Other Muslim Groups

A number of African Americans today are members of the Nation of Islam or of other Muslim groups such as Sunni Muslims. The Nation of Islam has provided spiritual guidance for many African Americans. The 1995 "Million Man March" in Washington, D.C., demonstrated the ability of the Nation of Islam to organize and inspire record numbers of African American men to be positive examples to their sons, families, communities, and the nation at large.

The Nation of Islam also has an extensive prison ministry. The power of their message has turned men's lives around from crime, drugs, and violence. One compelling example of this can be found in the life of Malcolm X. Those in the African American community who are concerned about the survival of young black men would do well to study the strategies employed by this group to empower African American men to be devoted husbands and fathers actively engaged in positive spiritual, economic, and community development whether or not they share this group's beliefs, or disagree with the teachings of its leaders.

Influence of African American Churches

Black churches have served a religious, spiritual, political, educational, cultural, and familial role in our communities. When many of us were growing up, they played a central role in black community life. Ministers were often respected community leaders. Churches today are experiencing a rebirth of interest and attendance on the part of adults and teenagers. This is especially true for African American churches. Young families are realizing the need for church in their lives and the lives of their children. For many, the challenge of raising black children in today's world leads them to want to seek all of the supports that they can for their children and families. In response to the needs of adolescents, more churches have created youth programs and services.

Finding a "Church Family"

Church has always been a source of solace, help, release, and relationships for black families. We rarely just praise the Lord and go home in the black church. There is a history of activities in our houses of worship—from meeting social needs to offering services of all kinds to members and the community. Today many churches offer special support for parents with children in the form of youth ministries, sports programs, men's groups, and fellowship times just for single moms. Many African Americans tell us that their closest friendships are nurtured through their church affiliation.

If you regularly attend a church you enjoy, you are in a great position to give and receive support. If you have children, choose a church that has services for them, such as a well-staffed nursery, Sunday school, or youth choir. If none of these services exist at your church, maybe you and a friend can start a ministry to parents, or begin a youth program. Don't be afraid to get involved and develop relationships with people beyond the "God bless you!" and a kiss on the cheek. Get involved in other activities besides Sunday service. Church is supposed to be a place where people of like mind meet together for fellowship, pray for one another, and seek to meet one another's needs as they are able. Carol, in the story below, illustrates how beneficial her church was to her family.

When she rang in the New Year, Carol found herself newly divorced with three teenage children and no reliable support. Her sisters-in-law and the mothers of her children's friends were okay, but many didn't share the beliefs she had about parenting. They often cursed and drank in front of their children, and would do the same when her children visited their homes. One day her fifteen-year-old daughter came home drunk from a day-long visit to Aunt Dottie, who was supposed to "baby-sit." When Carol demanded an explanation, she was told she was overreacting. She was often the butt of their friendly jokes and called "Miss Perfect Mother." Carol wasn't perfect, she just knew that she wanted more for her children than what she saw around her.

The bright light in Carol's life was her volunteer work at her church. There she was surrounded by other parents of teenagers who were trying to raise their children the same way she was. She talked with these parents as they ministered side by side. She observed how their children behaved and

*how they handled situations. These like-minded people told her about
church-based programs designed for teenagers. Now her son attends the
youth basketball league and her daughters attend an afternoon "homework club." All her children attend the church sleep-away camp. These
activities keep them busy after school and over the summer, nurture their
relationships with "good" kids, and put them in an environment where
moral principles are taught and exampled.*

Just as the sense of collective unity extends to the family and
community, it can extend to the church family as well. This is
such an ingrained belief that many African American families
readily seek out a "church family" when they move to a new community. This certainly has been true for us.

We were both raised in families with strong religious and spiritual beliefs. A.J.'s father was a Baptist minister; his mother and
grandmother were a central part of their church. Nancy's mother
is a deeply spiritual Catholic; her father was originally raised as a
Baptist but converted to Catholicism when he married her
mother. Although we both always had strong spiritual beliefs, we
had moved away from organized church involvement. Although
we shared our spiritual beliefs with our older kids and they often
attended services at their grandmother's church, we did not formally join a church as a family.

We became aware of how important this involvement was
when our older son wrote an essay for his college application in
which he talked about how he wished that he had had more of an
emphasis on spirituality and religious training in his upbringing.
His words touched us and influenced how we have raised our
younger son and the decisions we have made in his life. We
joined a church in Brooklyn when he was very young. Our
description of the process of our move to New Jersey will help you
to see how important this focus has now become.

As native New Yorkers, our view of the world for many years
was narrowly defined by "The City." When Nancy accepted a position at Rutgers University, we began to consider a move to New
Jersey. This prospect filled us with concern. Would we find a
viable black community there? A friend had told us that to define
the "African American community" in New Jersey often meant
asking yourself, "How many black people can we drive to in a half
hour?" This was a new concept for us. How could we ensure that

our younger son (our last child at home) would have strong black role models in his life?

With these concerns in mind, we searched for a "church home" or "church family." Many of Nancy's coworkers at Rutgers were surprised by the fact that we sought and found a church home even before we found our own home. We had felt very supported in our church home in Brooklyn, and we wanted that sense of connection for ourselves and our family in a new community.

African American churches can provide an anchor for our sons as well. We felt we had to find a church that had a strong youth ministry with activities and an atmosphere that would interest our teenage son. We found a wonderful Baptist church. This church, in addition to the traditional offerings of Sunday school, Junior Usher Board, and the Young Adult Choir, has a one o'clock service conducted by the Youth Ministry, ski trips, basketball league, plays, talent shows, and special singing groups. These opportunities for our young people to speak and be recognized are a part of the fabric of black churches everywhere. They also keep young people, particularly our young men, engaged in church as they become adolescents.

Music with a relevant message and hip flavor, such as the work of artists like Kirk Franklin, Fred Hammond, Dawkins and Dawkins, Yolanda Adams, BeBe and CeCe Winans, Lauryn Hill, and others inspires our youth and people all over the world. Christian comedians such as Sister Cantaloupe serve the same purpose. Whether it's the beat or the humor that "gets them in the door," they end up hearing a message behind the music. Our pastor has encouraged many groups of young people in the community to develop their talents and to perform and praise God at our church services. This provides the very strong messages adolescents need to hear from us: "You are gifted and talented," "You can do it," "We believe in you," "We value you," and "You are somebody."

We take up a collection every year for a scholarship fund for our grads who are going on to college. During various vacation times throughout the year, all college students are asked to stand and are welcomed home. Our pastor stays in touch with some of them when they are away at college by E-mail. He also acknowledges them in front of the congregation for special achievements, such as graduating from college.

If you are a parent who is searching for positive influences for your sons (children), even if you aren't a regular churchgoer, you may want to consider finding a church as a way to introduce your children to spiritual values and positive African American cultural values. There will probably be a small community church nearby where you can get individual attention. There are also large churches that offer a variety of services and programs. Visit places of worship that have positive youth programs in your community. You might take your cue from your children. Tell them that you want them to be a part of a church but that they can have some input in making the choice. Take the whole family, including the younger children, or visit different places of worship and then have a family discussion about which place each found most welcoming. Let them know in advance that although everyone will have input, you, as parents, will have the final vote.

If you have been part of a church home for a long time, ask yourself if the church is meeting your son's needs as he grows older. If not, push your church to create a positive youth ministry. Volunteer to help create it. If you are still unsatisfied, consider a change to a church that is more responsive to the needs of its youth. Here are some suggestions:

- Search for and find a supportive church family. Visit churches in your area and see where you feel comfortable.
- Seek out someone at church whom you admire or have heard about, or who just seems warm and friendly, and ask for their prayers on a problem.
- Go up to your minister, one of the deaconesses, deacons, or elders after the service and ask for help and prayers for your son and for you. You do not have to tell people your whole life story in order to ask for their prayers. Just ask them to "lift me and my son up in prayer."

Adolescent Rebellion and Spirituality

Many parents are surprised that religion or spirituality are often the "family values" against which teenagers rebel. We have heard many times from parents who were able to get their children to attend church when they were younger, but are now experiencing battles as they get older. This may be a very difficult period. We become alarmed when we feel that, in moving away from core spiritual beliefs, our kids will be more vulnerable to street influences. Studies have shown that young men who had gone to church as children were less likely to become involved in gangs, drugs, and crime as adults.

It is very important that we continue to encourage our sons to attend church with us as a family, even when Sunday morning church attendance begins to compete with Saturday night partying or hanging out. There are certain behaviors that parents can insist upon as long as children are living in their home, and this is one of them.

C. Eric Lincoln and Lawrence H. Mimiya, both professors of religion, wrote a compelling book based on their study of *The Black Church in the African American Experience*. When asked why black youth pulled away from the church during their teenage and young adult years, the majority of clergy attributed reasons for their growing disinterest to three areas:

1. They believed youth got bored and/or the church does not have relevant programs for them.
2. Adults do not give youth a chance for meaningful participation in church programs.
3. This is a stage of life where youth search for their independence.

In spite of the tendency for kids, particularly our sons, to become disinterested and seemingly drift away from our religious and spiritual guidance, we can be comforted by the knowledge that "the apple doesn't fall too far from the tree"—in other words, that they will not stray too far from the values we have taught them. In fact, many of the teens who drift away from the church in their youth return once they have children of their own, if not sooner.

Teenage years are a time when young people question *everything*. This is very hard when it takes the form of rebellion against the spiritual values that we hold dear. Our fear gets in the way and we begin to worry about all of the trouble that our kids can encounter. One of the greatest tendencies during this time is to continue treating them like they are young children rather than respect their increasing ability to make some decisions on their own. We should guide their thinking and decision making in a responsible way, but should also give them an opportunity to express their opinions and views and not suppress them. Encourage them to tell you the questions (and doubts) that they are experiencing about their spiritual beliefs. Listen to them.

Have open discussions with them about your spiritual beliefs. Resist the urge to preach at them, or they will tune you out. Have faith in the spiritual foundation you have given them. They need your prayers and support during this time. Remember the African proverb, "No one can uproot the tree which God has planted."

Start Young

As with all of the values discussed in this book, religious and spiritual beliefs should be taught from a very young age. One of the best ways to do this is informally in your normal family activities. Say grace before meals. Have discussions over meals about your spiritual values. Bedtime for younger kids is a great time to pray together and talk about the events of the day and teach spiritual lessons. This can also be done through regular, weekly family time where you sit down and teach your child a different spiritual value. This can include personal sharing of one's spiritual view of the world, prayer, Bible study, discussing the reasons behind your values, or what's right and wrong behavior and why. There are numerous materials available at bookstores on spiritual, religious, or popular self-empowerment literature that can help you along. Also check out the young adult book series that profiles famous black heroes in sports and other fields and their faith in God.

Be a Role Model

It is important to be a good role model for your sons in the spiritual arena. This is particularly true for African American men. Fathers have a very powerful role to play. As discussed in the last chapter, we often encourage our daughters to attend church but become less insistent with our sons as they get older. This is a mistake. We need to give all our children both the emphasis and the push. All the better if Dad and Mom attend and are active in church also. This is one of the most important ways to be a good role model.

Be a Witness

Talk openly to your son about the role of your spirituality in your life. Even if you are not religious, share your spiritual beliefs with your son. Tell him stories of how you overcame adversity or worked out tough decisions because of your faith. These messages mold and shape the man that he will become. This sharing is particularly important for African American men because many young men equate spirituality with women. Be sure to tell them about important black religious figures such as Martin Luther King Jr. and Malcolm X who became powerful African American leaders. Give them a more complete view of male spirituality and an understanding of positive manhood, anchored in spiritual beliefs.

Spiritual *and* Relevant?
Messages for Our Sons

African American youth can often be overwhelmed by the negative messages that are conveyed by society. As important as it is to educate our children about the realities of racism so that they will be prepared and not personalize these negative messages, it is just as vital that we give positive, affirming spiritual messages to our sons from a very early age. The messages of "we shall overcome" and "nothing is impossible" become not just a matter of racial or cultural pride but strategies for building positive spiritual values, self-esteem, and self-image.

Our emphasis on spiritual values should also include helping young men and women to learn how to have a positive view about life. Teenage years are a time when young people believe that they are unique in their struggle against troubling circumstances. Too often the view held by many African American male teens is:

"I'm not going to live to see twenty-five." They have to believe that life is worth living, that they have a future to prepare for. One way to help cultivate a better attitude is to use the history of people of African descent and your specific family history as tools for teaching about life.

Tell them stories often of how your family members used their spiritual beliefs to overcome problems and to survive. Give them the value of respect for life as an important spiritual belief. If enough important people in young black men's lives give them that message, then it will go a long way to counteracting the violence in our communities.

Using African American history can be helpful in teaching black male teens about developing an inner spiritual center that guides their lives and helps them to make their unique contribution to society. There are many examples in our history of persons struggling and surviving difficult times. Biographies of historic and contemporary figures are replete with lessons about life as a black man. Herb Boyd and Robert L. Allen published a prize-winning anthology entitled *Brotherman; The Odyssey of Black Men in America,* which is an inspiring source of lessons on survival. Learning from our history develops not only respect for what others have managed to overcome but also an understanding and appreciation of how important their spiritual beliefs were through it all.

You also have to remember to be patient with your son. There is a saying in black churches that has special meaning for all African American parents: "God may not come when you want him to, but he always comes on time." When our sons get in trouble or are giving us trouble, we tend to want to fix them right away. We also want them to change their behavior right away. Unfortunately, things don't always work out on our own personal timetable.

Our sons are growing more independent and their peers support this growth, encouraging them to explore new experiences away from home and parents' watchful eye. It is difficult as parents to allow our sons to cut the apron strings and feel confident that they will not be swayed by all the temptations that exist. A parent can be patient in a responsible way by continuing to provide guiding suggestions, register concern, and be supportive and protective while allowing her son to make errors and learn from his mistakes. Neglect occurs when you throw up your hands and completely walk away from the duties of parenting. We advocate "responsible patience." Rely on your own good judgment to know when to intervene and when to leave him alone and give him time to come around.

A spiritual foundation is one of the most important supports during this time for both parent and son to guide them through these new experiences. Because each child is unique and approaches the challenges of life differently, these will be *new experiences*, even if you have gone through this stage with other children.

For many African American parents, grandparents, aunts, and uncles, raising a black male child is a cause for almost constant worry and anxiety. But if we don't keep our anxiety in check, it may contaminate our relationship with our sons and our relationship with God. For some parents (particularly mothers and grandmothers), worry causes us to hold on too tight, love too much, or do too much for them. As we discussed in the last chapter, this is what can lead us to "raise our daughters and love our sons."

Have you ever noticed that when you begin to worry, your thoughts go from bad to worse? This is not uncommon. One African American mom once told us that her son had gotten an F on a test, and after a few hours of "worry," she had gone from this one F to his failing every subject, dropping out of school, and becoming homeless on the street by age thirty.

The Power of Positive Thinking

Parents have to stay focused on a positive outcome even when things are not going well. One of our favorite books is *The Power of Positive Thinking* by Norman Vincent Peale. Its message is as relevant and powerful today as it was when it was first published almost fifty years ago. Our favorite chapters have powerful upbeat titles like "Believe in Yourself," "I Don't Believe in Defeat," and "Try Prayer Power." Books by Bishop T. D. Jakes, Reverend Samuel DeWitt Proctor, and others speak to the issues of self-esteem and the power of faith from a black male perspective. For parents with a spiritual orientation, a prayer approach can help us keep focused on the positive and fight anxiety and "fear thoughts." Reading the Psalms can also help to calm our fears.

In *The Power of Positive Thinking*, Peale points out that when we hold on to "fear thoughts," they tend to grow and fester. In the worst-case scenario, they can become self-fulfilling prophecies. Therefore, we must nip them in the bud quickly and effectively. We recommend telling yourself firmly to *stop it*. Then substitute Peale's "prayer formula": (1) *Prayerize*, (2) *Picturize*, and (3) *Actualize*. He encourages us to pray by actively using this system of creative prayer. When you have a problem with your son or begin to worry excessively about the harm that can befall him as a black man, talk this problem over with God. Tell him honestly what your worries are. Do this in a simple and direct manner, as if you were talking to a very trusted friend (which you are). Put your current concern in your own words:

"Sometimes I get so down I just don't know what to do. So I read my favorite Bible passage over and over. It's from Philippians 4:13, 'I can do all things through Christ, who strengthens me.' When I'm desperate I will even write it twenty-five times until it sinks in." (Paula, mother of a fourteen- and a seventeen-year-old son)

Praying for Our Sons

Many of us are fortunate enough to remember a special person(s) who believed in us "no matter what," and continued to pray for us all through our rebellious years in adolescence and young adulthood. You often hear, "My mama (or grandma or father) prayed for me." These prayers are often "bread cast upon the water" and are never wasted. Our sons need the protection of our daily prayers as they go out the door, and we need the comfort of knowing that our prayers are heard so we can get through the day.

We have also found it particularly powerful to write prayer affirmations. You can write them anytime you begin to worry. Tape them on the dashboard of your car or over your workstation at your job, or keep them in a drawer that you open often. Read them on the bus or train on your way to work or at stoplights while driving. For example, you can say or write:

- Thank you, dear God, for keeping Kareem safe.
- Thank you, dear God, for protecting Hakim as he starts his new job.
- Thank you, dear God, for helping me to find help for Steven.
- Thank you, dear God, for protecting my children and all of my family today and every day.
- Thank you, dear God, for allowing David to pass all of his exams and graduate this year.

This is also a way to develop confidence in yourself and focus your efforts. The following are examples of statements of faith:

- I believe I will be guided toward the best answer for John and for all of us.
- I have faith that I will be guided toward the best decision.
- Thank you, dear God, for filling me with your wisdom and guidance as I prepare for tomorrow.

As you pray, focus on the positive outcome you want for your son. Try to avoid allowing negative images to form in your head or to slip into your prayers. If this happens, some of these negative images may be created. Don't pray the problem, pray the solution.

Nancy tells the following story:

A black mom came to me for help with her son, who was addicted to drugs and in trouble with the police. When I asked this mother what she had done to try to help her son, she responded, "I prayed for him." I then asked her to give me some examples of how she might pray. Her response was, "Dear Lord, thank you for keeping me from killing this child!" I smiled at her sense of humor and then worked with her to make her prayers for her son even more powerful by focusing on positive wording and affirmations.

When I asked her what she was doing to deal with this situation, she replied, "I have turned him over to the Lord." I admired her faith. What I found out in the following conversation, however, was that in giving the situation to God, this mom had stopped being a parent. She had given up on trying to monitor him or have an influence in his life, saying that it was in God's hands. But God's direction always involves our active participation in some form. This mother was relying on God to perform a miracle without performing her part of the bargain—taking the practical steps needed to see that her prayers were answered. I asked her to go home and pray out loud over her son each morning before she left home and each evening when she first saw him. She was to ask him about his day and find out what he had been up to. I encouraged her to thank God for helping her son and for showing her how to help him.

A month later, her son was arrested for possession of drugs. She was very angry in her session and at God because she perceived this as a negative answer to her prayers. I pointed out that God may have given the answer in a form that she did not expect. This proved to be the case. The judge sentenced her son to a residential drug rehab program. This was the beginning of the "miracle" that got him off drugs, turned his life around, and answered his mother's prayers.

Try to make sure your image for your son and God's plan for him match. We have often found it helpful to add: "This or something better we ask in Your Name" at the end of our prayers. God is likely to have an even better idea or plan for your son than the one you have imagined.

The Payoff

At the end of the rainbow, when you have sown the seeds of spirituality into your son's life, have been role models for him, and have provided a positive spiritual environment in which he can grow, you still must exercise faith that the payoff will come. But we will not pray this in fear. We will be praying confidently in faith and expectancy, knowing that if he has been raised with these principles, he will come back to them and they will sustain him through the period of rebellion. The payoff is a son you are proud to call your own. He makes decisions you can have more confidence in as he grows older and you can no longer control him. He will choose his friends wisely and think before he acts. He can handle life's pressures with grace (or he at least calls home for advice!). He will make a good husband to the right woman, and a worthy father to a child someday (but not too soon!); and, of course, the moment we're all waiting for, he will become independent and can also acknowledge the spiritual lessons you have taught him and practice them in his own life.

RESOURCES

Hopson, Darlene, and Derek Hopson. *The Power of Soul: Pathways to Psychological and Spiritual Growth for African Americans.* New York: William Morrow, 1998.

Jakes, T.D. *Water in the Wilderness.* Lanham, MD: Pneuma Life, 1996.

Mbiti, John S. *African Religions and Philosophy.* New York: Doubleday, 1970.

Peale, Norman Vincent. *The Power of Positive Thinking.* New York: Ballantine, 1996.

Proctor, Samuel D., and William D. Watley. *Sermons from the Black Pulpit.* Valley Forge, PA: Judson Press, 1984.

4

◆

THE BELL RINGS LOUDEST IN YOUR OWN HOME.
—YORUBA PROVERB

Positive Parenting, Love, Communication, and Discipline

In African American culture and in our history as a people, we have always viewed good parenting and strong family values as a protection against the many evils our children will encounter. When parents are faced with all the things that can go wrong or harm our kids, we can become overwhelmed and feel powerless. Parenting is a very humbling experience. It is important to remember (and remind ourselves often) that we are *the* most important influence in our children's lives. We can make a difference for them. Good parenting combines love, communication, clear consequences, and discipline. If you begin with this combination and stick to it, you will produce a son you can be proud of.

◆ ◆ ◆

If you want to know the end look at the beginning.

—African proverb

◆ ◆ ◆

Love Your Son

Love, unconditional and frequently stated, is the cornerstone in any parent-child relationship. Clear parental messages of love and understanding have a very powerful effect on our children. African American parents are often very affectionate with our children when they are younger, but as our sons grow up, they still need to be told often that we love them, even when they are taller than we are: Stating our love out loud has a positive effect on us too, because it focuses us on the positive aspects of our sons. This is especially important when we are involved in a struggle with them.

Remember that the job of an adolescent is to grow up. In order to do this they have to become more independent. Knowing, feeling, and hearing that they are loved provides a safety net as they venture out on their own. Physical affection is also important. A hug can go a long way to remind your son of your caring and may cause him to remember the positive aspects of his love for you.

For African American males, the message of love also should help validate them as young black men. They must be constantly told and shown that they are somebody (and that their ancestors were somebody) and that they can achieve anything they want to in this world.

Be Available—Take the Time

In today's busy world, most parents are torn between the demands of work and family. This pressure is even greater for single parents, who carry the total burden—having to provide financial as well as emotional support for their children. It is very important, however, that you set aside regular and predictable times when you can spend time with your kids. Many families find it difficult even to eat a meal together today. Look at your schedule. Find a few evenings when you and your family can all share dinner. If this seems impossible, find a regular breakfast or brunch time when you can spend time eating together and talking.

Use time in the car, bus, or train while you're traveling to school or other activities to talk with your children. As native New

Yorkers who were used to walking or taking the subway, it was a rude awakening when we moved to New Jersey and had to drive our son everywhere. The silver lining, however, was discovering that this was a great time for talking, listening, and just being together. Although your son may never admit it, he enjoys this time as much as you do when he can have you all to himself.

If you have more than one child, try to find a special time to spend with each child regularly. This is particularly hard for single parents with two or more children. Although little kids often need and want this special time every day, teenagers often enjoy going on an outing with a parent. These rituals become occasions that our kids remember and talk about as they grow older. It's also a great time to tell stories about your childhood, find out what might be bothering your son, talk about what's going on, and have spontaneous "teaching moments." Keep these times fun, where you are both doing something you enjoy and being with someone you enjoy.

One of A.J.'s favorite father/son or daughter events is going to Knicks games. He shares tickets to Knicks games with some friends, and all of our children look forward to their special night. Some of our most important conversations have occurred during or traveling to or from the games.

In another example, Nancy and our younger son have very different taste in movies. At sixteen, he loves action films—the more explosions, the better. Nancy likes movies he describes as "mushy." But they enjoy going to the movies together, so they explore the listings together to find something that they can both enjoy.

It's worth the effort to compromise in this way. Our kids can tell when we are suffering through rather than enjoying an activity. Trade off interests on some evenings or take turns on finding activities. Make sure you do not use this special time to talk to your children in a way that they will perceive as lecturing them.

Simple things you can do to spend time with your son:

- Play video or computer games together.
- Watch his favorite TV show or watch a video.
- Watch a basketball or football game on TV together.

Teach Positive Racial and Male Identity

Throughout this book, we have stressed providing a positive racial and male identity for African American boys. It is essential that they know who they are and where they came from. Even in their high school years young men need to have positive images and words constantly before them. Our boys are often hungry for models of how to be strong, caring black men. We cannot be passive in this process.

It is very important that we pay attention to the fact that they are male as well as to the fact that they are black. We are well aware that being black and male places them at risk for mistreatment in the world. Our clear messages about positive male values including self-esteem, responsibility, courage in the face of evil, persistence, spirituality, inner strength, respect for women, and love and protection of family and children will have a profound effect on them and on their development as men.

Pride in their people, a knowledge of their history and culture, and the desire to make a difference for their community can also become protective factors that can help immunize them against street life, drugs and alcohol, gangs, and peer influences. Talk openly and often about the accomplishments of black people and encourage them to do so also. Tell them the stories of our African American heroes. Teach them their history.

Give Praise

Many African American parents pay a great deal of attention to discipline, but they forget one of the most important rules of parenting: praise is the most powerful reinforcement we have as parents. We must "catch them being good." Don't forget that your approval means a great deal to your sons. Research has shown that praise from parents can profoundly influence the behavior of children even as they get older.

In our work with families, many black parents have responded: "Why should I praise him for getting good grades or doing his chores? He is supposed to do that." We can only respond that it works—and can dramatically change their behavior. Often we become burdened by the things that are going wrong and forget about the positive efforts our children are making. Compare the two following examples:

Al, a tenth-grader, had gotten an F on his report card in geometry, and his parents were justifiably concerned. They gave him a good talking to and met with his teacher, and arranged for a friend of the family to tutor him. His grades began to improve. The next marking period, he got a C. But his parents were furious—they yelled at him, called him lazy, and told him that he was never going to get anywhere if he didn't start applying himself. As a result, he stopped trying and gave up on that year.

Will, also in tenth grade, was failing chemistry, largely because he had not been doing or handing in his lab reports. His mother was very angry and punished him by grounding him for the week and taking away his video game time. He worked hard and finished some of the reports. His grade for the next week was a C. His mother acknowledged what he had done: "You have definitely tried harder this week and have gotten in many more lab reports. Let's see if you can get them all done for next week and bring this grade up to an A."

In the first example, Al feels only his parents' criticism and he shuts down. Will hears validation for his efforts and a clear message to try harder. With his mother's encouragement, he is motivated to work toward a better grade.

Make the Praise Real

It is very important that praise be real and specific. Kids can see through phony praise or compliments that are too general. They tend to dismiss or not take seriously comments such as "You are such a good son." Specific praise gives a very clear message. Try something like, "I was very proud of you for studying so hard on that test. I know it was not easy." Specific praise is also your way of conveying the values that are most important to you. If you value honesty, for example, you can say, "I am very glad that you were honest with me about what really happened after school."

Praise should reward not only the end result (or grade), but also the effort that went into it. It is often in the early phases when kids are first trying to change a behavior that they are most likely to give up.

Good Listening: Tools for Effective Communication

Many parents are under the impression that communication involves mainly talking to their children, but positive communication involves another necessary component: listening. Some African American parents are particularly vulnerable to a form of communication called preaching. We come by it honestly—many of our parents preached at us. As we get older we forget our own response to that preaching—we often tuned our parents out. Our eyes were open but our minds were someplace else. Our son refers to this as "the light is on but there is no one home." Remember that our kids learn their communication skills from *us*!

Effective communication requires skills of speaking *and* listening. So often parents will say, "I talk to him all the time," not realizing that this may be part of the problem. Talking "to" and talking "with" are two very different things.

In his book *Parenting for Prevention,* David Wilmes discusses two kinds of listening: active and facilitative. As a parent, active listening means hearing the message and repeating it back to your son in your response. It means not just paying attention to what is being said, but also engaging in more of a dialogue, so that the person who is talking hears you repeat what they are saying in your own words. Asking questions, making sure you get all the important details, indicating your understanding of what they are saying, and providing the appropriate body language, such as eye contact, are all part of active listening. Using Wilmes's categories, the following examples illustrate how Tom's mother actively listens to his report of a fight in school:

- She asks appropriate questions: "Who started the fight?"; "Who was involved?"
- She makes sure she understands him correctly: "You're saying that Akil just hit you for no reason."
- She offers him verbal encouragement to continue: "I hear you," "Uh-huh," "I see what you mean."
- She looks at her son while he's talking, not at the television or her watch.

Wilmes's last category is very important because our kids can read our nonverbal "what we do" as clearly as "what we say." The same way we can tell when our kids are tuning us out, they can sense when our minds are on work, our problems, or other things. Active listening requires facial expressions that show you are paying attention to the other person and care about what they are saying.

With facilitative listening parents help kids to clarify their feelings and then figure out ways to deal with their problems rather than just serving as a sounding board. Facilitative listening is a true discussion that involves two partners in the conversation equally. Wilmes points out that facilitative listening on the part of parents assumes a level of maturity in their children to verbalize and act on their own feelings and life experiences. They will need your help when the problem is very upsetting or is a very emotional issue for them. Here's an example:

Son *(in angry tone)*: That teacher just dissed me.

Father: What do you mean?

Son: He said that I was never going to get into college.

Father *(trying to control his own anger)*: What did he mean by that?

Son: He said I don't apply myself enough.

Father: What do you think about that?

Son: I think he's wrong. He's going by my grade on one exam and putting me down.

Father: Sounds like you're angry at him for not seeing your potential.

Son: Darn right I am.

Father: So what are you going to do about it?

Son: I guess I'll blow him away on the next exam.

This is a good example because many black parents are so aware of negative messages to their sons and are quick to attribute them to racism. This father controlled his anger long enough to find out the circumstances, and then to help his son to find a solution for himself.

Be aware that as adolescents, our sons become very adept at testing us or getting a rise out of us. They can come out with provocative statements like:

- "It was only one exam."
- "I'll still get into college if I get C's."
- "Everyone else in my class does it!"
- "The cops have it in for me."
- "If I didn't have sex with her, I would have hurt her feelings."

These comments would provoke a reaction in most parents. The challenge is to keep from getting angry and help your son explain more fully what he means by his statement, and giving us the reasoning behind his conclusion. If we simply start preaching, a constructive dialogue never occurs.

In his book *Surviving Your Adolescents* Thomas Phelan advises parents to use self-restraint and gives three goals for these forms of communication: "(1) not killing the conversation; (2) not killing the kid, and (3) knowing how to help the conversation along."

Teenage Rebellion

If your son, who always listened to you, is now talking back, defiant, and "in your face," constantly breaking rules, and/or messing up in school, then he (and you) have arrived at that dreaded juncture called teenage rebellion. All parents of adolescents live with fear about the consequences. Signs of teenage rebellion such as school failure, trouble with the law, drug and alcohol abuse, sexual acting out, and gang involvement often are viewed much more harshly when committed by African American males. All kids rebel to some degree. This rebellion is a combination of the sexual, physical, and emotional changes that accompany the onset of puberty. Some parents breathe a sigh of relief when their well-behaved kids go off to college or graduate high school and get a job, only to discover that the rebellion comes in college or in their son's twenties.

So what should you do? Some parents panic in response to teenage rebellion and attempt to crack down by becoming overly controlling and punitive. This is understandable. We are scared (make that terrified) for our sons. We know that our sons often venture into "hostile territory" out in the world.

If you are a parent faced with rebellion, remember that it is normal for teens. Look at the behavior and realistically assess how serious it is. Pay attention to whether it is destructive or will lead to serious long-term consequences. In his book *Smart Parenting for African Americans,* Jeffrey Gardere encourages parents to:

- Calm down. Don't panic.
- Seek the advice of experienced parents whose children have turned out well.
- If bad behavior escalates, seek professional help from a counselor, therapist, or another trained practitioner. (See the Resources section at the end of Chapter 13 for information on how to get help.)
- "Pick your battles." Don't fight with your kids over everything or you will be worn out long before they finish adolescence. Prioritize the most serious problems and go after those first.
- "Never make a decision when angry." Dr. Gardere points out that "some of the most tragic and accidental cases of child abuse occur when a parent is angry and disciplining the child at the same time."
- Take the time to chill first.
- Let your son know that you will definitely deal with this behavior later. If you are unable to discipline him at the time you learn of the misbehavior, be sure not to let him get away with it, by forgetting to discipline him later.

Set Clear Limits

As parents, you must set strong, clear limits for your son. Setting limits is one of the parental tools that most differentiates the kids who make it from those who do not. If there is any ambiguity in the limits, adolescents may take advantage by twisting our words. Setting limits gives them clear guidelines on what they can and cannot do. This should start as early as possible. Some families post the rules on the refrigerator so that everyone in the household is aware of what they are.

The following guidelines from David Wilmes have been helpful to parents:

- Make sure that the limits are clear. Write them down. Ask your son to repeat them for you.
- The limit should be age appropriate. For example, kids should have a curfew. While ten o'clock might be an appropriate weekend curfew for a fourteen-year-old, a sixteen-year-old may be given the later curfew of midnight.
- Only by obeying the rules will a child earn trust and increased flexibility.
- Parents must agree on the limits. This is very important. The classic formula for teenage acting out is two parents who are in disagreement about the limits and who give different messages to the adolescent.

Remember that the word *parent* should not be taken narrowly. In African American families many blood and nonblood relatives help to "parent" our children. If Grandma has always been your child's caretaker and she disagrees with you on parenting issues, your child will get mixed messages. *Adults must agree on the rules, and on the consequences if a rule is broken.*

Effective Consequences and Discipline

Make sure that you set up appropriate consequences, punishments, and discipline for misbehavior and stick to them. In his book *Parenting for Prevention,* David Wilmes emphasizes that consequences should be:

- *Related to the misbehavior.* Give consequences that relate to the incident that you are trying to punish. If your son is late for curfew, an appropriate consequence would be grounding him for the weekend, rather than allowing him to continue to go out.
- *Reasonable.* Avoid excessive amounts of time for punishments, such as, "You're grounded for a year!"
- *Timely.* Enforce the consequences as soon as possible after the incident.
- *Simple.* If the rules and consequences are too complicated, the system can backfire.
- *Progressive.* The first time your son neglects his chores, you

might explain to him that the only way to earn privileges (like going away for the weekend or getting a new bike) is to first take care of his responsibilities. The second time, one of his privileges must be taken away. The third time he loses that privilege for a longer period of time.

- *Consistent.* Avoid making up new rules and new consequences. This shows inconsistency in your parenting style, a quality your son will spot quickly and take advantage of. Make sure that they are agreed to by all family members. If your rule as a mother is that your son cannot use your credit card, make sure Grandma doesn't slip him hers.
- *Enforced—with love.* Anger will not get you far in teaching your son discipline. It will only get you upset and the lesson behind the consequence will be lost.

Wilmes gives the following guidelines on what to avoid:

- *"Seeking revenge."* When our sons misbehave, we are embarrassed and hurt. This makes us angry. If that anger is not controlled and rechanneled, we will strike out at our sons, the objects of our hurt at that moment, with a revengeful heart instead of a loving, correcting one.
- *"Punishing ourselves."* Keeping your son in the house every evening and weekend for a month might be more torture for *you* than for him! Think about the effect certain consequences might have on you and the family before you enforce them.
- *"Rewarding inappropriate behavior."* This is a "throw up your hands" response to parenting. For example, Ty is always on the Internet when his parents tell him to shut it off, so they buy him his own computer for his own room. Now they have given up control of that area of his life.
- *Blowing up or getting explosively angry.* This can often backfire and lead to a physical fight or confrontation.
- *"Making threats or promises."* Statements that begin "If you don't, I'll . . ." or "If you do, I'll give you . . ." bring you down to the level of the child. You are no longer in charge; you are bargaining to get obedience.
- *"Shaming" your son.* Though you may not believe it, your son

feels guilty when he does something wrong. But he will feel ashamed when he thinks he is bad. You must make a distinction between bad behavior and being a bad person. The former teaches him responsibility for his actions; the latter damages his self-esteem. Remember to: (1) validate his needs as a person and (2) avoid dehumanizing punishment (such as name calling, physical abuse, humiliation).

- *Overdoing consequences.* If all that we do as parents is set consequences for behavior, this may signal more serious family problems. Make sure that punishing negative behavior and imposing consequences is not the only interaction you have with your son.

All kids test the limits—even good kids who try hard and have never been in any trouble. Many parents are not prepared for this difficult aspect of adolescence, and they say things in anger like, "You're going to be stuck in this house for life," or "No TV, video games, or CDs for the rest of the school year"—consequences that they cannot possibly enforce. Give a reasonable time frame like one week. The hardest part of parenting is to be true to your word. Teens become confused easily when they are given mixed messages.

Follow-through is extremely important. It is best if your son knows in advance what will happen if he does a certain thing, or acts a certain way. For example, let's say you have a "no drug or alcohol" rule and your seventeen-year-old son comes home drunk. You have told him that you will not allow him to use the family car and ground him for a month. You must follow through on it no matter how difficult it may be or whether his behavior dramatically improves within a week. This is a tactic adolescents use to get consequences reduced, only to go right back out and misbehave.

To Hit or Not to Hit

"I never thought I'd see the day when my son and I would come to blows. He was mouthing off at me, and I hit him across the mouth. He shocked me by hitting me right back. It was a mess. Somebody called the police. It was just bad news." (Bill, father of a seventeen-year-old son)

❖ ❖ ❖

With your hands you make your success. With your hands you destroy success.

—*Yoruba proverb*

❖ ❖ ❖

There is a major debate in the black community about spanking and other forms of physical punishment. Many of us were raised with the saying "Spare the rod, spoil the child." Some of our parents had strong religious beliefs about this. Others felt that if they did not discipline us harshly, society would. They wanted to protect us by punishing us for acting out before society did. This was particularly true of black sons, who are often at the greatest risk. Yes, we know that most of you got spanked by your parents when you were growing up. Both of us are no exception. In fact, both of our fathers would get so wrapped up in "preaching" to us about what we did wrong that we almost wished they would hurry up and spank us and get it over with.

We have all heard the favorite threats of black parents (the old folks used to love these):

- "I brought you into this world and I can take you out."
- "Boy, don't let me have to come over there and knock some sense into you."
- "Cut your eyes at me one more time and I'm gonna knock them right out of your head."

These make for interesting stories about the old folks, but they don't work in today's world. The problem with threats is that they make the situation worse. Also, they give our kids the wrong message.

Many African American parents today spank kids when they are young if they misbehave. Some use this as a part of other forms of discipline. The problem with spanking, particularly as they get older, is that it does not motivate kids to take responsibility for their own behavior. In their book *Raising Black Children,* James Comer and Alvin Poussaint state that many kids "are relieved and feel less guilty after a spanking. With a spanking they 'pay their debt' and often continue misbehavior. They have not been required to take any responsibility for controlling their troublesome impulses or acts." Spanking stops the behavior for a very brief time when they are very young, but they learn nothing from it. Within an hour they may repeat the same behavior. As they get older, they begin to rebel.

A good friend of ours, Rosemary Allwood, a former dean of Spelman College, reminded us recently, "Many parents forget that the word 'discipline' is derived from the biblical term 'disciple,' which means to teach. We must teach our kids and talk to them about taking responsibility for controlling themselves and their own behavior." In the parenting classes she conducts she emphasizes that our goal as parents is to help our children to learn to self-monitor their own behavior, develop good judgment skills, and be less influenced by peer pressure.

The problem is that many hitting strategies do not work in today's world and will often backfire, particularly by the time your son is fourteen or fifteen. Here are some reasons why:

- It teaches your son that violence is the way to resolve problems.
- Physical size—he's probably as big or bigger than you.
- It can build resentment, anger, and bitterness in your son.
- It may lead to a physical altercation between you and your child.
- Your son may get involved in violent, aggressive behavior in the community and more fights at school.
- Your son can become very secretive and close down communication with you.

Comer and Poussaint also point out that parents often hit when they are angry. They state, "By being hit by you when you are angry, children learn to hit others when they are angry." Later, particularly in the teenage years, this behavior is very difficult to change, and they can get in more trouble at school, in the streets, and with the police.

"I got hit as a kid and I turned out all right." Many black parents make this argument. This may have worked when we were kids, but the world has changed a lot from the one we grew up in. Few

kids stop at "hitting." Many quickly move on to knives, guns, and box cutters. Do you want to put your son at risk?

❖ ❖ ❖

If you always do what you always did, you will always get what you always got.
—Jackie "Moms" Mabley

❖ ❖ ❖

So many African American parents with whom we have worked try the same parenting strategies over and over, even if it is clear that they are not working. So we will go out on a limb and tell you that spanking does not work, particularly by the time your son is a teenager. In fact, it can teach kids that hitting or physical violence is the way to get results. Many of the kids who have been referred to us for aggressive behavior in school had parents who regularly hit them as their main form of discipline. These kids were often extremely resentful of their parents and all authority figures.

"My father is always yelling at me when I get into fights at school, but the first thing he says at home if I get him pissed off is, 'This fist is going to knock you through that wall.'" (Travis, age fifteen)

In *Smart Parenting for African Americans,* Dr. Jeffrey Gardere cites research evidence that "when parents use corporal punishment on their kids to reduce negative behavior, in the long run their efforts will backfire. As a matter of fact, the children will typically act out even more, resulting in aggression, violent criminal behavior, impaired learning, depression, and, in extreme cases, suicide."

The other problem, at this age, is that if you use physical punishment as your main form of discipline you will have to keep increasing it. Your teenage sons will begin to challenge you or they will go take it out on their peers at school. It is far better at this age to use the tough love and positive discipline strategies discussed below. Force and physical strength only create more resistance. See Chapter 11 on violence and gangs. It will help you to understand how serious the use of violence can become in your son's world.

Tough Love

We are definitely not advocating permissiveness, just the opposite. As black parents today we must use "tough love." Learn to develop alternative methods of discipline that can be effective with this age group. These can include taking away privileges such as hanging out with his friends, talking on the phone, buying new clothes, watching TV or videos, playing video games, listening to music CDs, driving the family car, going to a party or a special event. This should be done for a realistic period of time such as a week and should be tailored to the rule that was broken. Be firm. Don't let them off the hook. Follow through on your discipline.

Give Them More Responsibility

Make sure that your son has responsibilities from an early age and that he helps with chores around the house. Hold him accountable for these, and do not let it pass if they are not done. Some parents assign regular chores and then allow their kids to earn extra money by doing big jobs such as washing all the windows in the house. Do not give your son sexist messages by calling some jobs "women's work." Make sure he learns how to cook, clean, do the laundry, press his clothes, etc. You can have him set the table at night or help you cook. Make sure that you expect him to make his bed each day and take out the trash at night.

When your son is old enough, encourage him to get a summer job. Encourage him to save his money by helping him to open a savings account at your bank. Having a job and saving money build character and instill discipline. Even a young teen who cannot get working papers can volunteer at a local church food pantry, summer day camp, or community program. Try not to let him lay around all summer doing nothing.

Teach Kids Problem-Solving Skills

When many of us were growing up, our parents told us what to do and expected us to do it. The problem with this "top-down" approach is that it does not teach kids to think for themselves. We will not always be with them, so we need to problem-solve *with* our kids about situations where they will be called upon to make difficult decisions *for themselves*. Of course, for some activities that have dangerous consequences, such as drug or alcohol use, a firm stand forbidding these behaviors should be taken.

One of the best ways to teach your children ways in which to solve problems is to call regular family meetings where everyone is expected to gather without the common distractions of TV, music, or video or computer games. The meetings do not have to be a formal process and can be held for decisions that affect everyone such as family vacations or events, party planning, movies, etc. It does not have to center around a heavy topic or a major family crisis—though, unfortunately, it often takes a crisis before a meeting is called. As your son gets used to regularly participating in and listening to the family discussions, he learns about teamwork, compromise, and conflict resolution.

Your family meeting should include the following basic ideas or questions:

- What exactly is the problem or issue?
- What are new ways it can be solved/addressed that we haven't tried?
- What do we agree on as the possible solution?
- How will we put the solution into action?
- What didn't work before? What else can we do to solve or address the issue?

"I found a blunt [reefer or marijuana cigarette] in my son's room. I was ready to kill him. My wife calmed me down. We sat my son and all the kids down and talked to them. We had a family meeting, and I told them that I'd better not find any more drugs in my house.

I asked the other kids if they knew David was using. They all denied it. We talked about what they would do if they thought someone they loved was using. Having the family meeting calmed me down and helped us all talk about it. By the end, I was able to listen to them too! (Michael, father of three teenagers)

It is helpful to start on a positive note. Dick Schaffer recommends asking each member to say something positive about another family member or share something they are thankful for. Let family members know the agenda at the start of the meeting and which topics will be discussed. Give everyone a chance to give his or her opinion about a problem or issue, then ask everyone to come up with a possible solution. You can even make this fun by suggesting some outrageous alternative that will make everyone laugh. Have someone write down any ideas that are generated (even wild ones). Include the planning of a fun family activity about which everyone can vote, such as when to have a family barbecue or what movie to rent. In other situations, you may decide to make the final decision. Let your kids know this and that you want to hear everyone's opinion before a decision is made. Ask them to come up with pros and cons for the different ideas. Once a solution is agreed upon or you have made a final decision, tell everyone, and then decide how it will be implemented.

This can also be an important time to teach your kids how they can "learn from their mistakes" and how to take appropriate, thoughtful risks. They will begin to learn about themselves. They will also discover that their opinions are important and that they are valued—a step in building their self-esteem. Let your kids know that if a particular solution does not work, everyone will get together again and brainstorm (or renegotiate) a new solution. Let everyone in the family know that their input was important and that they made a contribution.

RESOURCES

Organizations

Children's Defense Fund, Black Community Crusade for Children, 25 E. Street, NW, Washington, DC 20001; telephone: (202) 628-8787; fax (202) 662-3530; Web site: www.childrensdefense.org; E-mail: cdfinfo@ childrensdefense.org. (The BCCC's mission is to ensure that no child is left behind and that every child has a healthy life, with caring parents and nurturing communities.)

National Black Child Development Institute, 1023 15th Street, NW, Washington, DC 20005; telephone: (202) 387-1281. (The institute works to improve child care, child welfare, education, and health services delivered to black children.)

Urban League Parents Center, Greater Washington Urban League, 3501 14th Street, NW, Washington, DC 20010; telephone: (202) 265-8200; fax: (202) 387-7019. (Seeks to help parents gain child rearing abilities and fosters parent/school partnerships.)

Books

Boyd-Franklin, Nancy. *Black Families in Therapy.* New York: Guilford Press, 1989.

Comer, James, and Alvin Poussaint. *Raising Black Children.* New York: Plume, 1992.

Gardere, Jeffrey. *Smart Parenting for African Americans: Helping Your Kids Thrive in a Difficult World.* Secaucus, NJ: Citadel Press, 1999.

Hopson, Darlene, and Derek Hopson. *Different and Wonderful: Raising Black Children in a Race-Conscious Society.* New York: Prentice Hall, 1990.

Phelan, Thomas. *Surviving Your Adolescents.* Glen Ellyn, IL: Child Management, 1998

Schaffer, Dick. *Choices and Consequences.* Minneapolis: Johnson Institute, 1996.

Wilmes, David. *Parenting for Prevention.* Minneapolis: Johnson Institute, 1989.

Many of these books can be ordered from the Johnson Institute, 7205 Ohms Lane, Minneapolis, MN 55439-2159. Phone (toll free) (800) 231-5165; (612) 831-1630; E-mail: info@johnsoninstitute.com; Web site: http://www.johnsoninstitute.com

These can also be ordered on the Internet if you have access to a computer.

5

◆

EDUCATION IS YOUR PASSPORT TO THE FUTURE, FOR TOMORROW BELONGS TO THE PEOPLE WHO PREPARE FOR IT TODAY.

—MALCOLM X

The tragedy of life doesn't lie in not reaching your goal. The tragedy lies in having no goal to reach. It isn't a calamity to die with dreams unfulfilled, but it is a calamity not to dream. It is not a disaster to be unable to capture your ideal, but it is a disaster to have no ideal to capture. It is not a disgrace not to reach the stars, but it is a disgrace to have no stars to reach for.

—DR. BENJAMIN MAYS, former president of Morehouse College

Far too many African American young men today have no goals, no dreams, no stars to reach for. As parents, it is so important that you give the dream of an education to your children from a very early age. If they have goals, they will be less distracted by all of the temptations that life can give them.

Ever since the days of slavery there has been a strong link between the goals of education and freedom. Many of our enslaved ancestors were maimed or killed when caught learning to read. Slave masters knew the power of knowledge, and feared that such power in the hands of African slaves would lead to rebellion. Today, education is still seen as the acquisition of skills and strengths that no one can take away from a person. Many African American parents view it as our greatest weapon against racism and oppression.

A good education has always been seen by black people as a key that opens up life's opportunities. In some African American families, the reality of a college education for their children—or even a good high school education—seems to be an impossible dream. Yet for some African American families college and even graduate education has been a staple for many generations, as Lawrence Otis Graham attests in his book *Our Kind of People*. Regardless of economic status and education, the orientation toward providing schooling and learning for our children has always been an important strength and value in our community.

In African American homes, there is a tradition of enormous sacrifice on the part of parents and other family members in order to educate children. Nancy's parents often talked about how "education poor" they were as they struggled to put four children through Catholic schools. We did not fully comprehend their meaning until our own three older children were in college at the same time. A willingness to make the sacrifices necessary for the sake of education was ingrained in all of us from an early age.

Our experiences are not unusual. Many generations of African Americans can relate to this tradition of sacrifice for education. Closely associated with this value is the notion that the individual is not alone in this struggle for education—that others have gone without in order to make it possible for them—and the benefit of an education is accompanied by the obligation to give something back, both to others in the family and to our people as a whole.

Nancy's parents struggled to send her off to college, even with a scholarship. During her second year they asked her to help with her younger brother's college admission fees out of the money she earned from a part-time campus job. She knew it was time to give something back to her family. As parents, we have tried to give our children the image of a pyramid described by the African proverb in which we all stand on one another's shoulders.

Beating the Odds

High school graduation rates for African Americans have risen sharply since the 1970s, so parents should understand what separates the successes from the failures in terms of our sons and their school careers.

Freeman Hrabowski, a black man who is the president of the University of Maryland, and his coauthors Kenneth Maton and Geoffrey Greif, did a tremendous service to the discussion of black boys and education in their book *Beating the Odds: Raising Academically Successful African American Males*. The authors studied young African American men in a program for talented students pursuing careers in engineering and science, and their parents, to find out what factors had contributed to their success.

The students came from diverse backgrounds. Some had come from poor, inner-city families; others were from middle-class urban and suburban neighborhoods. Some were raised by single parents, either mothers or fathers; others had two parents living in the home. Still others were raised by extended family members, such as grandparents. What the young men had in common was their families' stressing the importance of individual initiative as a component of success. The authors conclude, "The challenge facing black parents is to help their sons believe truly that, in spite of racism and societal barriers, their success will depend largely on their own efforts."

These authors caution us against the victim mentality. Racism and discrimination win when young men internalize the negative messages from society and allow them to corrode their self-esteem. Our job as African American parents is to hold on to the belief that our kids can also beat the odds and succeed. Even more important, we have to communicate this to our sons—they have to believe they have a future no matter what they face along the way.

This sense of resilience and the belief that education can make a difference in their lives can best be ingrained in them if we begin encouraging them to "be all they can be" from a very young age. The motto of the United Negro College Fund that "a mind is a terrible thing to waste" carries an important message. By the time that our kids are teenagers, they often tune us out, so the positive messages about education and achievement must be given from preschool age. These messages will help protect our sons when they are faced with challenges in school, such as some teachers who may expect them to fail, and members of their peer group who may attempt to sabotage their academic success by accusing them of "acting white."

As African American parents, it is very important that we communicate our high expectations for our children in terms of their school performance. In Chapter 4, when we talked about parenting practices, we emphasized the importance of "catching them being good." The same goes for their school success. Talk to your kids about college. No doubt, they will tire of hearing that they are expected to get As and Bs (and will tell you so often), but they will remember the underlying messages. Remind them of family members or friends who had successful school careers and went on to productive lives and even bigger achievements. In both of our families, we grew up hearing stories about how hard our relatives and ancestors struggled to get an education. These stories help our children to understand why we value education so much.

One of the unique aspects of the book *Beating the Odds* was being able to hear the voices of black fathers, a group that has been neglected in books on raising black children. These fathers—some of whom were biological fathers, others stepfathers—talked about giving time to their sons, talking to them early on in their lives, challenging them intellectually, and providing continual support. They emphasized their vigilance in monitoring their children's daily lives, even if they did not live in the same home and could only offer their support long-distance. This monitoring and attention to their lives at school, in the neighborhood, and among their friends is crucial. The young men in the study who did not have a father active in their lives were fortunate in finding role models in their communities, schools, or churches.

Although parents may think that the most intense time for parental monitoring is when kids are young, this monitoring has to continue through high school. Constant monitoring can cause conflict in a parent's relationship with a teenage son, who may object to your "being in his business," and is likely to test the limits. But be comforted by the fact that many of these hard-to-manage adolescents have gone on to become responsible young adults, and productive men, who are looked at with pride by the members of their communities. Stick with the close monitoring through high school, but give your son more responsibility and freedom as he earns your trust. The monitoring should not end when your son graduates. Continue to offer input, emphasizing that with increasing freedom comes increasing responsibility for his own behavior.

As parents, we must also advocate on their behalf with school administrators in terms of recognition and class placement. The mothers and fathers in the *Beating the Odds* study advocated for their children constantly. You can incorporate these steps taken directly from these proactive parents into your own parenting style. Here's how:

- Read to your son regularly at home from an early age, and practice counting and simple math.
- Talk to a teacher if there is a problem with your son at school.
- Pay close attention to his schoolwork.
- Make sure your son is placed in the proper classes and advocate for him if you see that he is placed below his ability.
- Encourage and facilitate extracurricular activities.
- Be available to help with homework.
- Get to know your son's teachers by being a presence in the school.
- Set high standards and encourage your son to do his best in school.
- Set limits on his behavior.
- Transfer your son to a different school if you feel his current school is failing him.

Staying Connected, Staying Involved

When we were growing up, mothers were so present in our schools we had to create signals to alert one another, "Mom's on the floor. Look out!" We knew that while another classmate's mom was at school checking in with her son's teacher, she would also be keeping an eye on us while she was there—and reporting back to our mothers about what she saw.

These visits also kept the school honest. Now that few parents regularly drop in on schools during the day, the collective concern for children has declined, and some school staff and administrators can become apathetic and unresponsive to parents' needs, particularly when they are unvoiced.

One way to stay connected to your son's school experience is to simply keep in touch with teachers and other parents by attending parent-teacher conferences and school events and functions and talking to other parents. Don't underestimate the power of the grapevine to alert you to the best teachers and classes. It can help your son learn about opportunities and avoid pitfalls that could hinder his school success.

To make the best use of parent-teacher conferences and open school night visits, have a specific goal in mind, i.e., asking Kwesi's math teacher why he is failing math or asking Johnny's English teacher why he wasn't recommended for the advanced English class, rather than expecting to have a more general discussion. Because of the time limits and the many parents attending, a separate, private meeting should be arranged with teachers and administrators if needed. If you make the effort to get to know the teachers, guidance counselors, and administrators at the beginning of each school year, they will be aware that you are a serious and concerned parent.

Many parents who are actively involved in their son's elementary school become less involved as their sons go on to junior high and high school. Sometimes parents are burned out or exhausted after eight or more years of monitoring for each child. Other parents, who became accustomed to communicating with one teacher in the lower grades, are overwhelmed and intimidated when they must now communicate with as many as five to eight different teachers, plus coaches, advisers, administrators, and guidance counselors. Contacting teachers and other key individuals on the telephone can be very difficult.

Sometimes the best way to get a teacher's attention is to just show up at the school, although the teacher may be teaching class and unable to meet with you right at that moment. Your son's guidance counselor may help you to arrange a meeting during a teacher's free period. If you try to contact a teacher by phone, be prepared to leave a message on voice mail giving daytime and evening phone numbers and times when they can reach you most easily.

Rearranging your schedule to see a teacher to discuss problems concerning your child is a worthwhile effort and far more productive than engaging in telephone tag. Finally, don't visit your son's school only when he's in trouble. He needs to see you there to support him in good as well as bad times. What a boost he will get if you show up to see the teacher of a class in which he's excelling, and publicly praise him in front of his teacher or solicit suggestions from his teacher on how you can help him continue to excel. (Just as long as you don't do it in front of his *friends.*)

Brenda, a recently divorced parent of three, made a point of visiting her kids' schools every year. She would often send notes to her kids' teachers by fax and spoke to them frequently by phone on her lunch hour or breaks at work. When her son was found to be cutting class, she set up a system with the guidance counselor where she received printouts of his attendance in each class every week. In addition, she bought a beeper and gave both her kids and their teachers the number so that she could always be reached immediately during her busy day.

Establishing a positive relationship with the schools our children attend is often a challenge for us as African American parents. Some of us need to resolve our fear of confrontation. Other African American parents feel what Grier and Cobbs call in their book *Black Rage* "healthy cultural paranoia." They are "on guard" for their kids because of the realities of racism. While our history warrants this vigilance, it must be tempered so that we do not approach these institutions with a chip on our shoulder. Remember that our sons are also taking their cues on how to respond to their teachers from us. Teenagers are already inclined to defy authority. If we are always in "ballistic" mode when we visit or talk about the school or its officials, they will do the same. This hostility toward authority figures at school can cause difficulties for your son that neither of you need.

If you find yourself in this position, seek out a supportive counselor, former teacher, or administrator and ask for their help. Sometimes another African American parent, teacher, or counselor can serve in this role or, especially in single-mother headed households, an interested uncle, grandfather, or godfather can provide a male presence for both the school and your son. If you cannot find such a person, you may want to seek an outside counselor or therapist to advocate for you and your child. Schools often see this as a sign that your child is trying, and that you are getting help. Sometimes just that knowledge can influence or change the way they view you and your child.

Monitoring Teacher Expectations: Ending the Fourth-Grade Failure Syndrome

In the 1970s, Rosenthal and Jacobson did a landmark study of teacher expectations. In this study the teachers were told that half of the children in their classes were very bright students and half were not. Not surprisingly, those children who had been identified as "very bright" did the best at the end of the year, irrespective of their former grades, test scores, or ability.

Jawanza Kunjufu, a noted African American educator and activist in Chicago, has written a number of books on the education of African American children. Among his most important works are four volumes entitled *Countering the Conspiracy to Destroy Black Boys*. In the first book in the series, Kunjufu documents the experience of some eager African American boys as they enter preschool. Their natural exuberance and energy level may often be misinterpreted and mislabeled by teachers and school officials as "aggressive," "hyperactive," and "too loud."

Some teachers' issues with black boys can lead to what Kunjufu describes as the "fourth-grade failure syndrome," which occurs when the combination of low teacher expectations, racism, and fear of these young black males leads them on a path toward school failure. Some teachers perceive black males as a threat and may misinterpret their learning styles. (This can happen even with some black teachers who may bring their own issues to the classroom.) Their increased physical activity gets twisted and labeled "negative behavior," and some teachers no longer respond to the raised hands of the young black boys in their classrooms, preferring to call on girls, or boys from racial, ethnic, and cultural groups other than African American.

In this way, the eagerness young black boys displayed in first grade begins to drop and has practically disappeared by the fourth grade.

We often make school visits for the kids and families with whom we work. One day Nancy went to observe Jabar, a fourteen-year-old ninth grader, in his history class. His teacher gave her permission to sit in the back of the classroom and observe. The class was divided into teams to play a history quiz game. The winning team would get a prize, and the kids were very involved. Jabar raised his hand a lot in the beginning. The teacher ignored him and called on one of the other kids (never on one of the other black males). At first Jabar tried hard to get the teacher's attention. He waved his hand, but still he was ignored. Finally he gave up. He shut down and "zoned out" for the rest of the class.

Because African American males are disproportionately labeled and placed in special education classes irrespective of area of the country, type of setting (urban, suburban, or rural), or the socioeconomic level of the family, parents must be proactive in monitoring our sons' school experiences. For example, in our family, when A.J. met with our older son's high school math teacher to discuss his performance and math placement for the next year, the teacher reflected that the quality of the students in the school had declined: previously the school had educated "the best and the brightest." He told A.J. that he felt our son's above-average grade was not adequate for advanced math placement. The implication was clear to us: as the student population changed from virtually all-white to include more students of color, his expectations of their abilities and potential changed as well. A.J. challenged his insinuation not only about our son but also about the other students of color in the school.

The young men who succeeded in school in the book *Beating the Odds* were able to surmount obstacles posed to them as African American boys due to the strong advocacy on their behalf by parents and other adults in their lives. We have found that this has worked for our children also, and we encourage you to take an active role in your sons' education.

The Importance of Checking In

One of the greatest challenges for all of us as parents is to monitor homework, schoolwork, and the home environment after school, especially when we have jobs that entail long hours.

Many African American children are "latchkey" kids who are unsupervised for considerable stretches of time after school (two to six hours, and sometimes more) until a parent arrives home. A baby-sitter is often impractical when our children are in their teens—not only is it costly, but teens also resent the implication that they are too immature and untrustworthy to be left alone. There are a number of things that working parents in this situation can do:

- Establish clear house rules about how and when homework is to be done. The most useful rule from elementary through high school is no television, video or computer games, Internet, or going outside with friends until homework is finished. In adolescence it also helps to add no talking on the phone or visits from friends.
- Be available to assist them with their homework if they need help, even if you don't understand it all. Many high-achieving people insist that their parents' showing an interest in their homework and making sure that it got done made all the difference between success and failure.
- Ask to see your son's completed homework. Pay attention to how much they are given and the quality of the work your son is turning in.
- Praise them liberally when they do a good job (even though they are expected to do it anyway).
- Call your children when they are due home, if you cannot be there when they arrive. Focus them on homework first.
- Arrange after-school or homework club programs for younger kids so that your oldest does not bear the total responsibility until you get home. Sometimes teenagers, who may have been very good about taking care of and supervising their brothers and sisters when they were younger, may understandably begin to resent all the extra responsibility.
- Get access to a computer. Today, most junior high and high school kids need access to a computer to do their required homework and reports. If you can afford to, buy one. If you cannot afford a computer of your own, check with other family members, neighbors, and friends to see whether your

son can use their computer for school assignments. One way to make a computer more affordable is to get the family to agree to forgo individual gifts throughout the year on birthdays, Christmas, and other special occasions so that a computer can be purchased to benefit the entire family. You can even ask other family members to forgo buying individual gifts for special occasions so that they can contribute to the family computer-buying fund. Computers are used in many classrooms, therefore our children may know how to use them before they are purchased for the home. As a matter of fact, our children usually know more about computers than we do.

- Find out about community resources. Many libraries provide computers that your son may use for free after school. He may also be able to access a school's computer lab during his free period, study hall, or after school. Check with local churches, community centers, tutoring, or mentoring programs to see if computers are available. In addition, local businesses often offer used, but fully operational, computers for sale at very affordable prices when they upgrade to more powerful models.

- Ask family members, friends, neighbors, and church members to see if there is someone who can tutor your son after school if he is having trouble with his homework.

- Know when to "say when." If your son is an A or B *high school* student, seems fairly responsible, and gets his work done, you may be able to give him more responsibility for his own work. Your actions should be guided by your son's performance.

Extracurricular Activities

When your children are still young, involve them in a range of extracurricular activities to develop their unique skills and talents and develop new interests. For many African American males, basketball can become such an obsession that they often need to be encouraged to try other sports in junior high and high school. They may also have talents in music, art, writing, or dance that are untapped or being wasted. Start early to encourage and involve your kids in a range of activities. When your kids are younger, you can place them in certain activities. Adolescents want and need some independence in deciding on their own activities. You can suggest new ideas, but pressuring them into participating in activities in which they have no interest is seldom useful.

If you are working full-time, *you do not want your kids alone for long periods of idle time in the evening.* A good idea is to require one planned after-school activity each day. Try to give them more independence in deciding which activity matches their interests and talents best. If your son is doing poorly academically, the activity might have to be tutoring until his grades improve.

Start with your son's school in deciding on extracurricular activities. Learn from the school what they offer, the skills he will learn, and the time commitment. You can also find good information from other parents who have enrolled their sons in programs sponsored by various organizations in the community (e.g., Boy Scouts, Boys Club, PAL, YMCA, basketball, football, or Little League). Sometimes you can utilize the help of a friend, a cousin, older brother or sister, or other members of your extended family to suggest new ideas and interests.

Sonny felt responsible for seeing that his nephews, ages twelve and thirteen, developed into the men his recently deceased brother would have wanted them to become. He and his brother had participated in the local basketball league when they were young, which helped them to develop physical and leadership skills. Sonny asked his coworkers and friends to recommend local organizations. He called the school, police, social service agencies, and looked up programs for youth in the yellow pages and on the Internet. He and the boys' mother then presented a range of activities to his nephews. They decided to enroll in a summer sports program. In addition, Sonny made sure that his schedule allowed him to make more time to be with them in the fall. He went to most of their games and cheered as loudly as any other "parent" there.

Downtime

Our sons are often so active and are presented with so many entertainment distractions, such as television and video games, that they have no alone time when they can think, relax, or take a nap when needed. This situation gets worse in adolescence as our kids join more activities on their own, get more homework, and make more friends. Don't let them overdo it. "Downtime" is a period when they can stop the pace of their daily routine, collect their thoughts, and refocus on what they are doing and why. It allows them the opportunity to reconnect with family members and helps reduce stress.

Schedule downtime for your children each day so that you can touch base with them and ask how things are going in school. It is best if this can become a looked-forward-to part of the evening routine. Maybe you can have a few quiet moments in the kitchen or bedroom, away from other children. Talking while walking to the store or while shooting some baskets with your son can be very helpful in connecting with him, and can count toward your quality time and help both of you to unwind from the pressures of the day.

Black Peer Group Messages: Smart Equals White

One of the struggles unique to African American adolescents is this message from their black peers. Jawanza Kunjufu points out, in his excellent book *To Be Popular or Smart: The Black Peer Group,* that "the phenomenon of peer pressure and its impact on academic achievement has reached catastrophic proportions. It has now reached a point that to do well academically in school is to be accused of 'acting white' and risk being called a nerd."

Many African American parents are surprised to discover that this peer pressure exists in all kinds of schools: in city neighborhoods, in suburban schools with small numbers of black peers, and in private schools where black peer contact may be a limited but very powerful influence. African American kids who do well are often called "stuck up," told that they are "suck-ups" to the teacher or worse, and are often ostracized, threatened by their peers, or teased relentlessly.

T.J.'s parents were worn out with his annual roller-coaster school performance. Although he was capable of doing A work, only doing extremely well on finals kept him from failing. Although his peers realized he was smart, T.J. tried to fit in with his friends by discussing rap stars, the music business, and dee-jaying. A school counselor finally explained to T.J.'s parents that this was his way of keeping his friends "off his back." He did not want to be accused of "acting white" because he was smart.

Parents often tell kids in this situation to ignore their friends, but at fourteen, sixteen, or eighteen it is very hard to follow that advice. Our sons want to belong and to be popular. To further complicate the issue, some African American students are unfamiliar with the tremendous accomplishments of our African ancestors in ancient Egypt (or Kimet) who excelled in math, science, medicine, architecture, and much more. Deep down inside, your son may feel inferior to white students. Unfortunately, and maybe unwittingly, they have "bought" and internalized a stereotype that blacks can't achieve in these areas. Jawanza Kunjufu has identified a number of strategies by which bright African American students cope with this peer pressure:

- *Clowning.* This often begins in the early grades when a very bright child gains acceptance through entertaining his peers in class. Although he may get outstanding grades in academic subjects, the "clown" often gets poor grades in conduct.
- *Refusing to study in public places.* This teenager doesn't carry his books in school and spends the time doing anything but studying. He does schoolwork only at home, away from the watchful eyes of his peers.
- *Independence.* This child is a loner who may achieve significant success academically but is at risk for depression. Independence may also appear to others as being "mad at the world" and rejecting.
- *Fighting.* Many African American kids become known as "good fighters" to keep other kids from "messing with them." Though this may be a successful strategy with peers, it may have severe consequences otherwise, as these kids are prone to be in "detention" or the "discipline room" in school and labeled as troublemakers by authorities.
- *"Tutoring bullies."* Some kids compensate for the stigma of

their academic success by tutoring the bullies who would otherwise torture them. Kunjufu points out that this is dangerous, as it may extend to doing the bullies' homework and even helping them to cheat on tests.

- *Using sports and "becoming an athlete."* If an academically successful high school student is also an excellent athlete, his peers may overlook his academic achievement.
- *"Becoming raceless."* Kunjufu discusses Signithia Fordham and John Ogbu's studies of high-achieving black kids. They found a disturbing process for some of these adolescents where, tragically, they "have learned the value of appearing to be raceless—a clear example of internalizing oppression—in their efforts to make it. Many of these kids become very isolated and may struggle throughout their lives with a negative sense of their racial identity."

The best remedy to combat any of the above negative consequences is to make sure that you talk to your son about the pressures he may be experiencing. Listen actively; resist the urge to rush to the solution. You can also look for special academic enrichment programs such as Upward Bound, ABC (A Better Chance), Prep for Prep, and other programs that encourage academic achievement and the goal of college entrance for African American youth (see resources at the end of the chapter). These programs offer special enrichment for bright African American kids to help them prepare for better educational opportunities. Some programs like Prep for Prep and ABC provide scholarships for private schools. Upward Bound helps to prepare minority kids for college. Church and community centers in your area may have youth programs that emphasize academic excellence.

Getting to the Root of School Behavior Problems

By third or fourth grade, many school systems have already labeled African American boys as hyperactive, too assertive, and too aggressive. They are often singled out by teachers because of racial stereotyping and the misunderstanding of some schools of our kids' often exuberant style. There are complex reasons for this, not the least of which is the threat that many teachers feel when our adolescent sons become bigger and taller than they are. One key area in which our male children can begin to have trouble in school is in the area of fighting.

The broader issue of violence will be addressed in Chapter 11. Here, we would like to address the specific issue of fighting in schools and the often mixed messages that we, as African American parents, give our sons about fighting.

Your son may be fighting in school because:

- He feels someone has insulted him or a member of his family.
- He is defending himself.
- He wants to defend or "stick up for his boys."
- He is involved in a gang or is a "gang wannabe."
- It helps prevent other kids from picking on him or seeing him as a "punk."
- He was verbally teased.
- He is in a conflict over a girl or a turf issue.

When many of us were growing up, kids played cruel games like the "dozens," where they brutally insulted one another and their "momma," or other family members. Learning how to handle and defend yourself against this form of ridicule has become a part of the male rite of passage. Some kids have never learned how to deal with this process of verbal insults and they resort to their fists—or worse. Today, fights are much more deadly—box cutters, knives, or guns are being used, and some students, who feel they have to be prepared for that possibility, carry such weapons for self-defense. Even safeguards such as metal detectors cannot guarantee that these weapons will not be brought into schools. Thus, concern about violence has become a top priority in many junior high and high schools, with the punishment often resulting in suspension or expulsion regardless of whether the fight involves weapons.

What you can do to help your son deal with this situation:

- Start early. Give your son clear messages about avoiding fighting.

- Get fathers or other male role models to teach them how to handle themselves in these situations.
- Teach them not to start fights, but also teach them how to defend themselves if they are attacked.
- Teach them conflict-resolution skills so that they can learn to defuse verbal arguments before they become physical.
- Find out if there is a violence-prevention program in your son's school or in your community and enroll your son. (See Chapters 11 and 12.)
- If your son is constantly picked on by others or beaten up by them, find a self-defense program in karate, kung fu, etc. Be sure to explore the philosophy of the program and make sure that it supports ways to avoid or deflect fights.
- Talk to school authorities. Help to organize a dialogue between other parents, kids, and school officials to resolve these issues.

Special Issues

Certain areas are of special concern to African American parents who are committed to insuring that their sons get the best education possible. These include testing, problems in school, college planning, and alternatives to college.

The Mislabeling of African American Males in School Systems

There is no question that a disproportionate number of African American boys get classified and placed in special education classes for educational and behavior problems. Parents must be vigilant about this process. In the history of testing, African American intelligence and ability have been consistently undervalued. The belief that we are less intelligent and more prone to hyperactive behavior than other ethnic groups still exists among a number of professionals and educators. The Association of Black Psychologists, the NAACP, and other organizations have cautioned for decades about the biases within standardized tests and the manner in which the results are used.

Once we are aware of the biases, and carefully monitor the

process, tests can sometimes be useful in helping us to better understand the learning needs of our kids and guiding decisions about how to best remedy problems.

Yet long before school failure is confirmed by a poor report card or lack of promotion, you have to pay attention to how your kids are doing in school. But sometimes the source of your son's trouble in school is hard to pinpoint. (This is where it helps to know your child's guidance counselor.) In adolescence, many kids begin to take less interest in their studies. The lure of sports, girls, and friends becomes very strong and distractions increase.

By eighth and ninth grade, and into the later high school years, a range of academic and learning issues can present themselves that are hard to categorize. You may have a very bright son who does extraordinarily well on school aptitude tests but whose grades are mediocre or even failing. The most common reaction of parents, teachers, and school officials is to attribute the discrepancy to your son's "laziness" or "lack of motivation." Before you accept this conclusion, explore other reasons why your child's academic performance and grades may be poor. These may include:

Learning Disabilities

You may be surprised to know that the definition of a learning-disabled child is one of average or above-average ability who has problems in one or more particular skills or academic area. According to Lynn Roa, Neil Gluckin, and Bernard Kripke, authors of the book *Learning Disabilities,* the legal definition states that a specific learning disability is "a disorder in one or more of the basic psychological processes involved in understanding or in using language, spoken or written, which may manifest itself in an imperfect ability to listen, think, speak, read, spell, or do mathematical calculations." If your son is learning disabled, it is very important to educate yourself as much as you can about his learning needs. (See our Resources section at the end of this chapter for additional books, Internet resources, and parent support organizations.)

Dyslexia or Reading Disorder

With this condition, according to the *Diagnostic and Statistical Manual of Mental Disorders (DSM IV),* oral reading is often "characterized by distortions, substitutions, or omissions, and slowness and errors in comprehension." Also, reading achievement is substantially below that which is expected for the child's age, measured intelligence, and age-appropriate education. Very bright or intelligent kids can often "fool" parents and teachers until about fourth grade, particularly if they have good memorization skills. Dyslexia, a specific reading disorder, often leads to letter reversals, such as *b* for *d*. A dyslexic boy may read *dat* for *bat,* for example, and he may visually distort a whole page of written words or have difficulty comprehending their meaning.

Attention Deficit/Hyperactivity Disorder (ADHD)

Great media attention has focused in recent years on the increased diagnosis of ADD or ADHD in children across the country. This disorder includes inattention, the inability to sit still, distractability, difficulty concentrating, hyperactivity, and impulsivity, such as blurting out answers or interrupting when others are speaking. African American males are disproportionally diagnosed in this way. As parents, however, we need to be cautious about both sides of the coin. While you cannot allow your child to be misdiagnosed, you also cannot dismiss real problems for which help is available. Remember also that as a parent, you have a great deal of power to determine your child's educational decisions. If you would like more information on this condition, see Barclay's book under Attention Deficit Hyperactivity Disorder in our Resources Section.

What you can do:

- Make sure the school tells you why your son is being tested and evaluated and what the process is supposed to accomplish.
- Find out if the results may lead to a special class placement that will have an impact on your son's school and academic progress.
- Learn your rights in reviewing test results, the decision-making process, and appealing any test results and/or special placement of your son.
- Find out how to have an independent test and evaluation

done for your son. If you have this done, find out if the school considers the results in its decision-making process.

- Seek out independent professionals and/or organizations competent to advise and/or advocate on your behalf in the interpretation of any testing and evaluation of your son.
- Contact an advocacy group for parents of kids with learning problems.
- Join a support group for parents of children with learning disabilities or dyslexia.
- See the Resources section at the end of this chapter for guidance in obtaining help.
- Seek tutoring outside of the school. (Ask your child's guidance counselor or other parents for referrals.)
- Your son can still go to college with learning disabilities and other special needs. (See our Resources section.)

The Ritalin Controversy

One treatment for ADHD used widely in recent years involves the drug Ritalin. Many African American parents, fearful of giving drugs to their sons or skeptical about the possibility of misdiagnosis, have resisted the use of Ritalin. In some cases, this has proven to be good parental advocacy. (Do not allow anyone to pressure you into giving medication to your son until you have done your own homework on it.) In others, such a parental stand can keep African American boys from getting the medical help they need early on in their school careers. When the diagnosis of ADHD is correct, Ritalin works quickly and your son will show dramatic improvement. Do not be surprised, however, if it takes some trial and error for your doctor to find the correct dosage. The best prescription is to make sure you are well informed about the drug and its effects so you and your doctor can make an informed decision. Routine monitoring of the medication's effectiveness for your son is essential. For more information on books about Ritalin and other medications for ADHD and their long-term effects, see the Resources section at the end of this chapter.

College Planning
for African American Students

"My father talked about college from the time I was born. There was never any question. I was going." (Martin, age sixteen)

As the wonderful quote from Benjamin Mays at the beginning of this chapter shows, you must give your son dreams and goals early on. Talk to your kids about going to college. Talk about your own experiences if you went to college. If no one in your family has gone on to college, let your kids know that they will be the first. Ask them at an early age what they want to be when they grow up. Introduce them to friends, relatives, church, or community members who have gone to college. Give them the stars to reach for.

College is a dream that many of us, as African American parents, share for our children. Unfortunately, many of the obstacles discussed in this chapter can interfere with this goal. Here are a number of ways to insure that your son gets there:

- Talk about a college education as a goal and an expectation for your son early on.
- Enlist the aid of African American male role models who have gone to college to talk to and help to motivate your son.
- Get your son a mentor (an adult or an African American college or graduate student). Most colleges today have an African American student group. Call the dean's office at your local college and contact this group. Also, ask your minister to suggest a young man who is in college who could serve as a mentor for your son. (See Chapter 12 for other suggestions.)
- Take your son to events at local colleges. Take a group of his friends to a basketball or football game on a local campus so that they can see colleges.
- Explore the summer and after-school enrichment classes that are available at local colleges in your area. Enroll your child as soon as possible.
- Visit colleges with your son when you go to different parts of the country for family vacations or reunions. Go with your

son to the admissions office. They like to see parents. Often they can arrange for your son to visit a student on campus or to stay overnight in a dorm.

- Visit local college fairs, starting in your son's sophomore and junior years of high school.
- Speak with your son's guidance counselor or college admissions counselor late in his sophomore year or early in his junior year in order to familiarize yourself with the process of college applications.
- Ask your son's guidance counselor to talk to him early in his junior year about the college application process.
- Enroll your son in a College Board or SAT review course. These can often help him to get used to the format of questions and get used to timed tests.
- Obtain a copy of an SAT review guide (see the Resources section at the end of this chapter) from your library or bookstore, and have your son complete the practice tests.
- Look into buying computer software for SAT preparation.
- Ask about college tours in your area. Black organizations such as sororities and fraternities often sponsor bus tours of black colleges.
- Help your son fill out college applications. Many of these are accessible through the Internet, either on your home computer or on a computer at school. Electronic submissions are easier for kids than writing applications out by hand or finding a working typewriter (remember them?) to type them on.
- Be a role model for your son. Go back to school, even if you only take one course. Let your son know that education is important for the whole family.
- Go with your son to interviews at colleges or visit campuses, whenever possible.
- For more ideas see *The Black Student's Guide to College Success* in our Resources section at the end of the chapter.

How to Pay for College

If you need help paying for college, you should explore all sources for scholarship aid:

- Talk to your child's guidance counselor about applying for scholarships.
- Check with your church, sorority, or fraternity.
- Have your child check the box on the PSAT (taken in October of his junior year) to be considered for an Achievement Scholarship.
- Contact the UNCF (United Negro College Fund) for information on funding from historically black colleges.
- Inquire about scholarship aid at the colleges to which your son is applying. Some colleges have special scholarships for African Americans and other minority students. (See *Financial Aid for African Americans,* listed in the Resources section at the end of the chapter.)

Alternatives to College

"I was messing up big time. I was in a gang. I was always getting picked up by the police for fights. One of my boys stole a car. I was just riding in it. We were picked up by the cops. My father talked to the cops and the judge. They gave me a choice. Go to jail or go into the army. I went into the army. It turned my life around." (Brad, age nineteen)

"I went to college in Virginia. I partied the whole time and flunked out. My folks were really disappointed, but they stuck by me. They forced me to get a job that summer and work full time the next year. Now I've got a girlfriend. We want to get married someday. I'm planning to go to the community college at night." (Carlton, age twenty)

The most important message for African American parents is to help and encourage our children to "be all that they can be" educationally and in their life goals. If your son is capable of going to college, encourage him to strive for it. Many African American males are not ready or willing for a variety of reasons to go on to college right after high school. Still others start college, have difficulty, and drop out. The important thing to remember as a parent is that your job is to motivate your son to do his best in life. College isn't for everyone. If your son fits this description, consider other options:

- Find out what he enjoys most and encourage him to consider a technical school or an area where he has a special skill. For example, many noted black chefs attended schools such as the Culinary Institute of America (CIA), which helped to prepare them for a very rewarding profession.
- If your son spends hours on the computer, consider a computer school. (This can lead to a very well-paid job.)
- The armed forces are an alternative for African American kids who are not motivated to go directly to college after high school. The armed forces offer extensive training opportunities for their service members and educational benefits so that when your son finishes his military service he can go on to college. Employers are also enthusiastic about hiring people with military service because they are disciplined and often have leadership skills.
- Insist that your son work if he doesn't continue his education or training after high school.
- If your son has dropped out of high school, consider a general equivalence diplomacy (GED) program. Once he is done, he will be able to get a job more easily, or enroll in a junior college.

In whatever community you find yourself, as long as African American parents are willing to devote the time and attention to advocating for our sons and helping and guiding them with their academic work and other activities, there is no reason why our young men cannot succeed in school and in life.

RESOURCES

Organizations

Call the Association of Black Psychologists, P.O. Box 55999, Washington, DC 20040-5999; telephone (202) 722-0808; fax: (202) 722-5941; Web site: www.abpsi.org. Ask for a local contact in your city or near your town.

Call your local mental health association.

New Grange Parent Outreach Center, (609) 924-6204.

Learning Disabilities Hotline, (212) 645-6730.

Association for Learning Disabilities, 27 W. 20th Street, Room 303, New York, NY.

Special Programs for African American Students

Upward Bound, Council for Opportunity in Education, 1025 Vermont Avenue, NW, Suite 900, Washington, DC 20005; telephone: (202) 347-7430; fax: (202) 347-0786. (Federally funded program aimed at increasing the academic and motivational skills of high school students.)

A Better Chance (ABC), National Office: 419 Boylston Street, Boston, MA 02116; telephone: (617) 421-0950; (800) 562-7865; Web site: www.abetterchance.org. (Provides educational opportunities to students of color with the talent and potential to excel academically through their recruitment and placement into some of the nation's most outstanding secondary schools.)

Prep for Prep, (212) 579-1390.

Advocacy Organizations for Children with Learning Disabilities and ADHD:

ADD Action Group, P.O. Box 1440, Ansonia Station, New York, NY 10023; telephone: (212) 769-2457; Web site: www.addgroup.com. (Nonprofit organization that helps people find alternative solutions for Attention Deficit Disorder, Learning Differences, Dyslexia and Autism.)

Children and Adults with Attention Deficit Disorder (CHADD). 8181 Professional Place, Suite 201, Landover, MD 20785; telephone: (800) 233-4050; (301) 306-7070; fax: (301) 306-7090; Web site: www.chadd. org. (Parent-based organization formed to better the lives of individuals with attention deficit disorders and their families. The Web site provides information about ADHD and will help to connect you with local chapters.)

Coordinated Campaign for Learning Disabilities: http://www.fusebox. com/ld/.

International Dyslexia Association: http://www.interdys.org/default. htm.

LD Online: Learning Disability Resources: http://ldonline.org/index. htm.

Learning Disability Association of America: http://www.ldanatl.org/

National Academy for Child Development, P.O. Box 380, Huntsville, UT 84317; telephone: (801) 621-8606; fax: (801) 621-8389; Web site: www.nacd.org; E-mail: nacdinfo@nacd.org. (An international organization of parents and professionals dedicated to helping children and adults overcome dyslexia, ADD, and ADHD.)

SAALD (Students with ADD, ADHD, Learning Disabilities); Web site: www.adult-add.org; E-mail: add@adult-add.org. (Provides information for college students and young adults about ADD, ADHD, LD, ADD and other disorders. On-line study tips are available.)

If you do not have access to a computer, go to your local library. Most have free Internet access. Ask a research librarian to help you.

Schools for Children with Learning Disabilities and Dyslexia

The Gow School for Dyslexia and Learning Disabilities (New York): http://www.gow.org/ (boarding school for children with dyslexia and learning disabilities).

Books for Parents

College Success

Hrabowski, Freeman A., et al. *Beating the Odds: Raising Academically Successful African American Males.* New York: Oxford University Press, 1998.

Higgins, Ruby D., ed. *The Black Student's Guide to College Success.* Westport, CT: Greenwood Press, 1993.

Financial Aid

Beckham, Barry, ed. *The Black Student's Guide to Scholarships: 700+ Private Money Sources for Black and Minority Students.* 5th ed. Lanham, MD: Madison Books, 1999.

Weber, R. David, and Gail Ann Schlachter. *Financial Aid for African Americans.* El Dorado, CA: Reference Service Press, 1997.

Learning Disabilities

Bowman-Kruhm, Mary, and Claudine G. Wirths. *Everything You Need to Know About Learning Disabilities* (Need to Know Library). New York: Rosen, 1999.

Duke, Robert E. *How to Help Your Learning-Challenged Child Be a Winner.* Far Hills, NJ: New Horizons Press, 1993.

Fisher, Gary L., and Rhoda Woods Cummings. *The Survival Guide for Kids with LD [learning differences].* Minneapolis, MN: Free Spirit, 1990.

Greene, Lawrence J. *Learning Disabilities and Your Child: A Survival Handbook.* 2nd rev. ed. New York: Ballantine, 1987.

McGuinness, Diane. *When Children Don't Learn: Understanding the Biology and Psychology of Learning Disabilities.* New York: Basic Books, 1985.

Shin, Linda M. *Learning Disabilities Sourcebook.* Detroit: Omnigraphics, 1998.

Vail, Priscilla L. *Smart Kids with School Problems: Things to Know and Ways to Help.* New York: Dutton, 1987.

Wong, Bernice Y.L. *The ABCs of Learning Disabilities.* San Diego: Academic Press, 1996.

Hyperactivity: Attention Deficit Hyperactivity Disorder

Barkley, Russell A. *Taking Charge of ADHD: The Complete, Authoritative Guide for Parents.* New York: Guilford Press, 1995.

Block, Dr. Mary Ann. *No More Ritalin: Treating ADHD Without Drugs.* New York: Kensington, 1997.

Crook, William G. *Help for the Hyperactive Child: A Good Sense Guide for Parents of Children with Hyperactivity, Attention Deficits and Other Behavior and Learning Problems.* Jackson, TN: Professional Books, 1991.

Dendy, Chris A. *Teenagers with ADD: A Parents' Guide.* Bethesda, Md: Woodbine House, 1995.

Ingersoll, Barbara D. *Attention Deficit Disorder and Learning Disabilities: Realities, Myths, and Controversial Treatments.* New York: Doubleday, 1993.

Johnston, Robert B. *Attention Deficits, Learning Disabilities, and Ritalin: A Practical Guide.* San Diego: Singular, 1991.

Millichap, J. Gordon. *Attention Deficit Hyperactivity and Learning Activities.* Chicago: PNB Publishers, 1998.

Munden, Alison, Jon Arcelus. *The AD/HD Handbook: A Guide for Parents and Professionals on Attention Deficit/Hyperactivity Disorder.* Bristol, PA: Taylor & Francis, 1999.

Smith, Corinne Roth, and Lisa Strick. *Learning Disabilities: A to Z: A Parent's Complete Guide to Learning Disabilities from Preschool to Adulthood.* New York: Free Press, 1997.

Weissberg, Lynn W. *When Acting Out Isn't Acting: Understanding Attention-Deficit Hyperactivity and Conduct Disorders in Children and Adolescents.* New York: Bantam, 1991.

College Preparation

Green, Sharon Weiner, and Ira K. Wolf. *Barron's SAT: How to Prepare for the SAT.* Hauppauge, NY. Barron's Educational Series, 1998.

Claman, Cathy, ed. "10 Real SATs." College Entrance Examination Board, 1997.

Peterson's Guide to Colleges. Princeton, NJ: Peterson's, 1999. There are guides for each area of the country and specific career areas such as science, computers, health fields, etc.

Rimal, Rajiv N., and Peter Z. Orton. *30 Days to the SAT* (30 Day Guides). New York: Macmillan, 1996.

College Choices for African American Students

Custard, Edward T. *Best 311 Colleges, 2000 ed.* (CD-ROM). New York: Random House, 1999.

Parham, Marisa et al. *African American Student's Guide to College: 1999.* New York: Random House, 1998.

Wilson, Erlene B. *The 100 Best Colleges for African-American Students.* New York: Plume, 1993.

Colleges for Kids with Learning Disabilities and ADHD

Bramer, Jennifer. *Succeeding in College with Attention Deficit Disorders.* Plantation, FL: Specialty Press, 1996; (800) 233-9273.

Barros-Bailey, Mary, and Dawn Boyd. *Internet Disability Resources '98.* White Plains, NY: AHAB Press, 1998; 2 Gannett Drive, Suite 200, White Plains, NY 10604-3404; telephone: (914) 696-0708, toll-free: (800) 696-7090; E-mail: AHAB4@aol.com or www.ahabpress.com.

Mangrum Charles T., ed., et al. *Peterson's Colleges with Programs for Students with Learning Disabilities.* Princeton, NJs: Peterson's, 1997.

6

◆

WHEN I DISCOVER WHO I AM, I'LL BE FREE.
—RALPH ELLISON

Black Kids in White Schools and Communities

Melvia is a forty-year-old single mother from Harlem, whose son Melvin attended a local public school for his first two years of high school. Melvin, who was very bright, was not being challenged at his high school and did only what he needed to do to get by. Melvia was also frightened by the number of gang fights that occurred at his school. She became very excited when a friend told her about a number of boarding schools that offered scholarships for bright African American kids. With her friend's help and advice, Melvia helped Melvin to apply to a number of schools. He was accepted at a predominantly white boarding school in a small New England town where there were few African American residents.

Melvin was initially happy at the boarding school—he was on the basketball and track teams, and this athletic success made him very popular. Toward the end of his first semester, Melvin went to a local grocery store to buy snacks. The storeowner followed Melvin around the store, and after Melvin paid for his purchases, the storeowner accused him of adding candy that he had not paid for. A loud argument followed and the storeowner called the police. They took Melvin down to the police station, not believing that he was a student at the prestigious school, and proceeded to grill him.

When Melvin was permitted to call the school, his adviser came down to the police station and identified Melvin. He suggested that Melvin show the officers his purchases and the sales slip. When they compared the two, it was obvious that Melvin had paid for all of his purchases. The police released him.

After that day Melvin's feelings about his new school and the town changed. He was uncomfortable for the remaining year and a half until graduation when he went on to a historically black college. He shared with Melvia years later that he was miserable a good deal of the time he was at the school. When Melvia asked why he had not told her about the incident when it occurred, he replied that there was "nothing you could do anyway," and "I just handled it."

Many African American adolescents, faced with Melvin's experience in predominantly white schools and communities, "just handle it." Often that means that they attempt to cope by themselves with the impotent rage they feel. This rage often manifests itself in withdrawal, further isolation from peers, depression, and sometimes volatile outbursts and fighting.

When Your Son Attends a Predominantly White School

The belief in the power of education is so strong in many African American families that parents will go to great lengths to secure the best education available. For some parents that has meant paying for, or seeking scholarship aid from, a private or church-affiliated school. Still other parents seek better schools by enrolling their children in magnet schools with enriched curricula, having their kids compete for places in gifted programs in city high schools, or moving to suburban communities, which are often predominantly white. All of these experiences present both children and parents with a number of unique challenges. Many black parents find that motivating their deep commitment to the development of their children's racial identity becomes more complicated in a predominantly white setting. Some of these parents have encouraged their kids to consider a historically black college or university after high school graduation.

"I used to want fine black girls in my school. Now I'll take any black girls." (Jamal, age fifteen)

"The Only One . . ."

When very young African American kids attend predominantly white schools, they often find acceptance. But at around age nine or ten (sometimes sooner), a change may occur. The young boy who was invited to every classmate's birthday party may now find himself excluded from social activities. This can become even more pronounced by eighth or ninth grade, when dating issues become a factor. If there are not enough black girls to date, these boys often find themselves deciding between interracial dating or no social life. This process is very hard for many African American parents, who would prefer for their sons to date black girls. In addition, some white parents may be very reluctant to permit interracial friendships, some because they project their fears, often sexual in nature, onto African American male teenagers. Stigmas about interracial dating from black and white folks abound. The parents of these boys can also become conflicted when they realize just how isolated their son's life has become. In many ways, African American girls in these communities often feel even more isolated, as they often go through high school with no dates or social life. (See the end of this chapter for ideas on how you can help your kids to cope with this.)

Academic and Curriculum Issues

Another challenge for black teenagers and their parents in predominantly white schools is that teacher expectations often become "self-fulfilling prophecies." Teachers and school officials may bring their own stereotypes about African American boys to the classroom. In some situations, this may result in an African American boy receiving negative messages about his abilities, strengths, and performance. This can be played out in a variety of ways.

When our older son was in his senior year of high school, he went to see his college adviser with the list of colleges he intended to apply to. Although our son had excellent grades, the adviser crossed the three most competitive colleges off the list, stating that he would never get in. We were furious when we heard this and made an appointment to meet with the adviser and let him know how destructive his action was to our son. Once this was done, we had to engage in damage control with our son and help him to understand that he should not let the racism and low expectations of others define him or his belief in himself.

Many black parents whose children attend predominantly white schools also report that they struggle with the lack of African and African American history and books in the curriculum. When these issues are raised with teachers or librarians, they often become defensive. Some parents have also found that their children are assigned books that they consider degrading to Africans or African Americans, and when they seek to discuss this issue with teachers and school officials, they are, along with their children, labeled as troublemakers. It is very helpful for African American parents in this position to seek the support of and have a dialogue with other parents of color. You may find that your collective voices may have more power and will more likely be heard.

"I sacrificed a lot to put my son in a private school. He got locks in his hair and the assistant principal suspended him. I was furious. I went up to the school a number of times, but they just blew me off.

I got to talking to my son's guidance counselor. She told me that many of the other black kids and parents were running into these problems. I got a list of phone numbers and called some of the other parents. Some of them acted funny, but most were glad to hear from me. I called a meeting at my house. Five African American parents showed up. We made a plan to meet with the principal and talk about our concerns.

It was like night and day. He listened to us. It wasn't just my son; we were talking about how to improve things for all of our kids." (Richard, father of a sixteen-year-old son)

Often there is a conflict between African American kids and the school administration on cultural differences such as clothing, including the wearing of hats in school, music, and styles of communication. Many African American boys in predominantly white public and private schools have reported that their way of dressing is perceived by the school as inappropriate at best and threatening at worst. Of course, as white teenagers have increasingly embraced baggy pants, rap music, hip-hop, and other aspects of "street culture," such clothing, behaviors and styles are no longer perceived as threatening, however "gangster-ish" they may appear to some white and black adults.

Living in Two Worlds

For some African American kids, school is predominantly white but the home neighborhood is predominantly black or mixed. If this is your son's reality, it has its advantages because he has a black peer group to relate to. On the other hand, many kids have told us how hard it is to go back and forth between these two worlds.

Joe, a six-foot-tall ninth grader, has been attending a Catholic all-boys' school at his father's insistence, since the beginning of this school year. He is required to wear a uniform to school. This is a big problem because he becomes a "mark" in his neighborhood. He has adjusted by refusing to wear a backpack with his school's name on it. He leaves home in the morning in typical "homeboy" attire of baggy jeans, Nikes, baggy shirts, and his hat turned around. He changes into his uniform at a gas station men's room close to his school. At the end of the day, he reverses this process.

All of this exacts a price on Joe, but he considers it better than getting harassed or beaten up every day. He is very aware that he lives in two worlds and tries hard to cope, but admits that he doesn't always know how.

If your son is living in two worlds like Joe, talk to him. Ask him what it's like for him. Show him this story and this chapter and ask him if any of these things ring true for him. This will get the communication going between you so he doesn't feel so alone.

Living in a Predominantly White Community

Black kids who have spent their entire lives in predominantly white communities often feel awkward around other African American kids. Many of these kids spend their early life with no black peers and interact with other blacks only as adolescents. Parents who may have seen other black students while visiting their son's high school may not realize that the other black kids may be in other grades, or other classes if in the same grade. For parents who are concerned about their son's development of a positive black racial identity, his exclusively white peer group may present a problem, especially when their sons begin dating, as previously discussed. Such children may experience a conflict between their parents' expectations and the realities of their daily lives at home and in school.

Don, a seventeen-year-old African American living in a white middle-class community, angrily told his parents that he is repeatedly stopped by police when he is driving the family car alone.

Philip, a very friendly fifteen-year-old African American living in a suburban community near a large city in the South, has always been well liked and has felt accepted in his community. Suddenly, since he's become a six-footer, he finds that he is being followed in supermarkets and convenience stores. He feels watched all of the time.

William is a sixteen-year-old black male living in suburban Maryland. He lives in a white community and attends a predominantly white school. There is one other African American boy in his class. His parents are always pushing him to invite this kid over or "hook up" with him. The problem is that William can't stand this guy and feels very pressured to interact and be friends with him.

If you are raising your children in a predominantly white school and/or community or an area in which the black community is very spread out, realize that their experience in the community may be very different from your own. Parents in many cases leave the local community for their jobs every day, and it is the children who spend the bulk of their time in the neighborhood. As African American males, they often begin to experience subtle and not so subtle experiences of being singled out.

What you can do:

- Ask your kids about their experiences. Find out how they have been received and/or accepted in their school and neighborhood.
- Ask other black parents how they have been received or accepted in the community.
- Some black parents whose kids have been raised in predominantly white communities and who have attended predominantly white schools have encouraged their kids to consider a historically black college or university (HBCU's).
- Network with other black families with teenagers in your community. Throw some get-togethers to pull these families together so that the kids can meet one another.

- Find organizations for black families in your community, such as Jack and Jill.

Jack and Jill

Jack and Jill is a national black family organization with chapters in most areas of the country. New members need to be nominated by a family that has children in Jack and Jill. It was started by African American parents wanting to ensure that their children could have a black peer group who valued African American history and culture, educational achievement, and the spirit of giving back to the community. Prior to the 1960s and 1970s, Jack and Jill had a reputation for being restricted to blacks with light skin color as well as educational and professional status.

In recent years, however, the organization has become more inclusive and has developed a more positive black focus (although this may not be true of every chapter). Many younger African American mothers have brought a more Afrocentric focus to their Jack and Jill chapters. Although the organization was started when schools and communities were racially segregated (whether through Jim Crow laws in the South, or restrictive housing policies in other locations), it has particular relevance today for African American children who live in predominantly white communities.

For some black teens where the black community is defined by "how many black folks you can drive to in a half hour," Jack and Jill has provided a social lifeline of black friends and activities. It has helped in the development of racial identity for some black adolescents. For others, it has provided black peers, dates, and prom escorts. Some kids, particularly teenage boys, may resist participation in activities when young (early teenage years and younger), but this may change as they enter their late high school years and begin to benefit from the social networking opportunities the organization offers.

In today's mobile society in which families often move because of job demands, Jack and Jill has sometimes provided friends for kids in a new community. Jack and Jill is still primarily run by mothers, although many chapters have made an effort to involve fathers. Family activities, talent shows, dinners, and "black family" celebrations are a part of most chapters. The organization provides many Jack and Jill parents with other black parents to talk to about your worries about your kids. For single parents, this can be a particularly important support in a predominantly white area. It can also be an opportunity for black parents and adolescents to develop their leadership and organizational skills.

RESOURCES

Organizations

Jack and Jill of America, Inc. Barbara Newton, Executive Director, Jack and Jill of America, Inc., 7091 Grand National Drive, Suite 102, Orlando, FL 32819; telephone: (407) 248-8523; fax: (407) 248-8533.

National Association of Independent Schools, 1620 L Street, NW, Washington, DC 20036; telephone: (202) 973-9700; Web site: www.nais. org. This organization has diversity and multicultural services for students of color in independent schools and their parents. Contact Randolph Carter or Betty Ann Workman at the above telephone number or at rcarter@nais.org.

Special Programs for African American Students

Upward Bound, Council for Opportunity in Education, 1025 Vermont Avenue, NW, Suite 900, Washington, DC 20005; telephone: (202) 347-7430; fax: (202) 347-0786. (Federally funded program aimed at increasing the academic and motivational skills of high school students.)

A Better Chance (ABC), National Office: 419 Boylston Street, Boston, MA 02116; telephone: (617) 421-0950; (800) 562-7865; Web site: www.abetterchance.org. (Provides educational opportunities to students of color with the talent and potential to excel academically through their recruitment and placement into some of the nation's most outstanding secondary schools.)

Prep for Prep, (212) 579-1390.

Books

Tatum, Beverly Daniel. *Why Do Black Kids Sit Together in the Cafeteria*. New York: Basic Books, 1997.

7

OUR FUTURE LIES CHIEFLY
IN OUR OWN HANDS.

—PAUL ROBESON

The Journey to Manhood
and Peer Pressure

There is no question that successfully raising a black boy to manhood is a challenge. But we must keep within our vision that high-achieving, well-grounded, black teenage boys become responsible, productive adults. If it were left up to many of us, our sons' childhood days would go on forever, but we have to face the fact that our boys are becoming young men. We often ask ourselves where the time has gone.

We remember the morning when we looked at our youngest son and said to ourselves, Oh, my God, he's growing up. As he got dressed he walked around in his usual attire, which meant not much at all. Half dressed, he began the never ending search for the rest of his clothes in the midst of the piles in his room, wanting to know if anyone had seen his favorite pants. We bumped into him in the hallway as we competed for the bathroom, and it hit us that he was almost a foot taller than his mom and almost as tall as his dad. We noticed that he had once again used our lotion and hair products. All of a sudden he was taking a new interest in his appearance. These were telltale signs that our boy was growing up.

As parents we can stand back and admire the physical changes our sons' bodies undergo. This generation appears taller, bigger, stronger, and very adult-looking at a younger age. During this period there seems to be no way to keep them in clothes that fit, which makes some of us dislike the "baggy look" a lot less.

The physical changes in our sons set so many things in motion. They trigger a chorus of demands, particularly from some male family members who may say, "You must stop being a mama's boy and be a man." As African American parents we want them to be men, but we worry about their safety in this new role. On the one hand, we know that they are still too young to have learned the wisdom required for adult life: making smart decisions, shouldering responsibility, and making sacrifices for the future. Yet we look around us and see so many of our children involved in situations that even adults should not have to face. We hope that our efforts up to this point to make them good and responsible men will pay off. We pray that our boys will remain safe when they are not with us.

As we looked at our son that morning, we realized that he was not only changing in size but also in personality. We were so used to viewing him through rose-colored glasses that converted him to an eight-year-old boy. Taking those glasses off would mean having to acknowledge changes that would take a lot of adjustment. Not only did he smell differently with our lotion on—but now the mirror was suddenly all-important. His personality, mood, and posture changed with each piece of clothing he draped on his body. One day we also noticed he knew how to shave! His voice deepened, something we noticed particularly when he was talking on the phone with his boys. One minute he would be speaking in his normal voice to us and the next minute he's speaking in low, husky tones to his friends. Sometimes those exchanges were all about interests in girls. Yet another sign that our boy was growing up.

Your son, who just yesterday you may have had to run behind to get him to take a bath, now looks like a man, is grooming himself like a man, and is hanging out with his boys the way some grown men do. Our boys seem so virile. It is these very signs that make a parent shudder. As we see and respond to their changes, we know that others in the community will also—some of whom may not treat him well. Recognizing their growth gives us pause about their future.

When he goes out the door dressed like the other kids in

baggy pants and all, we become aware that others are beginning to influence him and pull him away from us. His peer group, likely to include a girl who has his interest, is moving in and becoming more primary in his day-to-day life. At the same time, your role as a parent is changing fast.

Transforming the Manchild: Letting Them Grow

Realizing that our boys are becoming young adults has many implications. We wonder how much his friends are going to control him, and how much control we are going to maintain. Many black sons play an important role in the family. Some parents rely on them to meet their own emotional needs.

We not only expect our sons to be responsive to our beliefs on how a boy should grow into manhood but at times we also place him in the position of acting like a manchild before he is ready, physically or mentally. Some of us expect our sons to substitute for the lack of a relationship with a man. Fathers (or mothers) can make sons best buddies when they should be more parent than friend. At times we expect our sons to substitute for us as adults or as parents, perhaps encouraging him to assume child care and/or family protective roles that are too emotionally and intellectually challenging for him. We may think that he can handle it, as many of our children manage the responsibilities given to them. But at times we can put them into positions that no child should be placed in. We can act out of convenience, given our own daily struggles. We look at our son, observe the man he appears to be, and begin to believe what we see. Some of his behavior is manly, after all, as when he insists that he has "everything under control." But in fact we know he has neither the life experience nor wisdom to take on the responsibilities we sometimes place in his hands.

When we see our young men pulled in so many directions it makes us want to hold on tighter. For some, the task of parenting a young black male is daunting. We can feel inadequate as we struggle against the outside influences that often seem like they are working against our good parenting efforts. It's important to understand that teenagers, more than almost anything, want to belong. Wanting to be a part of a group that supports their interests and activities is typical of all adolescents. It is no less the case for black male teenagers. What we contend with are the circumstances we know so well as the temptations and pressures that accompany these new needs, new experiences, and these new people they let into their lives. Some things that put the "fear of God" in parents include: peers, girls, drugs, police, and peer violence. We wonder how our boy-turning-man will survive.

The "Cool Pose"

Many black boys learn how to put up a front when they are growing into manhood, something author Richard Majors has called a "cool pose." Our sons learn how to act big and bad in ways that protect them and help them cope with the assaults on their manhood. Some of these may come from society, others from their peers. As they venture outside their neighborhoods, and even on their own streets, many people may respond to them with fear. Majors points out that "the cool front of black masculinity is crucial for the preservation of pride, dignity and respect. It is also a way for the black male to express bitterness, anger and distrust toward the dominant society." As a part of the cool pose that Majors describes, young black men learn to act "calm, emotionless, fearless, aloof and tough" in the face of threats or challenges.

Although parents have tried to help their sons understand the challenges black men face on a daily basis, their sons begin to really experience this for themselves during their teenage years, a time when it is common to feel insecure and unsure of where they belong in the world. Being cool on the outside provides a way of masking the turmoil that all adolescents experience on the inside. Your son may suddenly resent being called by the family nickname because it doesn't fit with the new cool image he is trying to convey. As we discussed in Chapter 5, he may be receiving messages from his peers that it is uncool to be a good student, and your son, who had done well in elementary school, is all of a sudden in danger of failing his subjects in junior high. He may also try to act like he has no parents when he is with his peers and not want to introduce you to his friends. You are a parent; for many kids that equals an embarrassment.

Hidden under all of this upsetting behavior is the fact that our sons are in search of their identities as men—and as black men. They want the same self-esteem and respect, dignity and control, that others want. In many ways, the cool pose may be your son's way of trying to protect his self-esteem when he feels assaulted by society, schools, his peers, and sometimes us—his parents, and his family.

The Lure of the Streets

All teenagers want freedom from the prying eyes of their parents. At the same time, many hunger for clear limits and guidelines, hoping someone they consider cool will mentor them in the "ways of coolness." Enter the peer group and the lure of the streets. One of the ways in which peer activities change in adolescence is that our sons are more drawn to the streets than ever before. For many kids, this lure began as early as age seven or eight. By young adulthood the peer group becomes central in our kids' lives. Richard Majors describes the streets as "the school for life that easily competes with the dry, often irrelevant pap squeezed between the pages of books."

Your son's new love for the streets comes with a number of dangers of which you may be unaware. Large blocks of unsupervised time coupled with the tendency of adolescents to be risk takers leads many of our kids into peer activities that are not positive, some of which carry a penalty from the law.

Ask yourself: is your son streetwise? Can he sense when trouble is coming his way? Will he forsake his peers if they are trying to involve him in illegal activities? Or is he a follower who will "go along for the ride"? Kalif's story illustrates the risks of being a follower:

Kalif was thirteen years old. He thought he was "big and bad," dressed in "gangsta" clothes, and had begun hanging out with a much older group (sixteen to eighteen years old). He tried to win their approval by being like them. One day, some of the other boys snatched cakes, drinks, and chips off the shelves of a convenience store and ran out. Kalif wasn't as fast as the older boys and he was the only one caught by the store owner. He was arrested and did time in a juvenile detention center. For Kalif, his need to assert his manhood and copy the behavior of older boys he admired led him to follow them into trouble.

Styling: The Clothes Don't Make the Man

Have you noticed that after years of not caring about his appearance at all, your son is paying a lot of attention to how he looks? He may not like to shop, but he forces himself to, rather than wear anything his mother picked out for him. If this is happening in your home, take heart. It is not just you. This is one of the most common changes for parents of adolescents.

For African Americans, "styling" or dressing "cool" has always been a part of the adolescent passage. It becomes for many of our African American males a way of declaring their unique style. Ironically, as they strive for individuality, they dress exactly like their peers. If you are one of many parents who is embarrassed by a son whose pants hang so low he's in danger of showing parts of himself that should be covered up, you are in good company. Styling and clothes can sometimes take on a deadly significance, as you will see in our discussion of gangs in Chapter 11. Even if your son is not involved in a gang, for the first time his clothes can make him a "mark" or a target on the streets. Many African American parents are reluctant to make the financial sacrifice to buy their kids the status items they ask for, having heard stories about kids being robbed and even killed over a pair of Nike sneakers, a leather coat, or a gold chain.

Once again, pick your battles. Every generation has had to battle with kids about clothes, hairstyles, etc. (Just remember our parents' reactions to Afros, dashikis, etc.) Kids are very sensitive to looking weird or like outsiders to their peers. If your son is doing well in other areas, you may cut him some slack on his clothes.

The one exception has to do with gang colors. (See Chapter 11.) Many gangs have their own colors. For example, the Bloods' color is red and the Crips' color is blue. If gangs are an issue in your community, find out the gang colors. Talk to your kids honestly about how kids have been beaten up for wearing gang colors. Ask them about the gang colors in your community. Ask around yourself. Other parents or older guys often know a lot. Many black parents also have kids pay for some of their own clothes out of money from part-time or summer jobs, their allowance, or gifts.

Suck It Up and Be a Man

Boys learn what it means to become a man in general and a black man in particular from five main sources: what parents teach them, what the peer group teaches them, what they see in the media (rap and hip-hop videos, TV and movies), what other adult black men teach them, and what they observe about how black men are treated in society. The harsh circumstances of being black and male are not lost on our teenagers. Statistically, black males do more poorly in school, have more difficulty finding jobs, are disproportionately represented in the criminal-justice system, and are at greater risk for certain diseases, such as hypertension, which results in a shorter life expectancy, than other groups. They see and hear the reality of these statistics in the lives of their peers, on television and in the movies, in their music, and in their own life experiences. We reinforce this in no uncertain terms by our constant warnings and concerns. It doesn't take long for our boys to know the score.

Where we fail to interpret life for them, their peers step in to provide their own interpretation. Where we fail to be family, the peer group—or the gang—becomes family. Where we fail to provide physical and emotional protection, the peer group becomes the foundation of support. Where we fail to teach respect, the peer group teaches its own version: "the brotherhood."

When our boys become teenagers, hit the streets, and embrace their friends, one of the rites of passage for manhood is learning the code of the brotherhood. This code is an appeal to the common bond, the unique experiences of being a black male in America. It is a style that is used as much to weather confrontations as it is to protect them against self-doubts, bolstering their self-esteem. First and foremost, the code is about survival as black men. It defines how to gain respect and dignity. It teaches about rules of trust between brothers and others, how to respond to betrayal and distress (i.e., "I've got your back."), and how to be fearless and project that fearlessness to others through "the cool pose." No matter how much we may want to control our son's emergence as a man, each black male child must walk down his own path to becoming a black male adult. Adolescence powerfully ushers them to that crossroad.

Role Models

Having positive black male role models helps our kids to see manhood positively. There are numerous role models of black manhood to be found in black history books. (See Chapter 1 for ideas.) There are also programs that teach manhood using rites-of-passage models from both traditional African societies as well as from contemporary African American history.

Mentoring is another important means of exposing young black males to positive role models. But you don't have to find mentoring programs to achieve this goal. Right in our very backyards there are living role models for our sons. The local business owner, the mailman, the corporate executive, and the retired military sergeant (to name a few) can be overlooked sources of information and inspiration for young boys. But we must be willing to strike up relationships and seek them out. The more we can expose our sons to a variety of different types of positive black male role models, the better. One of the biggest challenges is that so many role models are out of the realm of our sons' everyday lives. Professional athletes like Michael Jordan who are doing positive things are great to point out to our sons, but they are so removed from their daily lives that it is often a cruel hoax to hold these men up as role models and lead our sons to believe that every good basketball player can be like them. In addition to the media stars and great athletes, we must also elevate role models exemplifying attainable achievements. Also, beware of using athletes who may have come from humble beginnings but whose present lives don't live up to your high standard as role models.

We must be able to elevate the work ethic, sweat, sacrifice, and dedication that got them where they are today as examples for our sons, not the flagrant materialism that many of them exhibit. All too often, it's the latter that's emphasized, providing false expectations and promoting dangerous values in our sons.

In sum, we may not be able to get our sons to listen to everything we say, but we can come prepared for the task of raising our sons. We often know more than we think: we take for granted our own knowledge and life experiences, which are so helpful in raising our children into the men—and women—we wish them to become. Talk with others, ask for advice, and continue to learn about how to help your son grow into a strong black man. Talk to different men about the high and low points in their journeys to manhood. Learn from their lessons and share them with your son. Seek out the elders in your community and listen to their stories of survival. Wisdom is often found where you least expect it.

RESOURCES

Boyd, Herb, and Robert L. Allen, eds. *Brotherman: The Odyssey of Black Men in America.* New York: Fawcett, 1996.

Canada, Geoffrey. *Reaching Up for Manhood.* Boston: Beacon Press, 1998.

Majors, Richard, and Janet Mancini Billson. *Cool Pose.* New York: Touchstone, 1993.

White, Joseph, and James Coñes III. *Black Men Emerging: Facing the Past and Seizing a Future in America.* New York: Routledge, 1999.

8

◆

WE CANNOT SILENCE THE VOICES THAT WE DO NOT LIKE HEARING.

—DEBORAH PROTHROW-STITH

Rap, Media Influences, and Hoop Dreams

Sometimes it seems that our kids are bombarded by media influences from all sides. Whether it is the sexy "bad girl" images of hip-hop artist Lil' Kim or the "gangsta" rap of Snoop Doggy Dog, we can barely keep up with the current names before a new generation comes along. The movies are also rampant with constant images of sex and violence. Even TV, which decades ago was considered a lesser evil, now has more violence and sexual themes than before. African American parents, who often sacrificed to buy their children computers, believing that computers would help their children to do better in school, now realize that they must monitor computer use, aware of the often dangerous world to which the Internet exposes our children. It seems crucial that we ask ourselves a question: can a steady diet of television, movies, and the Internet produce the next generation of healthy, well-balanced, productive African-American men?

Although the great success of black athletes has inspired some boys to stay in school and away from drugs, many parents struggle with the mixed messages that the sports world gives to African American youth. This chapter will explore the above media influences and their impact on your children.

For the Love of Rap and Hip-Hop

Some of the songs are about drug deals, gun battles, gang wars, violent death, "bitches," and "ho's." And our sons (and many of our daughters) love them. As parents we have to understand the purpose and appeal of rap so we can communicate with our kids.

When rap and hip-hop originated in the black neighborhoods in New York in the late 1970s, it was simply a way for local D.J.s to boast about their skills and their neighborhood. The criminal and woman-hating imagery became associated with rap via groups like Ice-T and Niggaz With Attitude (N.W.A), who set the most negative stereotypes of inner-city life to music. For some rappers, their lyrics are autobiographical, having survived lives in gangs and prison, heroin addiction, and homeless shelters—many before their eighteenth birthday. The CDs include titles like *Hard-Knock Life,* and *Thuggin.* One rapper is pictured on the cover of his album holding an Uzi (ironically, one of his songs is titled "Stop the Violence").

Other rap songs tell of the injustices endured by black men in America. Messages are conveyed about politics, the poor educational system, and, surprisingly, that staple of the late 1960s— world peace. Some rap songs are concerned with the teenage preoccupations that were such a torment in our day and our parents' day—loneliness and heartbreak. In the late 1980s, Will Smith, the group Kid 'n Play, and girl groups like Salt-n-Pepa made rap more appealing to middle-class (black and white) American youth.

This amazingly profitable music was started by young men with little reason for hope finding a way to express themselves through "street poetry." In the process they found local, national, and, for some, international fame, and great financial success. Today there are rich black producers, rappers, and record label moguls. Our black sons see rap as an area where they can be themselves, show their talent, "keep it real," achieve fame, and make huge amounts of money all at the same time.

Black artists have set the standard for American music whether that was the original rock 'n' roll of the 1950's, the Motown of the 1960s, or the disco of the 1970s. And although some rap and hip-hop artists—such as Queen Latifah, KRS - One, Will Smith, and, more recently, Black Star and Goodie Mob— have tried to include positive messages in their music, what upsets parents about rap is its many negative messages. It projects the most negative stereotypes of black men as violent, drug- and alcohol-dependent, and abusive to women.

African American parents are worried that some rap and hip-hop videos glorify the violent gang lifestyle and characterize women as "bitches" and "ho's," who exist solely to service men sexually and serve as punching bags. References to drugs and alcohol, especially "40's"—bottles of beer and malt liquor that come in a forty-ounce size, are rampant, which is bad enough in the music but becomes even more dangerous in the visual image of videos. The negative values presented by some rap and hip-hop videos are all the more powerful because we see them acted out by black role models that our kids embrace. We are afraid of the power of those songs to change our sons into "gangstas" or gang wannabes.

"Gangsta Images" or "Reality" Rap

The violent deaths of Tupac Shakur, Notorious B.I.G. ("Biggie") Smalls, and other rappers have brought a lot of attention to the gang image of many rap CDs and videos. Some rappers have been arrested repeatedly for violent incidents, which further fuels their "gangsta" reputations. Even when they are arrested for nonviolent offenses, such as speeding or running a red light, they are often found to have weapons in their possession.

Because so many kids have a Walkman today, it is hard to restrict the music they listen to. You can set limits on what they listen to in your home. But it is even more effective to talk openly with them about your concerns.

What Parents Can Do

As is often the case, communication can help lessen the fear and the generation gap when it comes to rap and hip-hop music and our sons. Here are some strategies identified by Dr. Jeffrey Gardere that can help:

- Listen to some rap songs that your son likes. You may need to play them a few times to understand the lyrics. Be as open-minded as possible about what you hear.
- Watch rap and hip-hop videos with your son.
- Read some of the urban rap magazines like *The Source* and *VIBE*. Familiarize yourself with the lingo and examine the stories behind the rappers.
- Watch BET (Black Entertainment Television) and MTV (Music TV) once in a while with your kids to see the latest videos.
- Talk to your son about the messages in the music he listens to. (You'll have plenty to talk about!) Make remarks that state facts and show empathy rather than condemn. Example: "The guy in that song really had a hard life" or "That girl sounds like she really had her heart broken." This shows your son that you are willing to listen to the messages, and distinguish among the songs rather than condemn them all.
- Be honest with your son about the negative messages that really concern you: violence, sex, abuse of women, etc. Talk to him and listen to his responses.
- Ask your son how he relates to the messages in the music. Does he feel the way the rapper does? In what ways? Through such conversations you may gain some insight into a son who usually does not express his emotions.
- Ask your son if he would like to write his own rap song and perform it for you. You will find out a lot about him in the process.
- Talk to your son about the importance of "his music" in his life. (Remember how important your music was to you growing up.) For many of our kids, their music is one of the most important things in their lives and one of the ways they cope when life gets rough or the pressure becomes great. Also, if your son shows musical talent—singing, rapping, as a D.J.— encourage it. Many parents are afraid to encourage kids because of the lifestyle of many in the music business. Talk openly with your son about this. Talk to him about the drugs, sex, and violence of some of his hip-hop and rap idols and talk to him about how he would deal with this.

TV and Movies

According to the Center for Media Education, most children watch about 1,500 hours of television each year (that's about four hours per day!). Add to that a movie on the weekend and a few nights of video game play, and there isn't much time that children are not sitting in front of some type of screen. Free time, which once meant drawing, riding a bike, playing outside, or just stretching one's imagination, is becoming an endangered notion.

Like many parents, we like to watch the TV news in the evening while preparing dinner. One day, when our younger son was eight or nine he abruptly turned the TV off. We asked him why. He replied, "You guys won't let me watch violent movies, but all that's in the news is violence." He made a lot of sense. The top stories were about murder and rape.

Violence dominates much of the television content older children and teenagers watch. While a direct link between violent behavior and television and movie watching on the part of children and teens can't be proven, experts agree that there is a connection. President Clinton initiated a federal study into the influence of media violence on children and challenged the film industry to better enforce its R and PG-13 movie ratings. *New York Daily News* critic Jack Mathews noted, "There is no doubt that children are exposed to graphic, excessive, indiscriminate violence in movies, from G-rated pictures on up; the question is whether parental attitudes in our culture can be made less tolerant of it."

In her book *The Plug-In Drug,* Marie Winn reminds us that the worst epidemic of juvenile violence in our nation's history occurred just as television was introduced into the American home in the 1950s. Over the last few years alone, we have seen horrifying crimes committed by teenagers who seemingly show no remorse. Experts term this new breed of young criminals "nonempathic murderers." It is not that our children are learning *how* to commit awful crimes from what they watch, but that they see human life as a valueless commodity. An experiment was conducted with boys aged five to fourteen; some had watched a great deal of television, some had watched little or no TV. A violent sequence in a movie was shown to both groups and their emotional responses were recorded. The first group was significantly less affected by what they saw, as their many years of television viewing had desensitized them. This is corroborated by experience. Many adolescents who have committed remorseless crimes have been described as "heavy television viewers."

For our sons, television viewing may include local newscasts, which operate according to the rule "If it bleeds, it leads." Not only is the coverage heavily weighted toward stories of crime and violence, our young men's self-image cannot be helped when so many of the black men he sees on television have their heads down and hands cuffed behind their backs. Violent activity, sex, and profanity have become commonplace in the media. Even we adults often choose programs with violence and sex in them over lighter viewing, even though we watch TV "to relax."

Better TV, Less TV, No TV

We have all experienced the almost hypnotic power television has over us. It is fascinating—and frightening—to learn some of the effects watching has on our minds. According to Marie Winn, our eyes have difficulty focusing on the steadily changing picture on the screen, thus resulting in a "trancelike" state of glazed eyes, where we become oblivious to things going on around us. Experts have even suggested that early television viewing can lead to a predisposition to drugs that produce similar trancelike states. Some parents use television as a baby-sitter so that they can get a moment's peace. Others have the television on virtually all their waking hours: One mother admits, "It seems that our television is on twelve hours a day, sometimes just for background noise."

In a study of five hundred fourth- and fifth-graders, all of them showed a preference for watching television over reading anything. Preadolescents in another study said they rarely read for pleasure. Flipping on the remote requires much less mental energy than picking up a book or magazine. One effect is that it has produced a generation of "lazy readers," kids who may be bright and able to read but are unable to absorb or comprehend the material. Television-educated children can repeat what they've heard and sometimes sound as if they know what they're talking about, but they have no idea how to apply the information they've gleaned to real-life situations.

Many parents report that kids often need to be told to "calm down" from their television or movie viewing experience because after several hours of such viewing their children have become irritable, anxious, angry, or bored.

As a group, blacks watch a disproportionately high amount of television and number of films. Children who have difficulty reading will turn to the television more than those who don't. For our children, particularly our sons, this is a tragedy. In an era of declining literacy, it is often our smart black sons who are branded "learning disabled" and funneled into special education.

Television lobbyists try to focus the discussion on improving the quality of what our children are watching, but most parents agree the answer lies less in improving the quality of programming our children watch and more in limiting the quantity of television allowed. Even educational programs that teach children valuable things require them to sit passively, except for the few times the child may be asked to participate while pictures flash in front of them.

Some child-advocacy groups recommend television-free homes as the best environment in which to grow healthy, imaginative children into productive adults. This would mean a personal sacrifice for many parents who enjoy television viewing. One compromise is to take "TV breaks," where the television is unplugged and removed for a week at a time. This is an annual event in Southern California, with good results. "No TV Week" promotes family unity and communication and reduces the dependence on the tube for entertainment. Jesse Jackson has recommended that parents turn off the TV for three to four hours every night and insist that homework and reading take place.

A Word on TV Talk Shows

Today, violent or sexually promiscuous teens have become a sought-after commodity on daytime talk shows, television fare very popular with teens, especially during after-school hours. A survey done by professors at the University of Pennsylvania showed older adolescents as more likely to be frequent talk show viewers. Their conclusion, after studying over two hundred teenagers, was that those who watched TV talk shows thought the guests—who are brought in specifically because their lifestyles violate societal norms, such as having frequent sex, running away from home, and getting pregnant—were typical teenagers. Similar studies show that heavy television use also leads to having unrealistic views of things like the number of athletes and entertainers in the "real world," and the chances that they might be physically attacked in a given week. Continuous television watching gave them a distorted vision of the world and made them more pessimistic about their safety and their futures. (Parents, take note: viewership increases a whopping 68 percent among adolescents during the summer when school is out.)

Rough Riding on the Net

The Internet and the World Wide Web have opened up a boundless cyber-universe. Approximately one in six black households owns a computer, and most computers have Internet access. Many of our children are online both in class and after school, learning new things, gathering information for projects and papers, playing games, accessing the latest sports news, exchanging E-mails, and "chatting." Although most of our children are engaged in this benign and even helpful activity, the Internet also offers access to pornography and other materials that are very offensive to most parents, such as sites giving information on bomb making and sites devoted to hate group organizations. Even when sites are "adult only," teenagers with computer expertise can hack into those sites. The magazine *Yahoo! Internet Life* featured a story about two young boys who had no trouble accessing an adults-only site. Take a deep breath and talk to your son calmly if you catch him on a porno site. You will only make it more enticing to him if he sees that you panic and rant and rave about it. (This may be a good time to talk to him about his sexuality. See Chapter 9.)

Since adolescent boys (and girls) are naturally curious about what is "forbidden," there are certain steps parents can take:

- Put the computer in a place where you can see and periodically monitor what your son is doing.
- Limit the amount of time he is allowed to be on the Internet. (Some of the Internet service providers, such as America Online, offer plans that restrict access to ten hours a month. This is less costly than unlimited service and provides a built-in check.)
- Use a software filter such as Net Nanny (www.netnanny. com) or Cyber Patrol (www.cyberpatrol.com), or America Online's Neighborhood Watch (keyword: parental controls) to block undesirable sites from your child's access.
- Watch your own Internet habits. Are you staying up late to peruse porno sites yourself? Remember that your son is like a sponge, soaking up all the things you do. You must lead by example, or your punishments will be in vain.

Hoop Dreams and the Lure of Sports

Sixty-six percent of African American boys say they want to become professional athletes, according to a statistic reported in the *Los Angeles Times*. As in the music industry, boys see many positive black male role models in professional sports, so it is only natural that they want to emulate them. Sports and music are glamorized industries that get lots of media attention, much of it targeted to teenagers. They are not exposed to the successful black businessmen we adults read about in *Black Enterprise* nearly as often. Moreover, they may not be seeing those successful men in their own neighborhood. But they are constantly seeing cool-looking black men playing basketball on TV.

There is nothing wrong with your son admiring a sports hero

or dreaming about having a career in professional basketball, football, or baseball. The problem occurs when he refuses to understand how much hard work, discipline, and sacrifice is involved in making his dreams come true.

Sherman Givens, former pro athlete, coach, and assistant coordinator for ICB Sports Network, talks to promising young African American ballplayers all the time. He sees the same story: boys who have natural talent on the court or on the field and feel that this alone will take them where they want to go. "A lot of kids don't understand that it didn't just happen for Michael Jordan overnight," notes Givens. "They don't hear about all of the work he put in even before he went to college, learning the fundamentals of the game, sharpening his talent, showing up at every practice, keeping up with his schoolwork, and learning how to be a team player. They think trash talking on the court and degrading other players is where it's at." These talented young players often end up frustrated and discouraged when they cannot qualify for college scholarships because the college coaches find them too undisciplined—on and off the court.

Sometimes the athlete is so desirable, however, that he will be the focus of coaches and recruiters who pursue him with great fervor. Spike Lee's movie *He Got Game* depicts this scenario. Givens tells of one recruiter who arranged to have an envelope with a hundred-dollar bill in it delivered to a prospective player's mother—every day! Others offer keys to cars, plane tickets, and even houses to get our sons to sign on the dotted line.

If you have an athletically gifted son, he is a commodity in today's world. But a smart and aware parent can prove a valuable asset to an athletically gifted and disciplined son, as was the case with Michael Jordan, Bo Jackson, and Tiger Woods.

Here are some ways to help your son truly be all that he can be:

- *Recognize his talent.* Talk to his gym teacher or coach and find out what he needs to succeed at the sport he has chosen.
- *Make sure he learns the fundamentals of the game he's playing.* Many volunteer coaches are well meaning but untrained, and therefore unable to teach our sons the basics. There are sports videos, books, and other resources to help you with this; take advantage of them and make them available to your son.

- *Teach him about the discipline of sports.* Talk continually about the need for practice, commitment, effort, being teachable, being a team player, and having a winning attitude.
- *Go to his games.* We were once told that there is nothing that thrills a boy more than someone cheering for him in the stands or on the sidelines as he "plays his game." Let your son know that you are there for him, win or lose.
- *Encourage him to attend a sports camp if he shows promise.* These camps will give your son a preview of what is involved in playing on a college team. He will also learn to compete with players who are just as talented as he is.
- *Be knowledgeable about the recruitment process.* There are only certain times of the year that coaches or recruiters can approach you or your son. There are also guidelines for what they can and cannot offer you. Don't sign anything without consulting your son's high school coach and an attorney.
- *Emphasize the importance of getting an education for a man's future "after his playing days."* Too many of our best athletes find themselves in their mid-twenties with no pro ball contract and no college degree to show for their efforts.

As black parents, the most important thing to remember is that you must stay involved. Know what music your kids are listening to, watch TV shows with them, find out who their heroes are. Talk to your kids honestly about your reactions, especially to the negative messages. If your son is big on sports, talk to him about his future early on. Encourage him but help him to understand the real deal about how few of our sons really become professional athletes. Be his "reality check" on all of the media influences in his life.

RESOURCES

AAU (Amateur Athletic Union), call (800) AAU-4USA or (407) 934-7200 for a list of contacts in your area.

NCAA (National Collegiate Athletic Association), P.O. Box 6222, Indianapolis, IN 46206-6222; telephone: (317) 917-6222; fax: (317) 917-6888; Web site: www.ncaa.org.

9

CHILDREN MAKE FOOLISH CHOICES WHEN THEY HAVE NOTHING TO LOSE.

—JAWANZA KUNJUFU

Sex and Sexuality

We remember the eventful day well. Our youngest son was eleven years old when we sat him down and said, "You know, son, we think it's time for us to have a talk about sex." This was followed by much protest, mumbling, and grumbling about "Why?" "Are you kidding?" "Do we have to?" "What's wrong?" and other don't-bother-me behavior. Finally, he gave in. And his first question was, "Okay, what do you want to know?"

All parents know that when our sons are about ten or eleven it is time for "the sex talk," but our own past experiences and insecurities sometimes get in the way of this important parenting function. In addition, our own experiences with our parents—talking to us or *not* talking to us—about this issue clash with the sense of urgency we may feel in an environment of much greater risk than our generation faced. We tell ourselves that we can handle this task, take a deep breath, say a prayer, and give it a whirl.

It is a wake-up call for many parents today that our preteen kids know much more about sex than we realize. Today, information about sex comes not only from peers, as it did in our day, but also from rap and hip-hop videos, movies, television, magazines, and the Internet. All of these are full of explicit details. Most schools offer sex education to our kids and this is very important, but parents don't agree as to what and how much information is appropriate to teach. Schools do not have the ability to transmit each parent's values. You cannot rely on schools to relieve you of your own parental responsibility—you must teach your children your views about sex and sexuality.

When we do discuss sex with our children, many of us leave it at the basics and do not prepare them for all the other thoughts, feelings, and confusion that surround sex, love, intimacy, and commitment in relationships. We may not feel that our experiences have equipped us to teach our sons about these areas, or we might find that we have more inhibitions about sex than we thought. Many parents have found success using books designed to "ease the pain" of talking to our sons (some are listed in the Resources section at the end of this chapter). It's best to begin to present the topic early, even before grade school, as a natural part of life. By the time your son is a preteen, talking about sexuality will not seem like such a big deal.

Martha, an African American mom, says: "I began talking to my sons about their bodies and about differences between boys and girls when they were five and six, using books appropriate for their age. When my oldest son turned thirteen, though, I handed the responsibility off to his father. The material was getting pretty graphic, and I realized I was more intimidated about sex talk than I thought!"

Another area that gives parents a great deal of concern is the subject of masturbation. You should not be alarmed if you discover that your son masturbates. It is normal sexual behavior, often discovered in adolescence by boys and girls. It usually is practiced in private as another form of exploring new sexual feelings and desires. Along with sexual fantasies, it is part of a process paving the way toward sexual experiences with partners.

Raging Hormones

Adolescence is a time when we see tremendous physical changes in our sons, such as a growth spurt similar to the one they went through when they grew from a toddler into a child. These physical changes are now happening much earlier than they did for many of us. Boys and girls are now beginning puberty as early as ten years old. This growth is triggered by hormonal changes in the body, most notably the growth of the sex glands, or gonads—testes in the male and ovaries in the female.

Genes play an important part in physical development. In boys, the penis and testes grow in relation to a boy's overall inherited growth potential. In other words, a boy's growth is going to be within the range of growth in size comparable to his father and other blood-related males in his family. A son with a tall, slim father and uncle is likely to be tall and slim himself, and so on. Poor health and nutrition, however, can compromise the physical development that nature intended for your son.

As healthy boys go through these normal bodily changes, it may strike panic in your heart. As one overwhelmed father once said to us bluntly, "My son is becoming a horny toad and is on the prowl for girls!" The low tones, secret discussions, and perked-up behavior when girls are around let us know his interests are shifting and moving in a sexual direction.

Our son and his boys were talking in the back of the car as we drove them home one day a couple of years ago. We were listening to music and hearing bits and pieces of their conversation. As we drove past some girls walking down the street, all of their talk suddenly stopped. They went immediately into coded conversation about the girls. They were "cool" about talking with adults in the car. They mumbled to one another about what they would do if they could get to meet those girls. It didn't take a rocket scientist to know that adolescence had begun on all fronts for these boys. And we realized that they were soon going to experience manhood as young African American males. The thought made us pause and wonder what the outcome of that journey would be for all of them.

Teaching Respect for Girls and Women

Mothers and fathers, sisters and brothers, grandmothers and grandfathers, and, of course, peers are major players in teaching a young brother about girls and women. Who the boy is close to determines who has the most influence in this important new area of his life. These attachments are going to be the source of either the inner conflict or clarity about how relationships work. It is in adolescence that peers put the greatest pressure on a boy to deviate from the expectations and wishes of parents. Also, the messages given to them by women may differ from those given by the men in their lives. From research we know that many fathers and close male role models will influence adolescent boys to be more sexually active, as compared to a mother's influence. The quality of the advice our sons get is determined by the condition of the hearts and minds of the advice givers. Be very careful who or what you're allowing to play that role in your son's life.

For example, our youth often get a negative message from the media that women are primarily objects of sexual pleasure and recreation, and that it is acceptable to speak in negative ways about them. A message gets across in the adolescence of some black men that black women can be disrespected. Think about it: for generations "mamas" have been the subject of all types of verbal abuse in the game called "the dozens." Though this game is not always played in the same way today, it has taken its toll on the relationships between black men and women.

Today, many rap songs fulfill that purpose. Many of today's MTV videos and other music cable TV stations include explicit references to women as "bitches" or "ho's." But black male-female relationships are talked about in blues lyrics and pop hits, too. Those songs often speak of either love, hate, or ambivalence. They send the messages that say "Beware of black women," and that warn of a struggle for dominant control in a relationship. And they tell of the importance of having a black woman's beauty and sex appeal as a prize, if only for others to envy. In any case, black women are portrayed as trouble more often than they are as loving partners whom men marry and raise children with. These negative and incorrect messages about girls and women are soon learned by our sons.

Black parents know perfectly well about these relationship messages. However, we often stand by and watch our sons repeat the same script as previous generations. Why do we do this? Here are some questions to consider that may help answer this. If we talk about one another "like a dog" in our homes, then why would we expect our teenage sons to think and feel any differently? If we use the *f*-word in our conversations about women, why wouldn't our son? If there is no father in the home, how we verbalize to our son our feelings about his father shapes his view of male-female relationships. Equally important for fathers, if we disrespect the women in the house, then our sons will do the same.

The old saying "If you want respect, you've got to give respect" is true. How African American male adolescents come to view and treat black women is a result of how the black men in their lives feel about black women. It also is related to how black women are viewed and treated by the larger society. Stereotypes are abundant about black women and the role they play in the family and in relationships with black men. Too often parents find themselves enacting the very assumptions they say appalled them and buying into the stereotypes that have been conveyed by others, including family, peers, and the media.

The legacy of attitudes and behavior characterizing the relationships between black men and women starts in childhood and in adolescence. Therefore as the parent of a black boy you need to be thoughtful about the way you conduct yourself around your children. This applies to the extended family also. Children watch how aunts and uncles, grandparents, all family members treat one another. Being part of friendship and organizational networks that model positive values about male and female relationships can be extremely helpful. Churches and other religious institutions can be a place in which a positive force can be found. Likewise, after-school activities, summer camps, sports, boys clubs, rites-of-passage and mentoring programs are also good arenas to find people who represent your values and will model positive relationships for your son.

Peer Pressure

The type of friends and the kind of risks they take, their values, and their behavior are going to affect your son either positively or negatively. Monitoring your son's friends is reassuring and helpful but no guarantee. Do not kid yourself. Teenagers are teenagers, and depending on how much your son is a risk taker and follower, some exploration is going to occur. This does not mean that you should ignore the friends your son makes, but do not expect to have complete control and therefore knowledge of all the things your son is getting into. One consolation, or just a point of information, is the fact that "the apple doesn't fall too far from the tree." Your son is going to be mindful of what you tell him if you have reinforced it from day one and modeled it to the best of your ability. If you have done your best to train him right, when he is older "it will not depart from him," as Proverbs tells us.

In his book *Makes Me Wanna Holler,* Nathan McCall has described his teenage years and the path that led him to prison. In their book *Black Man Emerging,* Joe White and James Coñes describe McCall's early attitudes toward women:

In Nathan's teenage macho world, women are objects of pleasure and sex is a source of release of tension. His initiation into sex at age thirteen is through a gang rape, referred to in street language as "running a train." Nathan and his peers lure unsuspecting neighborhood girls into vulnerable situations and rape them. Gang rape consolidates the group's identity. Nathan and his cohorts separate girls into two groups: mothers and sisters and "bitches and "ho's." Bitches and ho's are sex objects to be conquered by macho power or by manipulation and cunning. There is no room in the gang philosophy for love. Love means weakness and being controlled by women. The object of relationships with women is to get sex without falling in love, but making the woman believe you are in love.

"Did You Get Some?" Having Sex . . . Already

Sexual intercourse for black adolescents, boys in particular, is happening at an earlier age in general than previous generations. Surveys come across our desk that show some black boys having sexual experiences very early (some as young as age ten), compared to adolescents from other ethnic groups. A boy and his peers will create their own definitions of manhood, especially when there is a physically or emotionally absent father. Peers have ways of pressuring our sons into early sexual activity. The threat of embarrassment and challenge to his manhood is an age-old tradition. As one adolescent crudely expressed it: "No pussy, no respect." Being successful with girls is important to teenage boys. One of the "codes of the brotherhood" hinges on bragging about sexual conquests, real and imagined. "Getting some" and then bragging about it to other brothers is a merit badge of masculinity that permits entry into black "manhood."

Our sons not only have sexual encounters at earlier ages, but they also look like adult men earlier than other boys. This of course is a concern for parents, who think of the risks in the street, the troubles from other youth or police who will treat them like men even though they are still boys. Early physical and sexual development can bring special pressures to young black men. The challenges of the street are obvious, but early physical development also presents emotional challenges. If the peer group also "honors" your early physical development by granting you adult status, then you are expected to behave the way they think a "man" ought to behave.

Looking mature doesn't mean acting mature. The fact is that most adolescents do not have the social and emotional skills to enter and manage a sexual relationship. But his "boys" may put the pressure on him "to produce" according to their expectations and fantasies. This may mean more than being able to "get next to a girl," but it can mean "making it" with an older girl (e.g., ninth grader with a twelfth grader) or perhaps a mature woman. Your son's unwillingness to comply or inability to achieve conquests violates the code of the brotherhood and puts his manhood in question in the eyes of his peers, whose opinion means so much to him at this stage. His loyalty to the brotherhood may also come under suspicion.

The pressures are different for a boy who is small in stature, or delayed in his physical development compared to his friends, but they also can be emotionally damaging. His peers may have less of an expectation of his success in wooing women or proving his sexuality because he is considered by the brothers as still a kid. They may put him in the "watch and learn" program, which can be a deadly position of humiliation for a youngster who wants to be part of the cool group. The embarrassment and blow to his self-esteem can lead to overcompensation on the part of the "kid," promoting exaggerated sexual behavior, such as promiscuity, to prove to friends that he is "down." He may also withdraw from his friends and from social settings, branding himself an outcast.

Physical development brings changes in behavior, temperament, and attitudes for youth. Thus, as a parent you should watch the physical development of your son with interest instead of horror. Watch the time and rate of physical development at various points, taking note of growth in height, appearance of facial hair, and body build so you can consider the possible influence it has on peer relations, his interests in girls, and his performance in school. As we physically changed from childhood to adolescence to adult, people treated us differently and had new expectations of us. Things haven't changed. Which is why the old saying that adolescents are "too young to be treated as adults, but too old to be treated as children" represents a classic dilemma for parents and the teenager during this period.

Teaching Sexual Responsibility

Teaching sexual responsibility includes not only the physical mechanics of having sex but the total experiences that come with it. This includes understanding the emotional demands of intimacy. Most teenage boys have no idea what it means to be emotionally close to another person. Start early by talking to them about the connection between sex and love. Talking to your son about how women should be treated is very important. This is a special role for black fathers to assume. Many black women with close relationships with their sons also do this well. Grandparents and other older people can do this as well, teaching their grandsons to open doors and show respect for their mothers and other women early on. Of course, if the talk is laced with sarcasm and bitterness about black men as "dogs," you will only reinforce the message their peers give them, that "black women see black men as no good." It is a vicious cycle, but one that can be broken with thoughtful and sincere parenting.

Teaching sexual responsibility also includes helping your son learn he does not have to prove his manhood by sexual encounters and escapades. Helping him to understand the way peer pressure works is often the meat of communication for parents during adolescence. It's teaching, trusting, and giving the freedom of responsible choice, that is, letting him make decisions that teach him responsibility for his actions without putting him at unnecessary risk.

Sexual responsibility requires that your son learn to love and respect himself. Only then can he love a woman and treat her properly. For an increasing number of African American parents with strong spiritual beliefs, sexual responsibility also involves talking to our sons about sexual abstinence until marriage. What that means is loving themselves and the woman they are with enough to wait. Today, many more African American youth, alarmed by the rise of AIDS in the black community, are beginning to see the wisdom of waiting until they are mature and ready to make a commitment to marriage and life partnership.

One mother of a thirteen-year-old son stated: "My son was part of a True Love Waits program for youth at our church. He asked a lot of questions, and it really helped him understand things about sexuality better than I could ever have explained them."

AIDS in the Black Community

Teaching about condom use and the risk of AIDS and other sexually transmitted diseases (STDs) is also essential in today's world. While morally and spiritually we may preach abstinence to our kids, we cannot lose track of the reality that even the best-behaved adolescents rebel against their parents' beliefs in some way. As responsible parents, you need to be frank about the risks and consequences of AIDS (and other STDs) from sexual behavior. You need to make it clear that condom use is still not 100 percent protection (they sometimes break during sex). Be frank with your sons and give them this and other important information.

The facts below should be shared honestly with your son. Be encouraged by the fact that young African Americans are more likely than whites to change their sexual behavior in an effort to prevent the spread of HIV, according to a study cited in Farai Chideya's *Don't Believe the Hype.*

AIDS is an insidious killer. At first there may be no symptoms, as our bodies attempt to fight the HIV virus. This asymptomatic state may last for years. The next stage is characterized by infections of all types that won't go away, even with treatment. And the final stage, full-blown AIDS, develops when an HIV-infected person is hit with various serious infections or cancers. A simple blood test can determine whether or not you have HIV. Here are some facts about AIDS:

- AIDS (acquired immune deficiency syndrome) is the number one killer of black males between the ages of twenty-four to forty-four. African Americans represent about 13 percent of the total U.S. population, but they account for 36 percent of the nation's 216,980 AIDS cases reported to the Centers for Disease Control and Prevention and 43 percent of the AIDS cases diagnosed in 1996. According to the Centers for Disease Control, one in 50 black men are HIV positive.
- AIDS can be transmitted through "needle sharing," which is common among certain drug users (especially heroin addicts) and by sex with a man or a woman.
- AIDS has the fastest-growing infection rate among young women of color, many of whom get the virus from IV drug-using men.
- AIDS curricula, offered in many public high school systems, teach adolescents about AIDS and its dangers. If your son is learning about this in school, it can be used as a springboard for further discussion in your home about sexuality.

STDs in the Black Community

Sexually transmitted diseases are viral and bacterial infections that are passed via sexual intercourse and oral sex. Most are treatable if detected at a reasonable time after infection (except as noted). Though most boys and men think STDs are a "woman thing," think again. Men generally suffer from symptoms of STDs as much or more often than women. This is largely because the penis is an "outside" organ, where changes can be seen more readily than on the inside of a woman's vagina. If infections persist, even with treatment, an HIV test is strongly recommended. It's key that you make your son aware of the consequences to *his* body of irresponsible sexual activity, as well as that of his partner. Here are some of the most common STDs and their symptoms:

- *Chlamydia* is the most common bacterial STD with little or no symptoms, though some include abdominal pain, abnormal discharge, and painful urination.
- *Genital warts* are caused by the incurable human papillomavirus (HPV) and appear as cauliflowerlike warts on the penis shaft, head, and under the foreskin. The warts can be treated and removed, though the virus remains for life. They are often confused with herpes lesions.
- *Gonorrhea* is a bacterial infection that causes discharge from the penis and painful urination. It can invade the genitals as well as the eyes and throat.
- *Hepatitis B* is the most contagious of all STDs and is incurable. It can cause fever, nausea, dark-colored urine, rashes, and yellowing of the whites of the eyes.
- *Herpes* is an incurable viral infection that causes small, painful blisters and sores to appear on the genitals or mouth, as well as flulike symptoms and painful urination. Often confused with genital warts.
- *Syphilis* is caused by bacteria and presents itself as a chancre (kan-ker) sore on the genitals, anus, or mouth. The sores ooze clear liquid and last about a month. Untreated, it causes flulike symptoms and rashes on the hands and feet. If untreated, it may result in organ invasion, serious illness, or death.
- For more information, see the book *Sexually Transmitted Diseases* in our Resources section at the end of this chapter.

Teenage Pregnancy and Fatherhood

Nathan McCall's story continues as follows:

In his senior year in high school, Nathan does fall in love. He and his girlfriend conceive a child. He wants to be responsible, cares for his girlfriend and infant son, but is not ready for responsibility. His girlfriend's parents provide financial support and medical care for the baby. (Excerpted with permission from White and Coñes' *Black Man Emerging*)

Most of the literature and programs on teenage pregnancy

have focused on teenage mothers; fathers are almost totally ignored. This is unfortunate because it can contribute to the cycle of fathers not being involved in their children's lives. A number of programs around the country, including the National Institute for Responsible Fatherhood founded by Charles Ballard in Cleveland, have focused on helping teen fathers to become responsible parents.

For many African American parents, learning that their teenage son has gotten a girl pregnant is cause for great shame:

Kenyatta's parents were very religious Christians who had struggled to put him through school. He was in his senior year in high school and had been accepted at a college when he came home and told them that his girlfriend was pregnant. They were devastated and saw all of their dreams for him slipping away.

Some parents have unfortunately accepted teenage pregnancy as a way of life:

Atif's girlfriend was pregnant at fifteen. Her mother acted as if it was no big deal, as both she and her mother had been pregnant at the same age.

Other parents give a different message:

Karil's girlfriend became pregnant with his child, and he was very proud of his approaching fatherhood. His mom told him not to worry, that she would help them take care of the baby.

Even if you have given your son strong messages about sexual abstinence or safe sex, they often will experiment with sexuality at this age. Wherever you fall in your beliefs about teenage pregnancy, make sure you give your sons a strong message about the responsibility of fatherhood. Even though you may not approve of the pregnancy, encourage your son to be a father to his child. And remember that no matter how you may feel about your son's fatherhood, his child is innocent of all blame and needs your love and support as well as his.

Gay Sons: Secrets in Our Communities

Carla, a forty-year-old mom, was devastated. Her seventeen-year-old son Mwanza had just told her that he was gay. She was so torn that she went to see her minister. He prayed with her. She was a devout Christian, but she loved her son dearly. She told her son honestly what her religious beliefs were, but she also told him that he would always have her love and could always come to her and his family.

Earl was furious. He found out from his nephew that his son was gay. He confronted his son, and Jeffrey proudly stated that he was. Earl yelled at him, beat him up, and told him to get out of his house. That night Jeffrey attempted suicide.

Max was "out" to everyone at school. He had even told his sisters that he was gay, but he was afraid to tell his mom. She was a deaconness in her church, and he knew her beliefs about homosexuality. With his sisters' help and encouragement, he finally got up the nerve to tell his mom. His worst fears came true. She was horrified and called him a "sinner" and told him that he would "go to hell." She told him that she was ashamed of him. Max was devastated.

Because of deep religious beliefs, many African American parents find themselves very upset when they learn that their sons are gay. Some families keep their son's sexual orientation a secret or cut them off from the family.

If you are a parent in this position:

- No matter how strong your beliefs, don't reject your child.
- Remember that your son needs your love and support now more than ever.
- Remember that we are all God's children and that God loves your son. Pray for both of you for the strength to continue to show your love.
- Try to keep the communication open. Talk to him. Listen to him. Share your true beliefs and feelings honestly and calmly and in a sensitive way.
- Let your son know that he will always have your love and the love of his family whether or not you agree with or understand him.
- Seek the help and advice of a family therapist or counselor who can work with you and your son together to help you both understand each other better.
- Find a support group for parents (see the Fairchild and Hayward book in the Resources section).

You must talk to your kids about sex and sexuality in today's world. Don't feel that you have to do it "right." There is no one way. Just keep communication open and honest and let your kids know that they can come and talk to you as issues arise. You do not have to have all the answers. See the Resources below for ideas on where to learn more about discussing sex and sexuality with your sons.

RESOURCES

Books on Teenage Sexuality and Sexually Transmitted Diseases

Adimora, Adaora A., et al. *Sexually Transmitted Diseases*. New York: McGraw-Hill, 1993.

Bell, Ruth. *Changing Bodies, Changing Lives: A Book for Teens on Sex and Relationships*. New York: Vintage Books, 1988.

Bull, David. *Cool and Celibate?: Sex or No Sex*. Boston: Element Children's Books, 1998.

Devries, Mark. *True Love Waits*. Nashville, TN: Broadman & Holman, 1997.

Fairchild, Betty, and Nancy Hayward. *Now That You Know: A Parent's Guide to Understanding Their Gay and Lesbian Children*. San Diego: Harcourt Brace, 1998.

Gale, Jay. *A Parent's Guide to Teenage Sexuality*. New York: Henry Holt, 1989.

Johnson, Eric W. *Love and Sex and Growing Up*. New York: Bantam, 1990.

Lee, Michele. *Teenage Sexuality*. North Bellmore, NY: M. Cavendish, 1994.

Lewis, Howard R., and Martha E. Lewis. *The Parent's Guide to Teenage Sex and Pregnancy*. New York: St. Martin's Press, 1980.

McCoy, Kathy. *The Teenage Body Book Guide to Sexuality*. New York: Simon and Schuster, 1983.

McDowell, Josh, and Dick Day. *Why Wait? What You Need to Know about the Teen Sexuality Crisis*. Nashville, TN: Thomas Nelson, 1994.

Madaras, Lynda, and Dane Saavedra. *The What's Happening to My Body? Book for Boys: A Growing Up Guide for Parents and Sons*. New York: Newmarket Press, 1987.

Pollack, William. *Real Boys: Rescuing Our Sons from the Myths of Boyhood.* New York: Random House, 1998.

Ross, Linda M. *Sexually Transmitted Diseases Sourcebook.* Detroit: Omnigraphics, 1997.

Stark, Patty. *Sex Is More Than a Plumbing Lesson: A Parent's Guide to Sexuality Education for Infants Through the Teen Years.* Dallas: Preston Hollow Enterprises, 1997.

Swisher, Karin, Terry O'Neill, and Bruno Leone. *Teenage Sexuality: Opposing Viewpoints.* San Diego: Greenhaven Press, 1994.

Some of these books can be found most easily through the Internet.

10

◆

A MAN WHO STANDS FOR NOTHING WILL FALL FOR ANYTHING.
—MALCOLM X

Drug and Alcohol Abuse

One of the most common concerns expressed by parents, teachers, educators, guidance counselors, therapists, social workers, and psychologists about raising teenagers is the issue of drug and alcohol use and abuse. Parents of all ethnic and racial groups—rich and poor, urban and suburban—are struggling with these issues to varying degrees. It may surprise you to know that the most important things you can do to prevent drug and alcohol use in your kids are: be a role model by avoiding drug and alcohol use yourself; practice the positive parenting we discussed in Chapter 4; and give your kids good strong positive values that they can "stand for" and believe in.

You may also be surprised to know that our children are no more likely to use drugs than white children. The National Institutes on Drug Abuse agree that race/ethnicity is not a significant determinant of drug use. However, socioeconomic issues such as poverty, unemployment, and level of education, as well as neighborhood makeup, *are* significant determinants of drug use, according to Farai Chideya, author of the revealing book *Don't Believe the Hype.*

In some communities and schools, the availability of drugs and alcohol has reached epidemic proportions. Fifty-seven percent of all illicit drugs are sold on school grounds from the sixth grade through college, according to Sheila Fuller and Leigh Rudd, authors of *The Parents' Pipeline Guide.* Many parents are shocked and surprised to discover how early kids begin experimenting with drugs. The authors also state that:

- "Twenty-five percent of all fourth-graders in the United States are being pressured by their peers to try alcohol and other drugs.
- Illegal drug and alcohol use is rising fastest in the nine-to-thirteen-year-old age group.
- The national average age of first drug use is now twelve.
- Fifty-two percent of adolescents ages twelve to seventeen drink alcohol.
- Twenty-two percent aged twelve to seventeen are drug involved."

Alcohol is a sneakier threat to our adolescents. Because drinking is socially acceptable, alcohol is a component of some religious rituals, and alcohol use is not illegal and does not carry the stigma of drugs. Many parents will even allow a child or preadolescent to have a sip of an alcoholic beverage on special occasions. Although this may seem harmless, it is, in fact, dangerous because it gives kids the message that alcohol use is okay. African Americans are twice as likely to die from alcohol abuse than from drug abuse.

Many parents have told us that they are overwhelmed when they have tried to sort through the extensive literature on drug and alcohol abuse. In this chapter we have therefore assembled the advice of experts in this field that we feel will provide you with a guide to the prevention of substance abuse and intervention for your children. At the end of this chapter we have listed resources that can help you in this process.

The first part of this chapter focuses on the things African American parents can do to lessen the risk factors for drug and alcohol use and abuse among our children. It will discuss such topics as how to talk to our kids about these issues.

The second part offers important facts about adolescents and drugs.

The third part addresses the question of how you can tell if your son is involved with drugs or alcohol. Information is an important tool for parents in preventing drug use and getting help for teens who are using. This will include a section on each drug.

The last part addresses the issue of what to do if you suspect (or know) that your son is using drugs or alcohol, and it tells you how to get help for yourself, your family, and your son.

Prevention

The best way to help prevent a drug- or alcohol-abuse situation is to work on establishing a positive parent/child relationship with your son. As you strive for love, connection, and closeness, also bear in mind that all kids need—and want—clear limits and boundaries. We all have to be parents first to our children and show them positive, embracing love. Many parents have the mistaken notion that our job is to be friends with our kids. They already have friends, many of whom are as confused as they are. Kids actually welcome a feeling that someone (besides them) is in charge. Clear guidance, limits, and consequences give them the parameters they need and provide a safety net beneath them when they venture out into the world.

To this end, it is important that you give them "tough love"— that you say no to things that can be bad for them. In terms of drugs and alcohol, it is crucial that you give a clear "no use" rule in your home and in your son's life. This is very hard for many parents who were adolescents themselves in the 1960s and 1970s and who spent those years experimenting freely with drugs, alcohol, and sexuality.

The challenge for most of us is in learning when to reel our sons in and give input, and when to let them go to fly on their own. The best strategy of working toward letting them go is to gradually allow them to make more decisions about themselves. If kids show that they can be trusted, then they have earned more responsibility. If, on the other hand, they have difficulty following simple rules, such as a curfew, a no drug and alcohol rule, a no cutting school rule, and a "do your best in class" mandate, then they are asking for more limits, more rules, and clear consequences.

In Chapter 4, we described the guidelines for positive parenting practices recommended by experts such as David Wilmes and Dick Schaefer. These are the most effective tools for prevention of substance abuse. To summarize, they include:

- Establish positive communication with your son and keep the "talk lines" open. It is essential that your son feel that it is okay to talk to you about anything, including a temptation to do drugs, get drunk, have sex, etc. Enlist the help of a family member or friend to talk to him about these things if you and he don't have an open enough relationship (yet).
- Be parents, not just friends, to your kids. Enforce limits—they need them.
- Know your kid's friends. Peers often lead kids into drugs.
- Show love to your kids, physically and verbally. Give them a hug whenever you can, and tell them daily that you love them. They may say, "Oh, Ma!" and look embarrassed, but secretly they love it. (Just don't do it in front of others, particularly their friends.)
- Have clear limits, rules, and consequences in your home. Be clear about punishments for serious misbehavior.
- Be consistent. Follow through on what you say you are going to do.
- Establish a practice of waiting up for your kids, or having them come to your room and wake you to say good night.
- Keep your kids busy and involved in community activities, such as volunteering.
- Have clear curfews. Fuller and Rudd, authors of *The Parents' Pipeline Guide,* suggest the following guidelines for curfews and ending times for weekend teen activities:
     eighth grade   10:30 P.M.
     ninth grade   11:00
     high school   11:30–12:30
- Talk to other parents and swap parenting strategies. What works for someone else's child may not work for you. You need to determine these limits based on your knowledge of your child.

Specific to Drugs and Alcohol

In their book *Raising Drug-Free Kids in a Drug-Filled World,* William Mack Perkins and Nancy McMurtrie Perkins offer the following parenting practices:

- Start teaching your child about drugs and their effects in elementary school so that you talk to them before their peers do. Make sure you don't just describe the negative effects, but also mention that they may enjoy the high and feel they won't become "hooked." This way they will be aware that this is why drug and alcohol use is so tempting. Let them know that the high doesn't last and that there are aftereffects.
- Have a clear "no use" rule for drugs and alcohol.
- Set an example of abstinence from drugs and alcohol yourself.
- Read about drug and alcohol use among teens, and make sure your children know this information is available in the home. Leave it around where they can find it. Try leaving it in the bathroom.
- Have an honest discussion with your children about peer pressure to use drugs. How they would handle this could be the basis for a family meeting.
- Wear an inexpensive beeper or pager so that your kids can reach you at any time. We have found this very helpful in our family because we are often in different locations during the day and evening. In this way, they can feel that they have access to you at any time. (Cell phones are also a good but much more expensive way to be available. An inexpensive pager will do the job just as well.)
- Let your children know that they can call or page you and you will come get them anytime they are concerned about drugs, alcohol, or other inappropriate behaviors on the part of other kids.
- Write down all of your phone numbers and those of other family members and close friends who your kids can call if they can't reach you.
- Help your son develop a plan to "say no" to drugs. Role-play

with your kids, pretending a close friend at a party passes them drugs and then pressures them to use the drugs. Encourage your kids to use you (or anything else they can think of) to get out of pressured situations.

- Be aware of the patterns of drug use in the neighborhood and among your son's friends. Know what drugs are sold in his school and in other nearby places.
- Use the party guidelines below.
- Warn your kids that if they are with kids who are using drugs or have them in their possession, they could also be charged if they are stopped by the police.

Eric (age seventeen) was riding in a car with four of his homeboys headed to a party. Unbeknownst to Eric, Jamar, one of his boys, had some cocaine and marijuana hidden in his pants. The car was stopped and searched by the police. Jamar threw his bag of drugs on the floor. All of the kids were taken into the police station and booked for possession.

Party Guidelines

Drugs and alcohol may often be available at parties your son attends. He may think his friends look cool chugging down "40's" (forty-ounce bottles of malt liquor popular with black teenagers) and be tempted himself. In *The Parents' Pipeline Guide,* Sheila Fuller and Leigh Rudd offer guidelines that will help keep things under control if your son is attending or giving a party:

- Be sure that you know the address and telephone number of any party your son attends.
- Contact the parent and be sure that it's a real party and that an adult will be present.
- Carry a pager or cell phone.
- Tell your son that if he wants you to pick him up for any reason including drug and alcohol use or violence, you will come and get him.

If your son is giving a party, Fuller and Rudd recommend the following guidelines:

- "Keep it small. Larger parties invite gate crashers.
- Specify what time the party will end.
- Invite male adults to be present and help supervise and discourage crashers.
- Be present yourself for the whole party.
- Have an adult at the door to greet guests."

They also recommend that you agree on the following rules (in advance):

- "No alcohol or drugs
- No leaving the party and returning (kids sometimes 'stash' drugs or alcohol outside)
- No gate crashers
- One entrance and exit
- Define off-limits areas such as the garage, bedrooms, backyard, etc."

"On the drug thing, I made myself available to my kid as an excuse. If he gets to a party where they are doing drugs, I gave him the freedom to say, even if it's not true, 'My dad's an ornery SOB, and he'll kill me if he knows what's going on, and I have to get out of here.'" (From a father in *Beating the Odds*)

Important Facts about Drugs

One of the most effective ways to prevent drug and alcohol use and abuse is to educate yourself (and your kids) about the process. In order to help parents learn important drug- and alcohol-related information, we have divided this section into two key areas: (1) the differences between adult and adolescent drug use; (2) descriptions of each drug (including signs of use).

Differences Between Adolescent and Adult Alcohol and Drug Dependence

Many parents are very surprised to discover that there are differences between the paths and processes that lead to adult and adolescent chemical dependency. Dick Schaefer, an expert on adolescent drug use, describes many of them in his book *Choices and Consequences*:

- Teenagers experiment on the basis of "convenience"—what's easy to get and what their friends offer them. This is unlike adults, who often choose one specific drug or alcoholic beverage. For both adults and adolescents, alcohol is the most common drug of choice. Since alcohol is a legal substance for adults to buy, there is quality control—you know what you are getting when you purchase alcohol in a liquor or package store. With "street drugs," such as cocaine, crack, and heroin, you are taking an extra risk. These drugs are commonly diluted ("cut") with other substances, from PCP (an animal tranquilizer) to strychnine (rat poison), which can cause violent reactions such as illness, overdose, or death. Kids are often unaware of this extra risk.

- It is often hard to distinguish drug or alcohol use from depression in teenagers. Adolescence is a difficult time for many kids, and signs of seeming substance use, such as withdrawal from family and friends, may really be caused by depression. In addition, substance abuse might be a response to the teenager's depression—or anxiety—where he is attempting to "self-medicate" his uncomfortable emotional state through the use of drugs or alcohol. Dick Schaefer points out, "What may look like symptoms in adolescence may be special education concerns (such as poor concentration skills, moodiness, hyperactivity, or poor social skills) or behaviors traceable to growing up in an alcoholic home."

- The addiction process happens more quickly for adolescents. Schaefer notes that it can "take eight to ten years for a thirty-year-old male to reach the chronic stages of alcoholism. For a teenager, the time period to reach the chronic stage may be less than fifteen months. Cocaine and crack addiction can be particularly rapid for adolescents. People literally 'fall in love' with the high and graduate almost immediately from misuse to addiction. Crack, a form of cocaine that is smoked rather than snorted, works so quickly that a user gets high in seconds," and it is the drug that offers the most danger of a user becoming quickly addicted.

- Emotional development can be arrested by drug and alcohol use in adolescence. This is the time when boys are developing emotionally, particularly in terms of relationships, and drug and/or alcohol use may suspend this process. Once they stop using drugs, they may function emotionally at the stage they were before use.

- "It won't happen to me." Many adolescents have misconceptions about drug or alcohol abuse, e.g., that you have to be "falling down drunk" all the time to be an alcoholic. If the symptoms are not extreme—experiencing blackouts, severe hangovers, or behaving in an extremely weird way—they may fool themselves into thinking that they are not alcoholics.

Many kids have the delusion that they are smarter or more creative when on drugs. Nancy once asked an adolescent to read a paper he had written when he was high on marijuana. Though he insisted it was his "best work," it didn't take him long to realize that it now made absolutely no sense.

Question: "What kind of parent can have a drug- or alcohol-involved kid?"

Answer: "Every kind." (Bill and Nancy Perkins, *Raising Drug-Free Kids in a Drug-Filled World*)

To be an effective parent, you must be able to recognize the warning signs of drug and alcohol use. If you suspect that something is wrong, seek help from a professional to determine if your child is abusing drugs or alcohol or has another emotional problem. Be cautious about making accusations without first consulting a knowledgeable counselor.

Red Flags for Substance Abuse

- Has your son's behavior noticeably changed?
- Has he become more defiant with you or others?
- Is he doing poorly in school?
- Has he been truant from school?
- Is he secretive and rarely talks to you?
- Do you catch him lying to you?

- Has he been in trouble with the police or school authorities?
- Has he stopped taking care of his personal appearance and clothing?
- Does he seem to have a group of new friends whom you do not know?
- Are his eyes often red?
- Does he often seem dazed or "out of it"?

Reactions That Hurt

Most of us view taking responsibility for our children's behavior as a natural part of parenting. When our children succeed, we feel proud. And when they fail, we feel as if it's our own failure as a parent. Unfortunately, that feeling of failure can lead to guilt which can lead us to cover up for our children. When we step in to prevent our children from facing the consequences of their drug and alcohol use, it's called *enabling.*

The Perkinses list typical examples of parents' enabling: "not confronting drug use by allowing a child to use at home, by making excuses for inappropriate behavior, by bailing kids out of jail (when they're guilty), by getting their child out of trouble at school, by calling in sick for them at work or school, by giving them money and not keeping track of how they spend it, and by not questioning them when items are missing from the home."

African American families have a tradition of extended family involvement. Grandparents, aunts, uncles, cousins, brothers, and sisters can also become enablers. Schaefer points out that "in general youth tend to have far more enablers than adults. The average chemically dependent adult might have as many as ten to twelve enablers, including the family doctor, his boss, and maybe the court. In contrast, the average chemically dependent teenager might have fifty to sixty enablers, including immediate family, grandparents, uncles, aunts, school personnel, church staff, law enforcement officers, court personnel, medical staff, friends, and parents of friends—all making it easier for the teenager to keep using."

"Helpers" can also be included in this group of enablers. Teachers, ministers, counselors, social workers, psychologists, and therapists can become so "hooked into helping" that they are really making excuses instead of intervening appropriately to get help for the adolescent and his family.

Some parents feel so desperate when a son is abusing drugs or alcohol that they can't stop themselves from threatening or blowing up. The problem is that threats don't work. They will only alienate you further from your son.

Other parents, who are sick with worry, try to frighten their children into not using drugs by describing consequences that seem too extreme. Kids tend to be dismissive of tactics such as telling them that they may die. A more effective approach might be to tie drug use into something they look forward to or personally value, such as, "If you use drugs they will throw you off the basketball team."

◆　◆　◆

You cannot fix what you will not face.
—James Baldwin

◆　◆　◆

Parental (or family) denial is one of the most dangerous reactions to a substance-abusing teenager. One hardworking African American single-parent mother told us in tears how much she had sacrificed to move her son from an inner-city high school to a private school that she was sure was drug-free. Not until her son and three other boys were suspended for possession of cocaine at their school did she recognize the reality.

While we feel strongly that parents should not be in denial or procrastinate on getting help for their kids, overreaction can make the situation worse. If you have discovered signs that concern you and you find yourself following your son around, snooping in his room, screening his phone calls, *then it is definitely time to seek help! You need a counselor or therapist with special training in alcohol and drug abuse.* After a careful evaluation this person can help to validate your concerns. The counselor can do a urine drug screen as well as conduct a careful interview with you and your son to help you get the help he and the whole family needs. (See the Resources section at the end of this chapter for suggestions of how to find such a counselor or therapist.)

Feeding the Fire:
Adults Who Supply Kids with Alcohol or Drugs

A serious error that parents can make is providing alcohol or drugs for kids. This might include allowing them to use at home or even using with them in the mistaken belief that allowing use at home will keep them safe or off the streets. This often backfires and tacitly gives permission for drug or alcohol use.

If your son's friends' parents do this, talk to them directly about your concerns. If they are unwilling to change this practice, you may need to limit your child's access to those homes. This does not mean that your son's friendships with their children must end (though maybe some of them should). Make clear to your son and his friends what the rules are in your house and then have him invite them over, and provide good food, music, videos, and a drug- and alcohol-free environment for them to enjoy.

"Do as I Say, Not as I Do"

Numerous parents have told us that they are moderate drinkers who enjoy a glass of wine with a meal or a beer while watching a sports event on television and are reluctant to ban alcohol from their home. These parents often have frank discussions with their kids about responsible adult drinking. They point out to their kids that drinking is illegal below the age of eighteen (twenty-one in many states). They caution their kids about being careful and responsible when they are adults.

While we accept that there is a distinction between what an adolescent can do and what an adult can do, many of these parents do not understand that they are taking a big risk by using alcohol in front of their children. Kids tend to respond to what we do rather than what we say. By not having a ban on alcohol drinking in their home, many parents have had their teens throwing their own alcohol use in their faces as they get older. In addition, many instances of alcohol abuse begin with kids sneaking drinks from their parents' liquor cabinets.

Parents who use illegal drugs or abuse prescription drugs are providing dangerous models for their children. They run a very high risk of similar behavior in their kids, even if they think that they have kept their habit hidden or secret. These become toxic "secrets" that kids are aware of but cannot openly acknowledge without feeling that they are betraying their parent. *This type of modeling is one of the greatest risk factors for adolescent substance abuse.*

In addition, if there is a father, mother, older brother or sister, boyfriend or girlfriend, or other relative who lives in the home and is an alcoholic or substance abuser, he or she poses a significant risk to your son. This person may refuse to get help for himself but continue to burden the entire family with his addiction.

Descriptions of Drugs

If you are a family member in the position of observing any of the above behaviors and you are concerned about the risks it presents for your children, adolescents, yourself, or other family members, there are some things that you can do.

The best way to deal with adolescent drug and alcohol use is to educate yourself and your kids about drugs. The following section will describe different drugs and the signs of drug use. Because parents may overhear conversations in which they suspect that drug use is being discussed by their sons, or hear unfamiliar terms that they think might be related to drug use, we have included the common street names for various drugs. We have used Sheila Fuller and Leigh Rudd's book *The Parents' Pipeline Guide* for all of the "signs of use" sections in this chapter. The street names for drugs were found in Dr. Jeff Gardere's book *Smart Parenting for African Americans.* We recommend both of these excellent resources to you for further information.

Alcohol

Alcohol is one of the substances most frequently abused by teenagers. Remember that alcohol is a toxic drug. Many parents are more permissive in terms of beer drinking, assuming that the alcohol content of beer makes it less intoxicating than other drinks, such as vodka, scotch, etc. In reality, a twelve-ounce beer has as much alcohol content as a typical mixed drink. Malt liquor, a favorite among some African American kids, has an even higher alcohol content than beer. The situation is made worse by the fact that the preferred size is a forty-ounce bottle rather than a twelve-ounce can. Jeff Gardere points to one recent fad among black kids involving combining malt liquor with smoking pot for a quick strong high.

Signs of Use: Parents should be aware of the smell of alcohol on their son's breath, finding hidden bottles of alcohol, or discovering bottles missing from their liquor cabinet. Physical signs include blackouts, slurred speech, or staggering.

Tobacco

Recently, Mike Wallace did a powerful interview on *60 Minutes* with an expert on the effects of smoking. People across America were astounded to learn that there has been evidence for years that smoking may cause impotence and sexual dysfunction in men. Adolescents have not been impressed with the statistics about the contribution of smoking to deaths due to lung cancer, but they might be more influenced by its threat to their sexual potency and their "manhood." As Fuller and Rudd have shown, heavy cigarette smoking is closely linked to other forms of drug use: "84 percent of marijuana users and 89 percent of cocaine users also smoke cigarettes, according to the American Cancer Society."

Signs of Use: The smell of tobacco on your son's breath or in his clothes is an obvious sign that he is smoking; other signs are cigarette butts in empty bottles, hidden packs of cigarettes or matches, and a hacking cough.

Marijuana (cannabis)

Marijuana (also called grass, joint, pot, dope, weed, herb, rope, and Ganja) can be purchased readily and inexpensively in either loose form—a nickel bag ($5 worth) or a dime bag ($10 worth) are most common—or already rolled to look like cigarettes ("joints" or "blunts") for a few dollars. Marijuana looks like dry leaves, mixed with bits of stems and seeds. A much stronger form of pot, hashish or "hash," looks like a flat dark-colored cake.

Many teenagers like the high they get from marijuana. It makes them feel mellow or cool. This is the substance, other than alcohol, most often used by young black teens.

Signs of Use: Your son may have a "spaced-out" appearance or a disoriented or confused look. He may seem euphoric or laugh for no reason. Physical signs are bloodshot eyes and brown spots on fingertips. You may also notice your son's lack of motivation.

Cocaine and Crack

Cocaine (street names: coke, snow, blow) is made from the leaves of the coca plant and looks like a white powder. It is most commonly snorted through the nose using a small straw or, in some cases, injected. This is a very potent, immediate high that leads to feelings of excitement, rapid heartbeat, and euphoria. Cocaine is expensive (around $100 per gram).

Crack cocaine, or "crack," a rock-like crystalline substance, is produced by "cooking" cocaine over a flame and is cheap ($5 or less for a "hit") and readily available. It is one of the most addictive of all drugs and has had a devastating effect in black communities. It is usually packaged in a vial and is smoked through a pipe. Crack addicts often become aggressive and frequently steal from their family and loved ones.

Signs of Use:

Cocaine—The user may appear euphoric, "hyper," even giddy, and very restless. This is followed soon after by depression, sleeping long hours, and often weight loss. Look for constant "sniffling" (like a stuffy, runny nose from a cold), frequent nosebleeds, etc. Look for small straws, mirrors, razor blades, etc.

Crack—You may notice your son has lost weight and doesn't have much of an appetite. Other signs include mood swings, hyperactivity, and pacing. Sleep is severely affected by crack—your son may be wide awake for a number of days and then sleep for as many. Look for small white crystalline rocks, plastic vials, tiny pipes.

Other Stimulants

Amphetamines or stimulants (speed, pep pills, uppers, black beauties, meth) are man-made and are swallowed in pill or powder form. Ritalin, often prescribed for attention deficit hyperactivity disorder (ADHD) is also sold on the street and used, in larger doses, by some kids to get high.

Signs of Use: Your son may be unable to sleep (insomnia), extremely nervous, hyperactive, extremely talkative, manic, or unable to sit still.

Heroin

Heroin (smack, horse, and junk) is a narcotic that can be snorted through the nose or injected. Sharing dirty needles by heroin users is the direct or indirect cause of a large number of the HIV/AIDS infections in the black community.

Heroin is a white powder that is usually cut or diluted with sugar, starch, or powdered milk. Other narcotics, such as codeine and morphine, are not widely used among black adolescents.

Signs of Use: Parents should be alert for needle marks on arms or the backs of knees and watery eyes. Another sign of heroin use is finding bloodstains on your son's shirtsleeve. Behavior includes "nodding out"—where your son seems too tired to keep his eyes open and his head up, and too relaxed; or "withdrawal," where the user is craving the drug and is very agitated. The most obvious signs are syringes; burnt bottle caps; cords; and belts, which are used as tourniquets.

Ecstasy, China White, Ice

This group of mind-altering substances are known as "designer drugs." They are known as party drugs and have the high of cocaine but last for days. These are very dangerous drugs that can kill brain cells and cause brain damage and Parkinson's disease. China White is a synthetic form of heroin.

Ice (glass, batu, and snot) is also highly addictive. Kids who use this often engage in very risky behavior, feeling that they can do anything. They can become aggressive, paranoid.

Signs of Use:

Ecstasy—The person looks confused, has trouble sleeping, and is often paranoid. Pills are a little larger than an aspirin.

Ice—The person is likely to become very paranoid, aggressive, has frequent mood swings, stays up all night, loses weight, and has heavy sweats. Look for pipes and glass tubes, which are used to smoke it.

Hallucinogens

These drugs were known in the 1960s as psychedelic drugs. They include PCP (angel dust), LSD (acid) and mescaline (mesc).

PCP can cause bizarre experiences and can result in a person becoming violent or out of control. It can be obtained in a powdered, tablet, or crystalline form.

LSD is usually taken in a tablet or licked off of a paper. It is very powerful and produces bizarre images and experiences.

Mescaline comes in a tablet and is most often chewed or smoked. It has properties similar to LSD and can also cause hallucinations.

Of these three, PCP is the most commonly found in the black community.

Signs of Use:

PCP—Your son may have a "spaced-out" appearance, behave in a bizarre manner, stagger, or have slow body movements.

LSD—Your son may appear "spaced out" and incoherent. He may not make any sense when he talks. Hallucinations (seeing or hearing things) are a common sign of LSD use.

Mescaline—Hallucinations are also a sign of mescaline use. Your son may appear very confused.

Depressants

Depressants are legal drugs that are prescribed to relieve anxiety. The most common kinds are tranquilizers and barbiturates (downers, red devils, blue devils, etc.). Tranquilizers such as Valium and Librium (in pill form) may already be in the home medicine cabinet as the result of a parent's or other family member's legal prescription, and they can also be bought on the street. Excessive use or taking these in combination with alcohol can result in coma or death.

Signs of Use: Slowed-down movements, spacey behavior, pills disappearing from the medicine cabinet or found in your son's room.

Steroids

Years ago, anabolic steroid use among black teens was rare. As Dr. Jeff Gardere has pointed out, however, it has become more of a concern for African American parents because so many of our kids compete in (and excel at) sports. Steroids are used medically to treat certain cancers. They mimic the male sex hormone testosterone. Many athletes use anabolic steroids to increase their muscle and body size. Athletes who have tested positive for steroids have been disqualified from the Olympics and other sports events. Steroid usage is very dangerous and can result in liver cancer, impotence, sterility, and the growth of breasts in men.

Signs of Use: Steroids come in small tablets, liquid vials, or are injected. Look for quick weight gain, darkening of the skin, the development of "breasts" in a male, breath odor, and aggressiveness. The aggressiveness is so severe in some steroid users that the term "'roid rage" has been used to describe this reaction.

Inhalants

Parents used to worry more about drugs like cocaine and heroin. Many miss the obvious drugs that are available in every home. Today kids are inhaling everything from the "sniffing glue" era to nail polish remover, lighter and cleaning fluids. In *The Parents' Pipeline Guide,* Fuller and Rudd quote a young recovering addict: "We'd buy those cartridges, the ones for whipped cream or seltzer bottles. Then we'd puncture them and put the gas in a paper bag or balloon and sniff it." Kids as young as seven or eight have been reported to sniff aerosols such as paints, hairspray, etc. Fuller and Rudd report, "Kids say they spray the chemical onto their clothing before they go to school, so they can sniff the fumes all day." The National Institute on Drug Abuse reports that inhalant use is on the rise among young teens.

Nitrous oxide or "laughing gas" can be bought in many stores. Some kids use amyl nitrite "poppers" to inhale during sex to enhance orgasms.

Signs of Use: The most obvious signs are gas cartridges, aerosol spray, or paint cans lying around, paint thinner, glue, or rags that smell and are left around. You can sometimes smell this on your child, in his room, or in the garage. Kids using these often seem confused, dizzy, and talk in choppy sentences. In the most extreme cases, they may have hallucinations, believing they are seeing or hearing things.

Remember that most teenage addicts will not admit the fact that they are using. Do not be surprised if your son denies his alcohol or drug use initially, as adolescents resent the intrusion into their "private affairs." If you have any reason to suspect that your son may be using alcohol or drugs, do not hesitate to seek professional help from a drug and alcohol counselor immediately. If you are overreacting, they will tell you. Do not make this decision on your own.

Get Help for Yourself First

It surprises many parents that the first step in getting help for your son if you suspect that he may have a drug or alcohol problem is getting help *for yourself*. The process of getting help for a kid who is using and abusing drugs and/or alcohol can be a long, difficult process. As a parent, grandparent, or other concerned family member, you will need all of the help and support that you can pull together. Dick Schaefer, an expert on adolescent substance abuse, recommends the following five steps that you can take in getting support—for yourself:

1. *Become familiar with the problem and immediately stop any behavior that is enabling your son to use.*

2. *Seek support.* It will be crucial in those difficult moments for you to know that you are not alone, and to see that other parents are struggling with many of the same issues. It is not enough to talk to friends on the phone about it, or even to see a pastor or elder. There are support groups that were formed specifically to allow parents of substance-abusing children to vent, learn, find support, and heal. Contact your local branch of Alcoholics Anonymous (AA), Narcotics Anonymous (NA), Al-Anon, or Families Anonymous—all proven programs for recovery for chemically dependent people and their families. Families Anonymous, as its title suggests, offers help specifically to families using the same successful twelve-step methods the other organizations use (see the Resources section at the end of this chapter).

Many African American parents struggle initially with some of these meetings, particularly if they discover that the meeting in their area is predominantly white or mixed. Do not let this or anything stop you from getting help. Your child's life is too important. Call your local branch of Alcoholics Anonymous. They can supply you with the locations and times of meetings in communities where you are more likely to find more black members. Take a trusted friend or relative along with you to the first meeting if you feel more comfortable.

Don't feel that you have to speak the first few times. Just go and listen to other parents. Get a list of meetings in your city, town, or surrounding areas. Visit different meetings until you find one that works for you. Don't expect to feel comfortable immediately.

3. *Know where to find support.* Be sure that the professional you choose has a specialty in working with adolescents with drug/alcohol problems. A counselor may be a very competent psychologist, psychiatrist, psychotherapist, social worker, family therapist, or pastoral counselor, but they must have a specialty and *extensive* experience in alcohol/drug problems. It is best if this person is a Certified Alcohol and Drug Counselor (CADC). Schaefer suggests that you find assistance through your :

- County social services office
- The Division of Alcoholism and Drug Abuse, part of the Public Health Department
- Alcoholism information and treatment centers
- Drug abuse information and treatment centers
- Mental health centers
- Family service organizations

4. *Don't forget yourself.* If your life feels out of control right now and you are overcome with worry about your child—please slow down! Many African American parents tell us that they spend half of their lives running for one good cause or another, especially when it concerns the needs of our families, extended families, churches, workplace, or community. But in the midst of the major battle to get help for your child (or another family member) it will be even more difficult if you are constantly on the edge of burnout. (See Chapter 14 for more on avoiding burnout.) You must stay strong to help your son.

5. *Watch and listen carefully.* Keep a notebook of things that you have noticed that have led you to believe that your child might have a problem with drugs/alcohol. A part of the value of a journal is that it can keep you from second-guessing yourself or wondering if you are imagining things.

Confrontation and Intervention

The next step in the intervention is setting limits. You must begin to take back the control in your own home. Do not begin this process, particularly confrontation, without the help and advice of a trained alcohol and drug professional.

Kids are actually relieved when parents take back control and begin to set and enforce limits, as long as it is coupled with a clear message of love and caring. Because kids delude themselves about the effects of drugs/alcohol, they must stop using before they can be honest with themselves and you about how drugs/ alcohol are affecting them.

Parents and other family members also need to recognize that this is a very difficult process and requires a unified team approach. It is very important that you anticipate resistance from your adolescent. He may get angry, belligerent, deny everything, and even accuse you of not caring about him.

Schaefer has been very clear that confrontation should not include shouting, humiliation, threats, or violence. You should be respectful of your teenager and give him your feedback without forcing him to lose face or feel put down. You want your son to cooperate with the intervention process. He outlines essential components of successful confrontation, which include "choices, consequences, and contracts."

- *Choices.* Though it will be difficult, be prepared to offer choices to your child about how to handle the problem. This approach will be much more effective than threatening, moralizing, or humiliating him. For example, research two or three drug treatment programs that are good and that you approve of. You can then give him the final choice. Be sure to be clear that he does not have the choice of not getting help.
- *Consequences.* You must be willing to enforce consequences if your son breaks the agreed-upon rules.

- *Contracts.* Show your child respect. Many parents use signed contracts to pin their son or daughter down to an agreement.

No parent, even one knowledgeable about drug and alcohol issues, should be doing the above interventions alone. You will need the help of a *trained Certified Drug and Alcohol Counselor or a therapist with special training in this area.* This is especially true as you prepare for an intervention. An intervention is a series of planned meetings between a trained counselor and many of the people involved in your son's life. It might include close friends, school friends, "his boys," family and extended family members, close friends of the family, a trusted school counselor, teacher(s), school principal, your minister or members of your church family, or a member of your community your son respects. The group should include at least one (hopefully more than one) person your teenager really trusts. Without this person's input, confrontation may be seen as an attack.

The intervention sessions should all be led or facilitated by a drug and alcohol counselor or a therapist with a substance abuse specialty who can help educate the group about the disease of chemical dependency. He or she can also help everyone to discuss ways to present a clear united front to the adolescent. The purpose is to have a unified outpouring of love and support for the adolescent and to confront him on what his drug and alcohol use is doing to him and to all of the people who love and care about him. An experienced counselor can help to prepare everyone for the adolescent's possible reactions. The goal of the intervention is to get the adolescent into a drug treatment program.

Types of Drug Treatment

The counselor can help you to decide which method of treatment is best suited for your son and family.

- Consult with a certified drug and alcohol counselor when choosing a program for your son.

- Visit the program with and without your adolescent before you make this important decision.
- Investigate your health insurance options and coverage early in the process. You may be limited to certain facilities, and your health insurance, particularly if it is a managed care system, may have limits on how long he can stay in a hospital or program. Make sure that your information is current, as health insurance companies constantly revise their policies.

Here are some of the options you may consider:

Detox. Some drug and alcohol programs require detoxification from the chemical substances before they will accept your adolescent for further treatment. This involves a stay in the hospital of about a week (or a little less) in order to remove the toxic substance from his body. It is often helpful if you can find a program that offers detox and treatment in one facility.

Inpatient or residential treatment program. Often called "rehab," this is an intensive residential program that may range from twenty-eight days to eighteen months, depending on the facility and your medical insurance. One example is Phoenix House (which has locations in cities across the country). This program offers a very intensive six-to-nine-week program that includes drug education and individual and group counseling. Family counseling is also available to discuss family patterns that may enable substance abuse, educating family members about the disease model, and removing kids from the environment of friends, peers, and easy access to alcohol and drugs.

It is essential to find a good aftercare program in your community so that your son does not return without any supports. Lack of a plan could put him at high risk for resuming his alcohol and drug use. It is best to find a program that is geared to teenagers close to his age.

Outpatient or aftercare treatment program. For an adolescent who is just beginning to experiment with drugs, an outpatient treatment program may be sufficient. There are pros and cons to this model. For the young man whose drug or alcohol use has not become extreme, this may be an appropriate treatment because it allows for regular school attendance and activities.

Parents should be aware, however, that adolescents in outpatient drug treatment programs must be carefully monitored and supervised. Because they remain in their familiar environment they are at high risk for peer temptation and resumption of prior drug- and alcohol-abuse behaviors.

The most important part of this chapter is the first part—prevention. Start prevention activities early in your children's lives. By far the best guide for prevention are the guidelines for positive parenting, love, communication, and discipline discussed in Chapter 4.

The following Resources include important books, organizations, and information to aid you in gaining help for your adolescent, yourself, and your family.

RESOURCES

Books

Fuller, Sheila, and Leigh Rudd. *The Parents' Pipeline Guide: Plaintalk about Teens and Alcohol, Drugs, Sex, Eating Disorders and Depression*, 1995. Order from Parents Pipeline, Inc., P.O. Box 11037, Greenwich, CT 06831-1037.

Gardere, Jeffrey. *Smart Parenting for African Americans: Helping Your Kids Thrive in a Difficult World*. Secaucus, NJ: Citadel Press, 1999.

Perkins, William Mack, and Nancy McMurtrie Perkins. *Raising Drug-Free Kids in a Drug-Filled World*. New York: Harper & Row, 1986.

Schaefer, Dick. *Choices and Consequences*. Minneapolis: Johnson Institute, 1996.

Wilmes, David. *Parenting for Prevention*. Minneapolis: Johnson Institute, 1989.

All of these books can be ordered through Internet sites.

Treatment Information

Phoenix House, Jack R. Aron Center, 164 W. 74th Street, New York, NY 10023; telephone: (212) 595-5810. (Nation's leading nonprofit drug abuse service for adults and teens. Medical insurance is not necessary.)

Contact Johnson Institute for suggestions of treatment programs. 7205 Ohms Lane, Minneapolis, MN 55439-2159; telephone: (800) 231-5165.

Freedom Institute, 515 Madison Avenue, New York, NY 10017; telephone: (212) 838-0044. Books can be ordered through them.

Videos

All can be ordered from Johnson Institute, 7205 Ohms Lane, Minneapolis, MN 55439-2159; telephone: (800) 231-5165 or (612) 831-1630.

Another Chance to Change. Color, 30 min. Order #V422.

Choices & Consequences: Intervention with Youth in Trouble with Alcohol/Drugs. Color, 33 min. Order #V400.

Enabling: Masking Reality. Color, 22 min. Order #V409.

Good Intentions, Bad Results. Color, 30 min. Order #V410.

Kids at Risk: A Four-Part Video Series for Middle-School Children
    Covering Up for Kevin. Color, 18 min. Order #V428.
    Blaming Kitty. Color, 18 min. Order #V428.
    An Attitude Adjustment for Ramie. Color, 15 min. Order #V429.
    Double Bind. Color, 15 min. Order #V430.

Organizations That Can Help

Many of these resources were obtained from Jeffrey Gardere's book, *Smart Parenting for African Americans* and from Dick Schaefer's book, *Choices and Consequences*.

Al-Anon Family Group Headquarters
1600 Corporate Landing Parkway
Virginia Beach, VA 23454-5617
(800) 4AL-ANON
Web site: www.al-anon.alateen.org
(Al-Anon is for families and
    friends of alcoholics.)

Al-Ateen
1600 Corporate Landing Parkway
Virginia Beach, VA 23454-5617
(800) 4AL-ANON
(Al-Ateen is a fellowship of young
  Al-Anon members.)

Alcoholics Anonymous (AA)
General Service Office
P.O. Box 459
Grand Central Station
New York, NY 10163
(212) 686-3400

Alcoholics Anonymous World
  Services
475 Riverside Drive, 11th Floor
New York, NY 10115
(212) 870-3400
Web site: www.alcoholics-
  anonymous. org

American Council for Drug
Education
204 Monroe Street
Rockville, MD 20850
(301) 294-0600

CDC National AIDS
Clearinghouse
P.O. Box 6003
Rockville, MD 20849
(800) 458-5231

Center for Substance Abuse
Prevention (CSAP)
Substance Abuse and Mental
Health Services Administration
5600 Fishers Lane, Room 800
Rockville, MD 20857
(301) 443-0373
(800) 729-6686 (national
clearinghouse)

Center for Substance Abuse
Treatment (CSAT)
5600 Fishers Lane, Room 618
Rockville, MD 20857
(301) 443-5052

Children of Alcoholics
Foundation, Inc. (COAF)
555 Madison Avenue, 20th Floor
New York, NY 10022
(212) 754-0656

Clearinghouse on Family
Violence Information
P.O. Box 1182
Washington, DC 20013
(800) 394-3366

Cocaine Anonymous
P.O. Box 2000
Los Angeles, CA 90049-8000
National referral line: (800) 347-
8998
Telephone: (310) 556-5833; fax:
(310) 559-2554

Community Antidrug Coalitions
of America (CADCA)
901 N. Pitt Street, Suite 300
Alexandria, VA 22314
(703) 706-0560
(800) 54-CADCA

Families Anonymous
P.O. Box 3475
Culver City, CA 90231
(800) 736-9805

Hazelden Foundation
15251 Pleasant Valley Road
P.O. Box 176
Center City, MN 55012-0176
(800) 328-9000

Institute on Black Chemical
Abuse (IBCA)
2614 Nicollet Avenue South
Minneapolis, MN 55408
(612) 871-7878

Johnson Institute
7205 Ohms Lane
Minneapolis, MN 55439
(800) 231-5165

Join Together
441 Stuart Street, 6th Floor
Boston, MA 02116
(617) 437-1500

"Just Say No" International
1777 N. California Boulevard,
  Suite 210
Walnut Creek, CA 94596
(510) 939-6666
(800) 258-2766

Mothers Against Drunk Driving
  (MADD)
511 East John Carpenter Freeway,
  Suite 700
Irvington, TX 75062
(214) 744-6233
(800) GET-MADD

Nar-Anon Family Groups
P.O. Box 2562
Palos Verdes Peninsula, CA 90274
(213) 547-5800

Narcotics Anonymous (NA)
World Services Office, Inc.
P.O. Box 9999
Van Nuys, CA 91409
(818) 733-9999
fax: (818) 700-0700

National Association for Children
  of Alcoholics (NACoA)
11426 Rockville Pike
Suite 100
Rockville, MD 20852
(301) 468-0985

National Black Child
  Development Institute
463 Rhode Island Avenue, NW
Washington, DC 20005
(202) 387-1281
(800) 556-2234

National Center for Tobacco-Free
  Kids
1707 L Street, NW, Suite 800
Washington, DC
(800) 284-KIDS

National Clearinghouse for
  Alcohol and Drug Information
P.O. Box 2345
Rockville, MD 20847
(800) SAY-NOTO

National Coalition for the
  Prevention of Drug and
  Alcohol Abuse
537 Jones Road
Granville, OH 43023
(614) 587-2800

National Crime Prevention
  Council
1700 K Street, NW, 2nd Floor
Washington, DC 20006
(202) 466-6272
(800) 627-2911 (information
  requests)

National Domestic Violence
  Hotline
(800) 799-7233
Treatment facility referrals and
  help line
(800) HELP-1111

National Federation of Parents
  for Drug-Free Youth
8730 Georgia Avenue, Suite 200
Silver Spring, MD 20910
(301) 585-5437

National Head Start Association
201 N. Union Street, Suite 320
Alexandria, VA 22314
(703) 739-0875

National Inhalant Prevention
Coalition
1201 W. Sixth Street, Suite C-200
Austin, TX 78703
(800) 269-4237

National Institute on Alcohol
Abuse and Alcoholism
(NIAAA)
6000 Executive Boulevard, Suite
409
Bethesda, MD 20892-7003
(301) 443-3860
Web site: www.niaaa.nih.gov

National Institute on Drug Abuse
(NIDA)
6001 Executive Boulevard
Bethesda, MD 20892
(301) 443-4577

National Parents Resource
Institute on Drug Education
(PRIDE)
10 Park Place South, Suite 540
Atlanta, GA 30303
(404) 577-4500

National Urban League
Substance Abuse Program
500 E. 62nd Street
New York, NY 10021
(212) 310-9000

Office of Minority Health
Resource Center
P.O. Box 37337
Washington, DC 20013
(800) 444-6472

Office of National Drug Control
Policy (ONDCP)
P.O. Box 6000
Rockville, MD 20849
(800) 666-3332

Parents Anonymous
675 W. Foothill Boulevard, Suite
220
Claremont, CA 91711-3475
(909) 621-6184; (909) 625-6304
(nation's oldest child abuse prevention organization dedicated
to strengthening families)

Parents' Resource Institute for
Drug Education
50 Hurt Plaza, Suite 210
Atlanta, GA 30303
(404) 577-4500

Safe and Drug-Free Schools
Program
U.S. Department of Education
1250 Maryland Avenue, SW
Washington, DC 20024
(800) 624-0100

Students Against Drunk Driving
200 Pleasant Street
Marlboro, MA 01752
(800) 521-SADD

Toughlove
P.O. Box 1069
Doylestown, PA 18901
(215) 348-7090
(800) 333-1069
Web site: www.toughlove.org

11

FORCE AGAINST FORCE EQUALS MORE FORCE.
—ASHANTI PROVERB

Violence and Gangs

Carl was a seventeen-year-old, raised in a suburban black community. One Saturday night he and his friends went to a dance in a nearby city at a large club that held a hundred fifty to two hundred partygoers. Carl was tapped on the shoulder while he was dancing. As he turned around, he was shot in the head by someone he did not know. His killer fled.

When the police arrived, the young people were too afraid of retaliation to identify his killer or give the police any other information. Carl was rushed to the emergency room of a local hospital, but it was too late to save him. The outpouring of rage and grief at the time of Carl's death was tremendous. At his funeral, young people from all over his community shared in a collective sense of loss and trauma.

A local minister and an African American psychologist, skilled in violence prevention, did some work with these young people, helping them to resolve their anger, grief and profound sense of loss. Many have lost other friends and family members to these random acts of violence. They can result from cases of mistaken identity, intimidation campaigns, or turf wars between rival gangs, or sadly, just from looking for something to do on a Saturday night.

Incidents of random violence such as these are becoming all too common in America today. Carl's story proves that our sons don't have to be drug involved or gang involved to be victims of violence. Kids today are far more mobile as they get older, whether they live in a city or suburban area. News reports are full of young people like Carl who were simply in the wrong place at the wrong time. Carl was not a gang member. He was the only child of an African American mother who was raising him alone. He attended school every day, worked a part-time job, and was expected to graduate from high school the following May.

Youth violence in communities throughout the United States has increased in recent years. As we have talked with African American parents, we have repeatedly heard fears of violence toward our sons. Violence takes many forms—random violence (such as Carl's story above or "drive-by" shootings), "brothers killing brothers" (crime in the black community), and abuses of authority, such as police brutality and racial profiling. Some of our sons get involved with gangs.

Most youth violence has to do with everyday conflict. While the media have focused on isolated, yet horrendous cases of youth violence in certain predominantly white communities, such as Littleton, Colorado—where two high school students shot and killed twelve of their peers and one of their teachers, wounded many others, and planted bombs to blow up their school—little attention has been paid to violence that is part of everyday life for many of our sons.

Many kids today resort to fighting when they feel insulted by their peers. They often feel that they have to stand up for themselves or become victims, and commonly carry weapons, such as knives, guns, and box cutters, to uphold their reputations or defend themselves against attacks. These are not gang members but ordinary kids. Violence or fighting today rarely means fistfights.

This chapter will present the issues surrounding youth violence as well as strategies that you can use to protect your son from these threats. The last part of this chapter will also describe violence-prevention programs throughout this country that are making a difference for African American youth. If you find that your son is getting into fights at school and in the neighborhood, these sections on what you can do are an effective resource.

The Case of Amadou Diallo

One startling incident of mistaken identity and police brutality against black men is the February 1999 shooting of Amadou Diallo. Diallo was a twenty-two-year-old African immigrant living in New York. Police officers, members of an aggressive street crimes unit, were cruising Diallo's Bronx neighborhood looking for a serial rapist. They saw Mr. Diallo standing in the doorway of his apartment building and, thinking they saw a resemblance between him and the artist's sketch of the rapist, started to question him. Mr. Diallo fled toward the building. A police chase ensued, and the officers fired at Mr. Diallo forty-one times, killing him.

The Diallo shooting has been condemned by numerous officials and has brought national attention to the issue of aggressive police enforcement—a tactic that brings the crime rate down but creates a climate of hostility between people and officers that can breed more brutality, particularly against young black men.

Abuse of Authority: Mistaken Identity, Racial Profiling and Police Brutality

Marshall was an African American honor student on scholarship in his junior year at a private school. One Saturday night he was running through a Harlem train station near his home with a friend, racing to catch the train. A cop, mistaking him for a criminal who had just mugged an old woman outside the train station, yelled, "Stop," raised his gun, shot, and killed him.

Recently, on *The Today Show*, Alton Fitzgerald White, one of the stars of the Broadway show *Ragtime*, shared his story of how a run-in with the police affected his life. He was arrested in his apartment building in New York City by police officers looking for drug dealers. Although cocaine was being sold in his building, and officers found a considerable stash of it in the lobby, Mr. White had absolutely nothing to do with the crime and had never been involved with drug dealing. That did not stop him from spending the night in jail, missing a performance of the play, and bearing the indignity of being strip-searched. He talked about the ironic fact that *Ragtime* deals with a similar incident in the 1920s and argued convincingly that things had not changed very much.

As black parents, we worry about these cases of mistaken identity that can result in death or serious harm to our sons. Fears of this kind of incident or the "driving while black" racial profiling experiences that we described in the first chapter have prompted many parents to teach their sons ways to avoid a tragic outcome.

The following are strategies you can use to teach your son to avoid violence if he is stopped by the police.

- Talk to your son about the reality of racial profiling (the process whereby black males are targeted for searches and arrested because of their race). Let him know that his skin color and the fact of being black in America may lead to his being stopped, searched, and questioned by the police.
- Explain the realities of racism and some of these practices to your son and prepare him to address it.
- Have your son keep a list of numbers where he can reach you in his wallet so it is with him at all times.
- Buy (and make sure to carry) an inexpensive local beeper or pager to insure that you can always be reached by him.
- Have your son carry the phone numbers of extended family members or close friends who may be at home and can receive his call if he is unable to reach you.
- Some parents have told us that cell phones have been very helpful in providing a way for their children to stay in touch. This can be expensive, though, and is not necessary if other methods are used.
- Dr. Jeffrey Gardere recommends that you teach your son that if he is stopped by the police he should follow these guidelines:
  - Do not try to run away.
  - Do not make any sudden moves.
  - Keep his hands visible or raised in the air.
  - Say, "I am not armed."
  - Respond to directives from the police.
  - Do not resist arrest or resist being searched.

- Do not act smart or back talk. This can make him a target.
- Say "yes sir" and "no sir."
- As soon as possible ask to make a phone call to his parents or family for help.
- Tell him to ask for a lawyer to be present before he says anything.

If any experience such as this happens to your son, get a lawyer immediately. If you cannot afford one, contact your local Legal Aid organization. Dr. Gardere also recommends that you also request a copy of all paperwork on your child and keep notes of what has occurred. Be sure to get the name and badge number of the arresting officer(s). Take note of the time and place of the arrest. Even if you do not know the name of the arresting officer, this can help your lawyer trace it. He also suggests that you reach out to and support black police organizations such as the Guardians or One Hundred Black Men in Law Enforcement. (Call your local chapter of the NAACP or the Urban League to obtain the names of organizations in your area.) Many groups of black parents throughout the country have started to invite black police officers to speak to their children about these guidelines. Your son's life could depend on being aware of this information!

Brothers Killing Brothers

Some black youth experience anger, frustration, and rage at racism and the other conditions of poverty in their lives—poor schools, joblessness, lack of role models, lack of adequate housing, etc. According to Richard Majors, author of *Cool Pose,* these "pent-up emotions born of frustration and disappointment may explode in aggressive acts against those who are closest in his daily life—other black people."

African American males who are involved in gangs see violence as a way of proving their masculinity and their manhood. Some gang members are required to rob a store or do a series of violent acts before they are accepted as full gang members. For example, one gang has a "blood in–blood out" rule—a would-be member's blood must be shed as his entrance card into the gang, and he must spill someone else's blood to get out, often that of a rival gang member. Gang initiations often involve being beaten by the other gang members.

For many young black men who have already dropped out of school and do not have opportunities to succeed in other ways, these violent acts build their reputation in their community and their status with their "homeboys" in the gang.

Gang Appeal

When we read the horrific accounts of gang violence involving teenagers, many of us ask ourselves, "Why on earth would a kid want to join a gang?" Here are ten reasons why many African American boys (and girls) have found gangs so attractive: protection, self-esteem, status, racial or cultural identity, friendship, a sense of belonging, excitement, power, reputation, and in some cases, money (via the sale of drugs).

You may be surprised to learn that protection is an extremely important part of the lure of gangs for many African American youth. Many kids living in unsafe areas learn early on that their parents can't be with them all the time and feel that they must find ways to protect themselves. Even if you live in a safe neighborhood, where everyone watches out for everyone else, by adolescence our kids venture beyond that net of safety and are at risk among their own peers.

One mother told us the story of her son, who had been arrested for assault after a major gang fight in their community. This hardworking single parent had tried hard to "do right" by all of her kids and was at a loss as to what to do. She implored her son: "Why did you get involved in a gang? I did my best for you!" He replied, "Yes, Ma, you did your best in raising me, but you can't protect me on the streets. You can't be with me every minute, and even if you could, you're no defense against a nine-millimeter gun."

Many of our kids are scared not just on the streets, they are afraid for their safety in their own school hallways. But for young African American males it goes against what Richard Majors calls their "cool pose" to let their fears show. Gangs become a way to feel safe and protected and not get picked on in the neighborhood and at school. Many parents, like the mother above, are often surprised that their sons (and daughters) don't tell them their fears. Remember that there are two factors operating: first, it is very "uncool" to show fear even to your mother; and second, they don't believe that we can do anything to protect them from these realities.

All adolescents crave a sense of belonging, friendship, and acceptance by their peer group. This boosts their often shaky self-esteem and helps them to feel a part of something special. For many African American kids whose families are struggling, the gang provides an alternative family. As one young gang member said, "Your homeboys love you. They are there for you no matter what." For many kids, gangs provide acceptance and attention that they often don't feel they receive from busy parents.

Gangs also provide young African American males with a sense of identity as black men. When kids don't receive any instruction from parents about how to survive in a hostile world, gangs provide it. For many black teens who have been raised solely by their mothers, there is sometimes a "father hunger." In the absence of positive African American males to fill this void, older gang members model for these young men their own mis-guided version of what it is to be a man and what it takes to sur-vive as a black man.

If the adults in a boy's life have never held a job or have been on welfare for generations, it is easy for him to see the difference between the haves and the have-nots. The people he associates with in the gangs have "stuff"— jewelry, cars, designer clothes and shoes, even houses in the country. Gangs have "older gener-ation" members who are in their twenties and thirties—even for-ties—who often teach lessons to younger members about how earlier generations of black men have been treated. Illegal activ-ity appears to some black youth to be the only way a black man can get ahead in a white-dominated society. This powerful and destructive survival legacy is being passed down to our sons from these substitute "father figures" and is also sadly reinforced by the negative images black boys see of themselves in society at large.

Some boys who feel disenfranchised or left out by society find a way to achieve instant status and to build a "rep" (reputation) in the community by joining gangs. For many African American males, particularly those who don't do well in school and who cannot prove their manhood on an athletic field, joining a gang provides a place to say to the world, "I am somebody." Gang members gain even more status by proving that they are tough and aggressive through their violent acts.

Ironically, many kids turn to gangs looking for the structure, limits, and rules they do not find at home. In their book *Deadly Consequences,* Deborah Prothrow-Stith and Michaele Weissman quote a Los Angeles teacher: "The gangs have a structure that they gravitate towards because there are rules, there are colors, there are guidelines. And this is what all kids need. . . . And kids see it as a positive way to make a statement. . . . I was part of something."

Gangs capitalize on the need for young black males to survive the peer culture and the adult world. If a young black man has areas of his life unfulfilled by his parents, family, and the community, the gang steps in and fills those voids. The gang is a place where black youth can learn about controlling their destiny by doing things that we as parents would not allow. Gangs teach about handling "the man," whether we are talking about the police, white men, or authorities in general. The gang claims to have the prescription for black manhood, for solving the identity crisis, and for "making it" in a hostile society. It teaches recruits how to watch out for the police and how to learn to party, meet girls, fight for your woman, make money, get ahead, get over and feel safe while you do it.

Gang Wannabes: Middle-class African American Kids

In an attempt to protect their kids from the violence of gang culture, some African American parents have moved their families to what they think are safer, middle-class urban or suburban neighborhoods. They then may be shocked to discover that gangs still have a seductive influence over their children, largely via media and music. Joe White and James Coñes III in their book, *Black Man Emerging,* address the issue of the "spillover" of violence and gangs, noting: "The excitement, adventure, and macho image of gang life and go-for-bad street behavior exude a seductive aura. . . . It is difficult for many young Brothers from stable middle-class families to resist the lure of the steady bombardment of exciting video images of singsong rhymes of gangsta rap music. Gang wannabes reject their middle-class status and discount their parents' advice in order to identify with the grittier gangsta image, which includes emulating gang fashions and behaviors. By doing this they attempt to prove their masculinity, achieve notoriety, and gaining respect as a 'bad dude.' "

Portrait of a Middle-class Boy in Trouble: Could This Be Your Son?

In their book, Black Man Emerging, *Joe White and James Coñes III tell the story of Nathan McCall:*

Nathan McCall [author of *Makes Me Wanna Holler*] was not the product of a single-parent [family in the] inner city. He grew up in a home in a middle-class section of Virginia with a mother, a stepfather, a grandmother, and four brothers. He describes a pleasant childhood during which he played cowboys and Indians, skinny-dipped in a nearby lake, and did odd jobs to earn spending money. Most of the Black families in his neighborhood had two parents and manicured lawns.

As a young adolescent, Nathan starts drifting toward a go-for-bad street definition of masculinity and identity. By his midteens, he is fully aligned with a peer group that had turned into a gang. Beginning with petty theft, Nathan and his cohorts escalate into burglary, armed robbery, drug using [and] dealing, beatings and assaults, shoot-outs, drive-bys, and gang rapes. His life is a constant search for ecstasy, excitement, adventure, and danger. . . . Respect is built by becoming known as a bad brother, a "crazy nigger" who will not back down from a challenge or allow anyone to diss him without swift retaliation. Nathan shoots a young Black man in the chest at a point-blank range for insulting his girlfriend. The shooting made him feel powerful and enhanced his reputation as a bad brother who was not to be messed with. . . .

Nathan is consumed by feelings of rage, anger and hatred toward White society. A combination of specific racial events and general perceptions of how Whites control power and opportunity trigger his rage. He experiences racial slurs and humiliations at the hands of White boys at his newly integrated junior high school. Furthermore, his grandmother compares him unfavorably to the well-mannered White children she sees in homes where she works as a maid, and his mother repeatedly tells him not to act like ill-mannered or low-class Black folks. When he watches TV, he begins to realize that there are two worlds: a Black one, with limited opportunities and economic and political power, and a White one, with an endless supply of everything. Nathan cannot see any possibilities in the African-American way of being. He sees his father and other Black men working hard, but feels that they cannot serve as positive male role models because they are oppressed, frustrated and defeated. He feels that older Black men have resigned themselves to economic and social injustices, and spend their off time drowning their frustrations in alcohol. His inner voice tells him he is destroying himself, but it seems like it is in constant conflict with his experiences. The realization of life's inequities fuels his rage and feelings of low self-worth.

Nathan's parents try hard to protect him from the street life he embraced, but they didn't talk about critical issues like work, sex, drugs, and the future. He wants to initiate a conversation, but feels it is against his macho code. His family teaches by examples of hard work and responsibility, but there is no communication on these subjects, which Nathan desperately needs.

It takes a twelve-year jail sentence, much self-reflection, and encouragement from inmate mentors to turn Nathan around.

Twelve African American males between the ages of twelve and fourteen were arrested for gang violence in a New Jersey community. Their horrified parents were called in; many had no idea that their sons were involved in gangs. A local minister who attempted to intervene took the parents in one room while his assistant took the boys in another room. When the assistant asked the boys how many of them were involved in gangs, all of them admitted involvement. When the minister asked the parents, nine out of ten were outraged and responded, "Not my child!"

For some boys who live in integrated or predominantly white communities, joining a gang becomes a misguided way of seeking a black identity. These kids, like all adolescents, are hungry for guidance as to how to be as a black man and how to survive in this world. In their eagerness to identify with anything black, they may embrace negative images of black manhood, such as those seen on gangsta rap videos.

In many suburban communities, black parents may ignore important signs or indicators of their children's gang involvement because of their denial that the problem exists—and that it could involve *their* son. This denial may persist until, tragically, they are confronted by a violent incident in which their sons are arrested, hurt, or killed.

White and Coñes point out that many of these kids do not just emerge suddenly as gang members. Often they begin with relatively innocent imitations of gang life, such as adopting the gangsta look of baggy clothes, imitating the "walk," and using terms they learn from gangsta rap. It is in the next stage, when they begin hanging out and cruising around neighborhoods in cars looking for action, that the kids are really at risk. Look for signs such as involvement in vandalism, fistfights, or threats to other kids. This behavior can escalate quickly and culminate with a fight where a kid is wounded or killed. If drugs and money are involved, your son could be caught in a drive-by shooting, in which cruising cars full of boys (the posse) might riddle a house with bullets and speed off.

Gang Symbols and Styles

Gang members often use symbols such as colors, hats, jackets, sweatbands, bandannas, hairnets, and sneakers to signify membership. In addition, there are special handshakes, hairstyles, a certain walk, hand signals, language, and nicknames—such as "Monster" or "Killer"—that complete the show of solidarity.

Hand signals are also used by gang members to warn one another of danger. Some gangs require members to have a tattoo placed on their ankle or their arm. Many gang members, particularly those who are involved in dealing drugs, wear large amounts of gold jewelry as their signature.

It is not hard to imagine the tremendous appeal that all of these special symbols of belonging have for African American youth. Most of us remember wearing the same things our friends wore in order to be "in." Today, our kids become gang wannabes in order to be "down"—same issue, different words, yet more deadly consequences. Some kids are killed just for walking on the wrong street.

Two famous Los Angeles gangs, the Crips and the Bloods, are expanding into other areas of the country, such as New York. Crips members wear blue clothes, scarves, and bandannas over their heads. The Bloods wear red. As a result of kids having been killed for wearing the wrong color to school, many schools throughout the country have forbidden the wearing of gang colors.

African American men have always used handshakes, words, and signals to bond with and communicate with one another. The black power handshake of the 1960s and 1970s and the "giving skin" of high- and low-fives are examples of handshakes and hand signals used by black men to show solidarity and loyalty. Black fraternities have a long history of secret handshakes, special colors, and codes of honor. It is all part of identifying with the brotherhood of black men. The gang then is the ultimate "cool pose" and appeals to the black adolescent's need for the signs and symbols of belonging.

Gangs and the Drug Trade

Gangs have existed in this country for over a hundred years. With the increased availability of guns (particularly semiautomatics) and the introduction of crack cocaine, White and Coñes point out that gangs have gained a stronger foothold, becoming drug dealers, distributors, and recruiters.

The addictive nature of crack cocaine provides a steady stream of customers for dealers/gang members. (See Chapter 10 for a description of drugs.) The effects of smoking crack are also quite different from the drugs that preceded it. For example, heroin causes addicts to "nod out," so they are not as much of a danger to the community when they are high as when they are "craving" the drug. But after smoking crack, addicts often become violent and are therefore a danger to others when they are high *and* craving.

Many gang-related killings now are drug related, too. As the drug trade expanded into the crack cocaine big money business in the 1980s, more gang members began arming themselves with semiautomatic weapons in order to protect their turf. These weapons have an advantage over traditional handguns in that they do not need to be reloaded as frequently. The phrase drive-by shooting has become a household word, and images of such violence are frequent in the media. This type of violence has killed both gang members and innocent bystanders.

Selling drugs did not start with young black males in our communities. Adults who deal in drugs are often the ones who recruit youngsters, some as young as age seven, as "lookouts." People they know—uncles, aunts, mothers, fathers, and older siblings—often deputize small boys (and girls) into the drug scene. By age nine, kids can be "runners," making drug deliveries. And by age eleven, they can become dealers in their schools.

Guns for Sale: Easy Pickin's

Guns are everywhere today and are surprisingly available to our children. The American Red Cross estimates that at least one child is killed by a gun each day. For $15 many kids can buy guns on the streets of most inner-city communities. Some suburban kids have been able to buy guns illegally at gun shows. One of the guns used in the Littleton, Colorado, shooting was bought legally at a gun show by an older classmate and then given to the boys, who would not have been able to purchase them themselves. Tragically, many kids obtain guns in their own homes. The irony in this is the fact that many parents keep guns at home to protect their families against violence.

If you must have a gun in the house, keep it unloaded, locked away, and equipped with a trigger lock. The best prevention, however, is not to have guns in your home and to give your son clear messages about avoiding guns and violence. The best prevention for us as a society would be the passing of stronger gun-control laws.

The Experience of Death

For many inner-city African American youth and gang members, violence and death are almost constant, at times daily, events. A part of the cool pose is to not show fear—particularly of others, injury, or death. In her book *Voices from the Streets* Beth Atkin interviewed young former gang members. For some of them the funeral of a particular friend, or a whole series of deaths, can lead them to begin their difficult struggle to leave the gang.

Funerals of gang members are numerous and elaborate. The public had a view of these funerals after the deaths of Tupac Shakur and "Biggie" Smalls, gangsta rap stars who lived dangerously and died violently. Some would argue that they enjoy more celebrity today than they did when they were alive as a result of their tremendous following among black teens and young adults. White and Coñes describe a gang member's funeral reported in the *Los Angeles Times*:

> The funeral of Cadillac Jim, a twenty-nine-year-old, high-level, Rolling-Sixties Crip, was attended by 500 mourners. He was gunned down one night outside a cheap motel in Los Angeles. Befitting his status as an O.G. [original gangster] with a history of more than ten years of gangsterism, Jim's body rested in a casket fringed with a sparkling blue garland, the color of the Crips. Over his casket hung an eight-foot banner that bore his name. Young men with blue scarves hanging from their pockets bent to kiss his forehead and have their pictures taken with the fallen hero. . . . Gang members told reporters that homeboys are what they fight and die for.

We know we've bombarded you with more information about gangs than you might ever have wanted to know. We did so not to instill fear but to make you an informed parent, and therefore a better parent. Below are some suggestions for how to protect your son from involvement in violence.

Black Churches Versus Gangs

In June 1998, *Newsweek* magazine ran a very unusual story about Reverend Eugene Rivers, a preacher in Boston, who runs a gang and violence intervention program at the Ella J. Baker House. He remembers the early phases of his unusual work:

> During a funeral service for a young murder victim, a gang chased another kid into the church, beating and stabbing him in front of a crowd of mourners. "For the clergy," says Rev. Rivers, "this was a wake-up call. We had to be out on the streets. . . ." While the mainline Boston churches issued a denunciation of the violence, a group of ministers . . . met in Rev. Eugene Rivers's house to discuss a more radical response: walking the hoods, engaging the gangs, pulling kids out. Instead of bickering with the police, the ministers vowed to work with them. . . . Since . . . that alliance . . . juvenile crime has fallen dramatically.

This has now evolved into a coalition of dozens of churches in Boston that are actively involved in crime prevention and in taking kids back "one kid and one block at a time." It is one of many inspirational stories about the power of black churches and ministers to mobilize our communities to intervene and "take our kids back from the streets." (See Chapter 12 for more examples.)

Violence Prevention Programs

In her book *Coping with Weapons and Violence in Your Schools and on Your Streets,* Maryann Miller describes a number of violence- and gang-prevention programs. She describes many reasons why young people join gangs: "to have a place to belong, to be accepted, to be noticed—and sometimes just to have something to do."

Schools around the country have tried to address the problem of gangs by establishing programs that offer kids some of the same benefits they could derive from gang membership. One such program is the "Good Guys Gangs" in the T. J. Rusk Middle School in Dallas, Texas. Teachers there used some of the aspects of gang symbols that often appeal to adolescents. They have adopted the gang practice of greeting one another with secret signs, codes, and symbols. They meet regularly and wear similar colors and clothing. Their main purpose is to help kids to resist the pressure to join gangs.

Programs such as the Block Watch Program in Seattle, Neighborhood Watch in Detroit, and many others throughout the country have worked with the police crime prevention units to train parents and other concerned community members to "take back their streets."

Many violence prevention programs have targeted younger kids. The consensus of experts seems to be that the younger we start antiviolence messages, and the more consistent we are, the less likely our kids are to adopt a violent lifestyle. Miller describes a program called "Journey," a three-day violence- and gang-prevention program that teaches antiviolence messages and helps to build self-esteem and self-discipline. This program utilizes mentors, many of whom are ex-gang members.

Rahway State Prison in New Jersey and many other prisons throughout the country have "Scared Straight" programs in which inmates talk candidly to young men about the harsh realities of prison life. Their input helps to deglamorize "life on the inside." These inmates encourage youth to seek a better life for themselves.

Other alternatives are what Dr. Prothrow-Stith calls "second chance opportunities" for "high-risk" youth. She believes that "many kids could be saved if just one adult took an interest in them, made a commitment to them." In her book *Deadly Consequences,* she includes a number of stories of concerned community members who have given kids in trouble a "second chance" by becoming foster parents.

What Schools Can Do

Dr. Prothrow-Stith's research revealed a number of factors that have helped certain schools avoid violence:

"Schools with strong principals; schools that are not too large; schools where discipline is fair but firm; schools where teachers are imbued with high expectations for every child; schools where parents are drawn into the educational orbit, are schools where learning takes place. They are also schools that are safe."

She describes the Peacemakers program in a school in New York with racial tension. The program is a quarter African American, a quarter Latino, and the rest of the students are white. The key here is that teachers were trained in conflict resolution and are able to teach this to their students.

What you can do to support or create school violence prevention programs:

- Ask your principal if such a program exists in your son's school or in your district.
- Obtain information about violence-prevention programs. Contact one of the organizations listed in the Resources section at the end of this chapter.
- Make a formal request that your local school board add violence prevention to the core curriculum.
- Start a parent school patrol—patrolling the hallways of the school and the streets surrounding it.

Sankofa

Dr. Paulette Hines at University Behavioral Healthcare in New Jersey has developed a comprehensive violence prevention program called Sankofa, a West African term meaning "reaching back to our past in order to move forward." The program's goal is to change behavior and promote a message of youth responsibility and self-control through teaching life skills, such as anger management and conflict resolution, to adolescents and building cultural pride. Although it has been applied to many different cultural groups, Sankofa's Afrocentric focus is particularly sensitive to the needs of African American youth and families.

This program involves prevention as well as interventions that can be used to help kids to avoid violence in their communities. Sankofa utilizes an active training approach. The Sankofa program has two levels of training: violence-prevention training for youth and violence-prevention training for those involved with youth, including parents, teachers, school staff, administrators and counselors, and police. It has already been implemented throughout New Jersey in schools, community and faith-based organizations, as well as juvenile facilities. (See Resources section for further information.)

❖ ❖ ❖

Strategy is better than strength.

—*African proverb*

❖ ❖ ❖

Another program that Dr. Hines's office offers is the Sudden Violent Loss and Mediation Services Project, which has been designed as an intervention in schools and communities in the aftermath of traumatic deaths. This can involve the sudden killing of a youth in the community or random acts of school violence. If you are a concerned parent, teacher, school counselor or administrator, or community member, the manual *Managing Sudden Traumatic Loss in the Schools* is available and might be helpful. See the Resources section for more details.

Sankofa's effectiveness is greatly enhanced because it offers a student- and parent-intervention program. The Sankofa program offers the following tips to prevent and manage conflicts peacefully. Start young and teach them to your sons:

Sankofa's Tips for You to Teach Your Kids:

- "Anger is a normal, okay emotion.
- You can remain in control and not make hotheaded responses even when you are angry.
- Use your brains, not your fists or weapons!
- It is easier to prevent a fight than to stop one after it has started.
- Assess the level of risk involved before deciding how to handle a conflict situation.
- Don't make assumptions! There may be a difference

between what appears on the surface and what is going on below the surface.

- There is a difference between fighting and self-defense. Fighting involves intentionally attempting to inflict harm on another person.
- Be aware of the messages you receive about violence from your peers, your family, and the media. Make healthy choices!
- Taking a deep breath when you are feeling angry may help you calm down.
- There are many healthy and workable alternatives to violence. These include: back off, walk away; negotiate; agree to disagree; apologize; ask for help; refuse to get involved; use humor; throw a curve (do something unexpected).
- Take control of your anger before your anger takes control of you.
- Approach conflict with the notion of finding a solution that will be positive for everyone concerned.
- You can avoid fights and other violence without losing face or extending an invitation to others to take advantage of you.
- It is wise to build techniques into our lives that help us stay centered, feel healthy, and avoid overreaching or, as some say, "going off."
- The same strategy doesn't work all the time. What works for one person may not work for another.
- It takes more strength to use your head than your hands.
- It is important to realize you cannot control other people's behavior. It is helpful to determine which things are within your control and which things are not.
- You are responsible for your own behavior. This you can control.
- How you say what you want to communicate may be as important as WHAT you say."

The following is a list of things you can do to stem violence:

- Model positive, nonviolent behavior; children and teens learn what they observe.

- Talk to your children early on (age six or seven) about violence and the harm and loss of life it can cause.
- Give your children (from an early age) clear messages on avoiding violence, including specific how-tos.
- Monitor your kids constantly. Call and check in before you leave work; get an inexpensive local beeper, pager, or cellular phone so they can be in constant touch with you; make sure they are home after school and engaged in productive activities.
- Find out from the local police and from other concerned parents what areas in your community have the greatest amount of violence and/or drug dealing; discuss this with your sons and encourage them to avoid these areas.
- Contact your local United Way, Urban League, or NAACP for information on violence-prevention programs in your area.
- Invite representatives of local violence prevention organizations to your school, PTA, church, or community organization.
- Get to know your son's friends. Insist that he bring them home once in a while; allow your home to be a place where they can hang out occasionally.
- Get to know the parents of your son's friends.
- Take this book to school officials and community leaders and advocate for programs such as these. Join or help create community and school coalitions to develop and support programs to foster safer schools and communities.

Here are antiviolence messages to give your sons:

- Be clear about your position against fighting. Teach your son that there are better ways to resolve things than by fighting.
- Practice what you preach. Show your son that people can become angry without becoming violent. Say this directly to your sons. Model anger management and control.
- Teach your sons positive "self-talk." Example: "This may be rough, but I can handle it. I don't have to lose control. I will

not react based on the emotions I feel at this moment. I can stay cool. I don't have to take this personally."

• Start an anticrime patrol with other parents in your neighborhood.

RESOURCES

Books

Atkin, S. Beth. *Voices from the Streets: Former Gang Members Tell Their Stories.* Boston: Little, Brown, 1996.

Gardere, Jeffrey. *Smart Parenting for African Americans: Helping Your Kids Thrive in a Difficult World.* Secaucus, NJ: Citadel Press, 1999.

Hines, Paulette, and C. Sutton. "Sankofa: A Violence Prevention and Life Skills Curriculum." (800) 762-2989.

Hines, Paulette. "Managing Sudden Traumatic Loss in the Schools." (800) 762-2989.

Majors, Richard, and Janet Mancini Billson. *Cool Pose.* New York: Touchstone, 1993.

Miller, Maryann. *Coping with Weapons and Violence in Your Schools and on Your Streets.* New York: Rosen, 1993.

"Peace by Peace": Peer Mediator's Guide, Conflict Resolution Through Peer Mediation. (800) 99-YOUTH.

Prothrow-Stith, Deborah, with Michaele Weissman. *Deadly Consequences: How Violence Is Destroying Our Teenage Population and a Plan to Begin Solving the Problem.* New York: HarperCollins, 1993.

White, Joseph, and James Coñes III. *Black Men Emerging: Facing the Past and Seizing a Future in America.* New York: Routledge, 1999.

Programs

Centers for Disease Control Violence Prevention Programs. www.CDC. gov

Dr. Paulette Hines Sankofa, Program Director, Office of Prevention Services, University of Medicine and Dentistry of New Jersey, University Behavioral Healthcare, P.O. Box 1392, Piscataway, NJ 08855-1392. Toll-free: (800) 762-2989

A manual and trainer kit is available to provide group leaders with a step-by-step approach to violence-prevention exercises for children and parents.

School Mediation Associates, 72 Chester Road, Belmont, MA 02178

Violence Prevention Project, 1010 Massachusetts Avenue, Boston, MA 02118. (This is Dr. Prothrow-Stith's program.)

12

◆

IF YOU ARE ON A
ROAD TO NOWHERE,
FIND ANOTHER ROAD.
—ASHANTI PROVERB

Taking Our Sons Back from the Streets

Nancy: I was born in Harlem, and I grew up in a housing project in the Bronx where the buildings were about seven stories tall. Parents were always looking out of their windows to watch their children playing downstairs. If I got in trouble, my mother usually knew about it before I got upstairs.

A.J.: As a child growing up in Bedford-Stuyvesant in Brooklyn, most families on my block were friends and neighbors in the real sense of the word. They had one another's phone numbers and, in some instances, a key to one another's homes for emergencies. Other adults looked out for me and the other kids on the block. We were expected to respect them as the "guardians" of the neighborhood.

So many of us would have gotten into big trouble early on if someone hadn't snatched us back from the road to nowhere and put us on a different road. We all had lots of "parents" in our communities who would tell our folks if we were on the wrong path. Unfortunately, few communities today have the sense of connection we had in our childhoods decades ago. This is a big loss. People in African American communities used to feel free to discipline one another's children, and children were expected to respect "grown-ups" because they were your elders. Many parents are now afraid to speak critically to someone else's children, let alone discipline them, or to tell parents what their children are doing "in the street." One senior citizen recently remarked: "Years ago I would stop somebody's child and say, 'Hey, what are you doing?' Not today. I'm afraid somebody's child might pull out a nine-millimeter gun and put it in my face."

Fear of reprisal from kids—or their parents—keeps the elders in our communities, who are often home during the day and after school, from intervening when they see our children in problem situations. Many elders say that if you want to know why kids act the way they do, watch the behavior of their parents. One mother complained: "I used to feel comfortable going to a parent and saying, 'Your son got in a fight with mine.' Not anymore. These parents today will get up in your face as quick as their kids will." This fear has turned the streets of some African American communities where children used to play into war zones. But a remarkable turnaround has started to happen in some African American communities. Black parents and other concerned members of the community in many parts of this country have begun to actively fight to "take their sons back from the streets."

As African American parents, it is so easy to get discouraged when we think about the many street influences that our kids are vulnerable to: peers, gangs, drugs, alcohol, violence, crime, harassment by the police, etc. But we can't remain passive and allow our concerns to become reality in our own homes.

How do you know when "the street" has won your son over? Ask yourself the following questions about your son's recent behavior:

- Is he rarely at home?
- Does he stay out past curfew consistently?
- Does he sleep late and stay out late no matter what you say?
- Is truancy an issue? Does he pretend to go off to school and then return home after you leave for work?
- Is he secretive about his friends and where he goes?
- Does he have favorite clothes, colors, and jewelry he must wear all the time? Do his friends wear the same colors and clothes?
- Is he defensive, combative, and defiant about your regulating his time with friends?

- Do you find yourself increasingly defending his behavior with various people and authorities because of minor altercations and infractions? Does he have juvenile offenses?
- Has he seemed to grow more disrespectful of you, relatives, or other adults?
- Does he seem to know it all, believe only his friends, and dismiss any of your opinions and suggestions?
- Is he openly using drugs and alcohol, or do you have strong suspicions that he is?
- Is he sexually active or do you suspect that he is?

Allow your answers to the above questions to guide your actions. Just answering yes to two or more of these questions should sound an alarm for you to do something. Pay attention to those other parental instincts and vibes that go with knowing your children. If we are honest with ourselves, most of us are instinctively aware when our son has significantly strayed from the values and way of life we have labored to teach him. These behaviors are clear warning signs of future trouble for your son.

Taking our sons back from the street requires *time, energy,* and *commitment.* The first step is to develop a plan and make sure it happens. There is no other choice. Loving your sons under these circumstances requires commitment and dedication. You may have to take time off from your job, pay to get professional advice, and give up some of the leisure-time activities you enjoy. Make sure, however, to keep yourself in balance so you do not collapse. (See our last chapter.) Either you give the time now or you will be forced to give that time at another point—for things like court appearances, hospital visits, or trips to jail.

The following are the steps you as a parent can take to develop a "help plan" for your son:

- List the number and kind of problem behaviors you see your son engaged in. Your list will tell you how far he has gone into street life.
- List the areas where you believe you still have influence with your son.
- Identify how much time you spend talking and being with

your son and figure out ways to increase it. List the things that the two of you can still do and enjoy together.

- Write down some notes that describe the way you are when you are with your son. Do you have good times together, good conversations, or does the time you spend together become a setup for you to get your demands across?
- Identify and list those people who your son respects and you believe he will listen to. Talk with these people about your concerns for your son and ask for their help.

Clear demonstrations of your interest, determination, and willingness to reach out can show your commitment and can sometimes get his attention.

"My son was about to be kicked out of his second school mostly because he never showed up. I took a leave of absence from my job, and every day for two months I went to school with him and sat in the back of his class-room. The teacher said she never had so much cooperation from students in her entire teaching career. But I was just trying to show my son that his father would do anything to save him from the streets." (Randy, father of two teenage sons)

Valerie, a grandmother raising her grandson, stopped at her grand-son's hangout every day on her way home from work. She was respectful of his pride, and what she considered misguided male bravado, so she would not take him away from his friends to talk to him. She just wanted him to see her walk by to send the message she was watching and was there for him. He was always warning her of the risks of walking in that area, to which she responded, "If it's good enough for you, it's good enough for me." She counted on his attachment to her to act as a buffer against "the forces of evil."

The story above illustrates one family member who went it alone against "the street" in a young man's life. But don't believe that you can save your son alone. Sometimes the personal risks we are willing to take are too great for what we hope to achieve. Good judgment is knowing when you need help and having the wisdom to get it.

Taking Our Sons Back:
A Community Approach

Here is one example of a community approach to taking our kids back from the streets. We think it is an excellent model. Take note of the various components needed for a successful outcome.

The Problem: Twelve kids between the ages of twelve and fourteen were arrested in the local junior high school in New Jersey for "gang violence" in the hallway. The police were called and the kids were taken out of the school in handcuffs. The boys were subsequently suspended from school and required to attend an alternative school program with a violence prevention component.

The Response: One frantic parent called Reverend DeForest B. Soaries Jr., pastor of the First Baptist Church of Lincoln Gardens in Somerset, New Jersey. He mobilized the church and the community to take action on behalf of all of the kids, even though only one of the children was a member of his congregation. He enlisted the help of a lawyer who was a member of his congregation to provide pro bono legal services for the boys and their families. He volunteered his church to serve as the site of a temporary alternative school program for that school year. Nancy and two other local psychologists were also asked to help provide individual and family counseling and parent- and family-support groups. Men from the community volunteered to run violence prevention groups for the boys and provided them with mentoring and black male role models.

The Key Components: Community and church involvement, parent- and family-support groups, home-based family therapy, school intervention, proactive parent involvement, violence prevention groups, and mentoring by black male role models.

The Goal: To provide a forum to discuss the consequences of the fight and to offer assistance that addressed the needs of the boys and their families. To create a group effort that would get the boys the help they needed so they could be reintegrated back into the school. The larger goal was to empower the families to address the issues in the community threatening their children.

The Process: The families of the boys (including fathers, mothers, grandparents and other concerned family members), along with other members of the neighborhood, set up a series of meetings at a neutral place located between both "gang territories." Key figures involved in the incident, such as the superintendent of schools, the principal, guidance counselors from the school, and the head of the police department's juvenile division were invited to the first meetings to provide information to the parents.

The Chief Concerns: Many parents refused to believe that their sons were involved in gang activity and were very suspicious of the school officials' motives, believing their actions to have been motivated by racism. They were encouraged to discuss those angry feelings. This was followed by a number of heated sessions with the parents and family members about violence prevention and gangs. They discussed their fear of gunfights and offered differing opinions about what to tell a child about fighting. The parents were also uncomfortable initially with the "shrinks" and were not sure that they could be trusted.

The Turning Point: A clear, consistent message for the boys emerged once the parents vented their various opinions about violence prevention. One parent whose two sons had been arrested in the incident took on a leadership role in the group. She believed that together the parents could control the outcome of the crisis. The other members, encouraged by her, became empowered to create an action plan. Also, the parents finally began to trust the therapists because they saw their consistency in attendance, and they came to appreciate their listening skills and positive input. With their help, the parents were able to control their anger and channel it into constructive action.

The Results: The parents decided to make surprise visits on a rotating basis to the alternative school program. Each parent would prepare a report about the boys' progress to the school board, to avoid any miscommunication or delay in their return to their "regular" school. The parents exchanged the reports on the boys' progress and helped one another problem solve when necessary. The parents composed a letter to the presiding judge documenting the boys' progress at the alternative school.

The Epilogue: The boys went back to their regular school in the fall. The parents now intervened when they saw incidents occurring among the boys in the community. If any parent saw any of the boys on the street, they would drive them to their weekly probation meeting. The parent leader of the group got a security-related job in the local high school. When the boys entered high school the following year, the parents tried to prepare them with new rules for survival. They made more of an effort to participate in parents' night, class selections, and school events. The parent leader became a key figure in the resolution of disagreements between the boys in rival gangs at the school. She eventually developed joint meetings between the gang leaders, which resulted in a decision to make peace. The "peace treaty" was significant enough to be written up in the local newspaper. Some of the parents continued to meet for several months to discuss ongoing legal issues, school problems, violence-prevention messages for their sons, and various activities for boys in their community. After the boys' probation ended, the parents decided to continue to meet even though there was no official reason. They planned future workshops, kept abreast of one another's children, discussed pushing the local authorities to build a recreation center, and encouraged other concerned parents to attend the meetings. Many of the parents increased their sense of agency and empowerment as a result of participation in the group.

It Takes a Whole Village

The story above illustrates many lessons. It shows the central role that black churches and black ministers can play in mobilizing and focusing community efforts. It shows the power of community-based parent- and family-support groups, mentoring and violence-prevention groups, and the role of black men in the community as role models. The empowerment of these parents is evident. They organized to monitor their sons, to intervene in school, and to share responsibility for their welfare. Many different members of the African American community who were not related to the boys mobilized behind them and their families.

This story illustrates the second important aspect of this chapter. In order to take our sons back from the street, we must work together. In the words of the African proverb that has now become a political cliché, "It takes a whole village to raise a child." This is truer in today's world than ever for our African American sons. One parent, one family, one pastor, cannot do it alone. Our sons need time, individual attention, and personal care. This used to be provided by the family structure. Today, it requires a variety of people—many of whom are simply caring strangers.

Mentoring Programs

Mentoring programs for African American boys can take many forms and are sponsored by different groups and organizations, such as African American churches, fraternities, black men's organizations (such as 100 Black Men of America), black colleges, black professional organizations, and community organizations, such as Big Brothers and the Boys and Girls Clubs. Dr. Vernon Allwood at the Morehouse School of Medicine in Atlanta has helped to create a number of mentoring and rites-of-passage programs.

In his mentoring program African American medical students work with undergraduates who, in turn, work with kids in elementary through high school. As students receive mentoring from an older black role model, they are also "giving something back to their communities" by simultaneously mentoring a younger child. This builds a pyramid of mutual help, support, and role modeling. It also empowers young black people at all stages of life and educational development.

You should consider several things when evaluating a mentoring program:

- There should be a coordinator who can tell you how the program operates and how volunteers are utilized to mentor the youth.
- Ask how the mentors are recruited and trained to tutor and work with adolescents. Are they experienced? What is the program's success rate? Some of our sons will present a major challenge to a mentor's patience, skill, and ingenuity,

e.g., they may have dropped out of school, literally or figuratively; they may not be used to keeping regular appointments or seeking outside help; they may be resistant to the program structure, etc. You should inquire from the coordinator how their mentors deal with such challenges.

• Many mentoring programs consider their mentors as role models for youth and expect them to know how to serve in that capacity. Ask about the details of this relationship. What will be expected in terms of time, activities, and bonding between your son and the mentor? Some parents become anxious that they will end up competing with the mentor for their son's affection and it will pull him away from them. They don't want to lose him to a new group, even if it is positive. This is understandable, so find out if they encourage parental involvement in the mentoring process.

How to Find a Mentor for Your Son

Contact:
• Your son's school guidance department
• Local black churches or other places of worship in your area
• Local chapters of black fraternities
• Organizations such as 100 Black Men of America
• Local colleges
• Local community youth programs

Tutoring

The search for a tutoring program is similar to the search for a mentor. Many adolescents, even those who are very bright, experience difficulty in a particular high school subject. This often requires somewhat more specialized help. Here, contacting a local college and asking for a good student who can tutor your son in geometry, chemistry, or physics may yield excellent results.

Many parents concerned about the hours of unsupervised time after school have encouraged their teenagers to participate in after-school programs, which often have some tutoring component. Search carefully. Be sure that you start with your son's teacher and guidance counselor and with your own family-church-friend network.

Mentorship Behind Bars: Prison Ministries

Young men are being mentored behind prison walls. When the young Malcolm X was put in prison, he at first continued his street life on the inside. Then he was approached by another inmate and follower of the Nation of Islam whom he at first rejected. This man persisted. He gave him articles to read and began teaching him. A correspondence began between Malcolm and Elijah Muhammad, the founder of the Nation of Islam. These letters and the persistent efforts of the prison "ministry" altered the course of Malcolm's life from street hustler to one of the greatest African American leaders of all time. In Malcolm X's own words, we must continue efforts such as these and take back the minds of our young men "by any means necessary."

Both members of the Nation of Islam and Black Church Prison Ministries have had success running prison programs to help inmates relearn what manhood is all about. Through these prison outreach ministries more and more black men in prison are turning to spiritual solutions to solve their identity crisis; redirect their lives; and come to the realization that although racism exists, their rebellious and violent response to it will ultimately destroy them. As Malcolm X's story illustrates, older inmates—many of whom are serving long prison sentences—are enlisted to mentor younger men in prison. Today, older inmates are often gang veterans who have realized the futility of their former self-destructive lifestyles and help younger inmates prepare for a productive life after "lockdown."

Rites-of-Passage Programs

Rites-of-passage programs have begun to spring up in many African American communities throughout the United States.

Nsenga Warfield-Coppock, a researcher who has studied these programs, has found that they have in common the goal of promoting self-esteem through the development of a positive black racial identity based on Afrocentric principles. They help to develop an appreciation of the cultural and racial heritage of African Americans. Patrick McHenry and a group of other researchers studied seventy-six African American boys who participated in rites-of-passage programs. All of these youth were living in foster homes and were at risk for juvenile delinquency, drug and alcohol abuse, gangs, violence, and school failure. Their results clearly demonstrated that young men who participated in rites-of-passage programs were less likely to engage in these behaviors.

In Africa historically, children were considered great blessings, to be nurtured and protected. We had strong systems of socialization and rites-of-passage that enabled us to survive and resist oppression. Dr. Asa Hilliard states that the greatest damage done to African people worldwide as a result of slavery, colonization, segregation, and racism was the collapse of our independent systems of socialization for children. As a result, we have boys desperately in need of manhood training.

Rites-of-passage programs have developed out of the work of African American scholars such as Nathan and Julia Hare, Jawanza Kunjufu, Asa Hilliard, Nsenga Warfield-Coppock and Aminifu Harvey, Vernon Allwood, and Paul Hill. These Afrocentric scholars have called for a return to the manhood rituals of many African civilizations in order to prepare young African American men to embrace positive values in their racial identity and service to their communities. The programs are usually targeted to early and later adolescent boys.

In Chapter 7 we discussed the challenges and mixed messages that our sons receive on "how to become and be a man." Rites-of-passage programs, such as Onis and SIMBA described below, take charge of the process of clearly defining that transition to manhood. It takes the responsibility for that definition out of the streets and gives it back to adult male role models.

The typical format of a rites-of-passage program includes teaching African and African American history, providing black male mentors, emphasizing responsibility, education, respect for oneself and others, discipline, sexual responsibility, and unity and conflict management, among other positive values.

The Onis Program: Manhood Training

Dr. Vernon Allwood in Atlanta developed the Onis Program, a program designed to lead African American males through the rituals of manhood training. It is similar to the process many of us watched depicted in Alex Haley's acclaimed series, *Roots,* in which adolescent boys were taken into the woods for an extended period of time and given the rigorous physical and mental training considered important in the development of men. This training was conducted by respected older males and had as its purpose the development of attitudes and skills necessary for young boys to develop before assuming the responsibilities associated with the masculine role. If a boy successfully completed the training, he was formally acknowledged as a man among his people and accorded the rights and responsibilities that went along with being a man.

Onis is a rites-of-passage program based in a black church. Through a series of weekly group sessions, African American adolescents are taken through a similar process to help them achieve a clearer understanding of positive African American manhood. The goal is to strengthen their minds, bodies, and souls through activities designed to build self-esteem, positive black racial identity, and strong bonds with other men in the community. Sessions address cultural and historical traditions, and given the high rate of violence in our communities, special attention is paid to developing positive interpersonal skills, anger management, and violence prevention. Dr. Allwood also uses an assertiveness training model to teach African American youth how to effectively handle situations with police officers, teachers, parents, and other authority figures.

At the end of the training, the young men attend a rites-of-passage ceremony based on African traditions, to which their peers, parents, church members, and other residents of the community are invited. This ceremony acknowledges that they have been trained in values of positive African American manhood and are now ready to take their places as adults in the community.

Out of concern for the further development of boys beyond the rites-of-passage program, Dr. Allwood developed the Onis Graduate Program. African American men in the community volunteer to serve as mentors for the graduates, with priority given to those who do not have a father in the home. These mentors work closely with the young men in the areas of careers, college and financial aid, business opportunities, and developing entrepreneurial skills. There are also social activities, and the mentors participate in special outings such as camping trips.

Leadership skills are developed in the post-rites period, when the graduates take a major responsibility for the next group of young men preparing for the rites of passage. They can provide tutoring at a local elementary school's after-school program, clean up an eyesore in the neighborhood, or visit a housebound senior citizen. This community involvement, whereby the graduates take on a younger child to mentor, is key to building on the original effort and fosters giving something back to our community, a principle so essential for our future as a people.

SIMBA—Dr. Jawanza Kunjufu

Dr. Jawanza Kunjufu, the author of four volumes of *Countering the Conspiracy to Destroy Black Boys,* is another advocate of rites-of-passage programs in African American communities. In his books he provides guidelines for parents and communities eager to start these programs. He challenges black men to take our kids back from negative societal influences, such as "making a baby, fights, consumption of drugs, alcohol, clothes and cars." He developed the manhood training program SIMBA, which means "young lions" in Swahili.

In the development of the SIMBA program, Kunjufu drew on the work of Nathan and Julia Hare, who give requirements for rites of passage in their book *The Passage.* Their program links the generations by requiring these young men to give service to their neighborhood and community and to adopt a senior citizen. They also emphasize education, cultural pride and values, discipline, and responsibility. Kunjufu and Nathan and Julia Hare stress the importance of parental involvement.

Kunjufu reminds us that we can learn a lesson from the streets. A gang leader said to him, "We will always have the youth because we make them feel important." Parents and other community members who start these programs need to adapt the symbols of solidarity that gang membership accords young men—such as logos, T-shirts, jackets, caps, a chant, song or step routine—to a positive end. He reminds us of the success of fraternities in our communities and on black campuses. Vernon Allwood recommends that when we adopt these new symbols we should connect them in some way to Africa.

Finding Keepers of the Flame

All of these programs emphasize the importance of parental involvement. The leaders in the rites-of-passage movement voice concern over the difficulty of sustaining commitment and involvement on the part of volunteers and parents over time. But by paying a fee to those who conduct manhood training sessions, the consistency and continuity of the program can be assured. Dr. Allwood has been able to obtain grants from local funding sources for these men. Charles Ballard, founder of the National Institute for Responsible Fatherhood, recruits blue-collar workers and other professionals in the community to become mentors to the teen fathers he is trying to turn around. This group of working-class black men seem to be a forgotten but valuable source of good role models for our boys.

If you are planning to start a mentoring or rites-of-passage group, Joseph White and James Coñes suggest that potential volunteers should meet the following criteria:

- An expressed commitment to helping black youth
- Insight into the struggles facing black males
- An understanding of the educational and social challenges confronting black men
- A demonstrated success in reaching personal goals
- A strong sense of personal responsibility

What You Can Do: Have a Game Plan

As you have read, we as black parents can do many things to take our kids back from the streets. Our most important piece of advice is to develop a plan, get assistance, and be prepared to dedicate the time, energy, and commitment toward your goal. The size of the task will depend on how far your son has immersed himself in street life and is disconnected from you and the family, and what you are able to provide as an alternative. Let's summarize the considerations that should go into a master plan for taking your son back from the streets:

- Identify and list the signs in your son's behavior, attitude, and mood to determine how much he has drifted from home life to street life.
- Determine if there is a drug problem that includes using and/or selling. If there is, this becomes the primary focus. You will need to get assistance for substance-abuse treatment. (See Chapter 10.)
- Do not hesitate to take your son and your family for therapy or counseling to determine if there are any major emotional or behavioral problems. (See Chapter 13.) This becomes a major part of your plan and guides it accordingly.
- Be mindful of your son's history of juvenile offenses and contact with the court system. If he gets into trouble again, can it undermine your plan? Is he under court supervision? Your plan may involve your finding out the legal status of your son. (Is he still on probation? Does he have a court date pending?) It should be done not for threatening purposes but for developing plans to avoid future trouble.
- Identify family members, friends, or any other people who can help, either through their relationship with your son or their knowledge and experience. Having the rescue plan be a team effort can be very effective and stress reducing.
- Visit his school and determine what he must do to get back on track. See if the school has or knows of any special programs that can help your son in his schoolwork.
- Identify any mentoring, tutoring, and/or rites-of-passage programs in your community that can provide role models,

build skills, and provide grounding in traditional values. Contact schools, churches, professional organizations, or community groups to locate the network of youth programs.

- Look closely at your relationship with your son and the way the two of you communicate. See if you can adopt a way to approach him differently and more effectively. Don't be afraid to get some coaching from your therapist or counselor, family, or friends.
- Finalize and then review your plan. Make sure that everyone is working together to help your son.
- Mobilize your community, because it takes a whole village to make this work.

We caution everyone to be realistic. A plan should not be set in stone. Many conditions can come up that will require adjustments and creative changes. You must empower yourself to be proactive and organize if you are to take your son back from the streets.

RESOURCES

Hill, Paul. *Coming of Age: African American Male Rites-of-Passage.* Chicago: African American Images, 1992.

Kunjufu, Jawanza. *Countering the Conspiracy to Destroy Black Boys.* 4 vols. Chicago: African American Images.

13

THE ONE WHO ASKS QUESTIONS DOESN'T LOSE HIS WAY.

—AFRICAN PROVERB

Getting Past the Fear of Counseling

"I know something is wrong with my son. He is so sad and down all the time. He has pulled away from me and the family—won't talk to us. He stays to himself all the time. My mother and my sisters keep telling me, 'It's just a phase. He'll outgrow it,' but I know he needs help. I just don't know what to do—how to get help for him." (Karen, mother of James, age sixteen)

Adolescence is a very difficult time in life for all kids, and sometimes we are not sure whether our sons are experiencing a real problem or something that they will outgrow. In addition, many African Americans have grown up with what we call healthy cultural suspicion. After generations of dealing with racism and discrimination in this country, we have been taught to keep family business in the family and to avoid airing our dirty laundry in public. Sometimes we do not want to tell others—especially those outside of the family—about our problems at home because we are so embarrassed by our son's behavior. We are also afraid that it will appear as if we lack the ability to cope.

As African Americans, our definition of what is private and what is public has been very narrow. If our parents were concerned about us, they might have consulted trusted people in the family, extended family, a network of friends, neighborhood circle, or church family. Often a minister, minister's wife or a deacon, deaconess, or church elder would have been approached for their wisdom.

The same places our parents and grandparents looked to for help in a crisis are still good places to start. One of the worst things that you can do as a parent when you are worried about your son is to isolate yourself and not talk to others about your concerns. Although the desire to hide within in difficult times is perfectly normal, try not to get stuck there. Pick one person who you feel safe about telling. Maybe a friend would feel safer than a family member at first. Don't let the fear that someone will accuse you of being a bad parent paralyze you from seeking help.

Misconceptions about Therapy in the Black Community

Some African Americans are leery of seeking therapy or counseling. Part of this has to do with the myths about therapy or counseling in the black community. The following are just a few of the myths:

- It's only for "crazy" or "sick" folks.
- It's for weak folks.
- It's for white folks.
- It's for rich folks.
- It's not for us.

Anyone who is having problems in life can benefit from therapy. Going to a therapist does not label you sick or crazy. But holding on to this outdated belief causes some African American parents to lose out on opportunities that could help save their children and families—they either refuse to seek help or wait so long that their child's behavior has become much worse in the meantime.

Black people put a great premium on being strong. We see strength as a survival skill in a world that can sometimes be hostile. In our communities there is a tendency to see going for help as a sign of weakness. Many African Americans do not realize that going for help is a strength. Here's an example from Nancy's own family:

Nancy: My doctoral program in clinical psychology strongly advised students to go into therapy ourselves as part of our training. But I was not convinced that therapy was for me, so I put it off. When I experienced a very painful breakup with my boyfriend in my last year of training, I finally let go of my negative feelings about therapy long enough to seek help.

My parents were very proud when I became the first person in my family to pursue a Ph.D., but when I told my family that I had gone into therapy, my father was horrified. He said, "Oh, my God, baby—do you have to?" He then made me promise I wouldn't tell anybody.

My father later shared with me that, at the time, he had all of the misperceptions on the list above. He didn't realize that many people seek help for everyday problems, and he was afraid people would think that there was something seriously wrong with me (and that he and my mother were bad parents!) if they knew.

"God Is My Only Counselor"

One response that we sometimes hear from African American parents is that therapy or counseling is "antispiritual" or "against their religion." Many religious groups are suspicious of therapists or counselors because they fear that these practitioners may not respect their beliefs. Ministers, priests, and other religious leaders may therefore caution their congregation about seeking therapy or counseling. This is also true for some families in the Nation of Islam, Sunni Muslims, and Jehovah's Witnesses. If this is your concern, you should seek the help of your minister or religious leader to find someone in your faith who is also a trained therapist or counselor. Do not wait until your son is in serious trouble before you seek help. In the African American community, religious leaders, parents, family members, therapists, counselors, and schools need to work together to address the behavior of our children. Your counselor should respect your spiritual or religious beliefs and work with you toward a solution for your son.

Nancy: Some years ago a very distraught mother came to see me. Her son's school had threatened to expel him unless she took him to a psychologist immediately. She told me that she did not believe in therapy and was seeing me only because she was forced. I asked what she did believe in, and she responded: "I pray to the Lord, and my minister is praying for him."

I told her that I also believed in the power of prayer and that my grandmother often said, "God works in mysterious ways, his wonders to perform." She nodded and told me that she believed this also. I asked her if she had considered that therapy might be one of His mysterious ways. She paused for a moment, thinking about what I had said.

I then asked her if she would allow me to call her minister and to ask his help. With her reluctant permission, I called him and made arrangements to meet with him at his church. We talked a long time. I asked if he would be willing to meet with the mother and her son along with me. The four of us met for a number of sessions, and together we were able to help this mother to set limits for her son and to address his behavioral issues.

Recognizing Problems in Your Son

What are the signs that your child needs help? There are a number of issues that complicate recognizing the signs of problems in an adolescent:

- Adolescence is a difficult time, and all kids show some signs of distress during this period.
- The bodily and hormonal changes that occur during adolescence can trigger emotional reactions.
- Some adolescents are very good at disguising or hiding their problems from us.
- Some adolescent problems do not "look the same" as similar problems in adults.

Another dilemma for parents is that many well-meaning family members, friends, doctors, and school officials will minimize our concerns and tell us, "He's just going through a phase," or "All adolescents act that way," or "He'll outgrow it." They are either trying to make us feel better or they don't want to be bothered—neither of which helps. As a parent, learn to follow your own intuition. If you sense that something is wrong, seek a second opinion from a mental health professional. It is amazing that many parents who will beg, borrow, or steal to get the best medical doctor for their child will often hesitate to seek help from a mental health professional when their son is having behavioral or emotional trouble.

After many years of working with African American parents and teenagers whose problems had gotten to the crisis point before seeking help, we now advise parents to err on the side of getting help sooner rather than later. In the remainder of this chapter, we will cover a number of adolescent emotional and behavioral problems in question-and-answer format to help you as a parent recognize the signs that your son may be in serious emotional distress.

Depression

Don't all adolescents get depressed?

Yes, we know that adolescence is a time when many, if not most, adolescents experience some depressed thoughts and feelings. But if these feelings persist for more than a month, it is time to talk to your son about it. If the depressed feelings persist longer than two months, seek help from a mental health professional.

What are the signs that my son might be depressed?

This is a very important question. Depression does not always look the same in adolescents as it does in adults. They may show us that they are depressed in ways that make it hard to put two and two together. This problem is compounded by the fact that depression is often an underlying cause of a whole range of behaviors in adolescents. Dr. Ava Siegler, author of *The Essential Guide to the New Adolescence,* gives us the following signals to look for:

- Listlessness, always tired
- Constantly says, "I'm bored"
- Has a hard time concentrating
- Grades in school have dropped dramatically
- Drug and alcohol abuse

- Anger and violence
- Irritability
- Agitation
- Withdrawal
- Acting out
- Rebellion
- "Psychosomatic" symptoms that are limited to a psychological state rather than a medical illness, such as headaches, backaches, stomachaches. (Be sure that you have your doctor rule out medical causes.)
- Gaining or losing a great deal of weight.

Older adolescents begin to show signs that are more similar to "adult symptoms" cited in the *DSM* IV.

- Feelings of guilt
- Low self-esteem
- Feelings of hopelessness
- Loss of appetite/overeating
- Sleeplessness/being constantly sleepy
- Indecisiveness
- Inertia
- Feelings of worthlessness
- Sadness

What can cause depression?

Depression can be caused by many things, including grief or a loss, especially the death of a close family member or friend. For some kids, experiencing too many deaths in their community (even if they don't know the people personally) can trigger depressed feelings. Remember that there are many other losses besides death. In adolescence, peer pressure, conflicting values, fears for one's safety, and the loss of a close friend, particularly a girlfriend, can trigger feelings of depression and sadness.

Any of these can cause depression and low self-esteem. Adolescent boys may feel that they are "ugly" or "stupid" or "too skinny" or "too short." This is the most sensitive time in their lives.

Can depression run in the family or be inherited?

Yes, research shows that some forms of depression run in families. If you ask your parents and family members, particularly older members, if they can identify or remember other family members who suffered from this condition, you can probably see this pattern in your own family. One helpful aspect of counseling can be the creation of a genogram, which is like a family tree, but it tracks the illnesses and conditions that may run in the family. In some families, there is a genetic predisposition toward depression. It can also be caused by a chemical imbalance that can be helped by medication. (If you want to explore this possibility, you will need to take your son to a *psychiatrist*, who can prescribe medication.)

Can family problems cause depression?

Yes, family problems such as divorce, separation, remarriage, angry arguments, and physical or sexual abuse can trigger depression in adolescents.

Is withdrawal a sign of depression in teenagers?

Yes, it often is. If your son does not seem to have any friends or if he seems to keep to himself all the time and not want to participate in any activities, this may be a sign of depression. Many teens suffer from loneliness, even though they may seem to have outgoing, gregarious personalities.

Although it is normal, to some degree, for adolescents to withdraw a bit from family activities and "hide out in their rooms," extreme behavior of this type, particularly in the absence of friends or other outside activities, may be signs of depression.

What are the signs that a teenager may be considering suicide?

Severe feelings of depression can lead to suicidal feelings in adolescents. Dr. Siegler recommends that you look for the following signs:

- Statements such as "Who cares anyway?" or "What's the use of living?"

- Frequent "accidents" in which your son gets injured
- Pills or medicine disappearing from the family medicine cabinet
- Expressions or statements to you, his friends, or others of the wish to die
- Talk of a plan to hurt or kill himself
- An actual attempt to hurt himself such as cutting his wrists or taking a drug overdose
- Obsession over the death of a friend or schoolmate who committed suicide
- Giving away valued belongings
- High risk taking, such as driving recklessly

Any of these signals should be followed up immediately by seeking the help of a competent mental health professional. Another reason for getting help quickly is that teenage boys are likely to select more lethal options in planning suicide than girls.

The Trauma of First Love

It's bound to happen sooner or later—your son falls in love for the first time. He wants to see "his girl" twenty hours a day and spends the remaining four on the phone with her. His boys, who were ever so important last week, now take second place in his life. You have to repeat things when you talk to him because he is often "in another world." But then it happens. They break up. He is devastated. His hurt manifests itself in an anger that may well be taken out on you and anyone else who's around. He doesn't talk, barely eats, and may skip school (especially if "she" is there). If these behaviors continue, they may be the early signs of depression.

What are the signs of anxiety in an adolescent?

The *DSM* IV identifies the following:

- Nail biting, twitching, startled responses
- Excessive worry and apprehensive feelings

- Excessive concerns about appearance, school, friends, girl-friends, parents
- Restlessness, seeming on edge or very "keyed up." (Remember that this could also be a sign of attention deficit disorder with hyperactivity, ADHD.)
- Difficulty concentrating
- His mind "goes blank"
- Irritability
- Muscle tension (backaches, headaches, muscle spasms)
- Difficulty going to sleep at night
- Restlessness, inability to stay asleep
- Excessive fear

Duane is a seventeen-year-old who has always been an average student and had many friends. Recently, he was hanging out in a Burger King in his neighborhood when suddenly an angry group of guys came into the restaurant, "snatched" his friend from the group, and shot him at point-blank range.

Since this incident Duane has become very anxious. He has withdrawn from "his boys" and stopped going out. He is very nervous and jumpy, and is always afraid that he will be shot. He starts cutting school and sneaks back into the house when his mother leaves for work.

Duane does not feel that he can tell his mother and sister because he is afraid of making them worried. He can't talk to his friends because expressing fear is not a macho thing. He hides out in his room and becomes more and more sad. He is eating less and tosses and turns all night. He has flashbacks of the incident.

Many youths have been exposed to too much violence and death. These issues have negatively affected many communities and the teenagers who live and grow up within them. Some experts feel that kids who have witnessed violence of this type can have a post-traumatic stress disorder (PTSD) in which they have nightmares and daytime flashbacks of the incidents. Sometimes these kids experience a form of survivor guilt, asking themselves over and over, "Why was he killed and not me?"

What should you do if your son is showing these signs?

The first and most important step is to *talk to your son about your concerns.* Be sure to do this in a caring, supportive way. Notice the difference between the two approaches below:

- *Caring, supportive*—"Son, you know I love you very much and I've been worried about you because you seem very upset lately. Let's talk about it."
- *Confrontational*—"You've been moping around this house and snapping at all of us. What is your problem?" If you are confrontational, your son may pull back even further, and getting help will be even more difficult.

Talk to your son and ask him how he has been feeling. Listen to his response. Some parents are so busy talking at their kids that they have a hard time listening. Reread the material in Chapter 4 about facilitative listening. Force yourself to say less. Use leading comments like "Tell me more about it" or "I hear you" to encourage him to keep talking. You should be willing to try any approach—even if you must bite your lips raw while you do it—to have effective communication with a son who may be suicidal.

The next important step is to get help from a therapist or other mental health professional for your son. (See Resources section at the end of this chapter.)

My son won't talk to me about his feelings. What should I do?

Remember that boys are often socialized to hold their feelings in. Even kids who were very expressive when they were young and who may have talked to you a great deal in earlier years may clam up now. Often peers give macho messages to adolescent boys that it's not okay to express feelings. Sometimes the older male role models in their lives have also given them these messages. This is hard especially for African American mothers, who may have enjoyed a special communication with their sons in earlier years and are distressed to see the change in their relationship. First, remind yourself that this withdrawal is normal. The kids who are the closest to us often have to get some distance in order to grow up. Ask another family member, male friend, minister, coach, or favorite teacher who your son respects to talk to him. If not, explore suggestions in Chapter 12 for finding a mentor for him. If he continues to be withdrawn, see suggestions at the end of this chapter for seeking help from a mental health professional.

My son has begun to act out, talk back to me and is very rebellious—what causes this behavior?

Many adolescents go through periods of acting out and rebelliousness. Sometimes this is their way of testing the limits you have set for them. In some cases they are "raising the stakes," trying desperately to get your attention or to get you to take action. (See also our discussion of teenage rebellion in Chapter 4.)

Sometimes this behavior is an adolescent's reaction to stress in the family. Ask yourself the following questions:

- Have there been any major family changes recently?
- Has anyone been very sick or died in the last year?
- Are there constant arguments in your home?
- Has there been a divorce, separation, or end of a relationship in the last two years?
- Have your hours outside the home increased, or are you forced to travel more for your job?
- Has your son's peer group changed in the last year? Is he acting more like his friends?
- Have you moved to a new community recently?
- Do you have clear consequences for misbehavior in your home?
- Do you follow through on those consequences or just threaten?

If your answer to any of the above is yes, you may want to seek the help of a family therapist or counselor to help you, your spouse or partner, your son, and the rest of the family to sort it all out.

My son has been getting into fights recently in the neighborhood and at school. What should I do?

This fighting may have a number of different meanings. Have a frank discussion with your son about it. Make sure it is a calm discussion. Ask him: what were the fights about? Is he involved in a gang? Why does he feel he must fight? You may want him to be more specific and ask him to describe his last fight.

Find a violence-prevention and conflict-resolution program for your son. Check with the guidance counselor at your school. Many schools now have conflict-resolution, peer-mediation, or violence-prevention programs. (See Chapter 11.) If not, they may know of such a program at a mental health center in your community. (See Chapter 12 for further suggestions.) If you are involved in a church or mosque or Kingdom Hall, ask if there is a program such as this in the community with a spiritual base. Finally, call the local police station and ask if they know of a program in the community.

Check the messages you have given your son on fighting:

- Have you taught him that he should fight and that this is a way to resolve difficulties?
- Have you made him feel that he would be a wimp or a punk if he didn't fight?
- Have you ever had an honest discussion with him about self-defense versus instigation of violence?
- Do you know if he feels he has to fight to display his manhood or show his peers that he's a man?

What do I do if my son has been arrested or has been in trouble with the law?

- Find a lawyer.
- Contact the Legal Aid Society if you can't afford one.
- Go with your son to court and show your willingness to help him. Take along a trusted male family member or friend if possible.
- Talk to your lawyer, the judge, the police, and the parole

officer about good delinquency prevention programs in your area. Don't wait until he is in jail!

Having a child arrested is one of the most upsetting and frightening experiences for African American parents. If this has happened to your son, try to stay calm. (See Chapter 11 on what to tell your son to do if he is stopped by the police.) For some parents this is so devastating that they feel like giving up. If this has happened to your son, take heart, there are things that you can do to get help for him. See Chapter 14 for some things you can do to help get yourself through this crisis.

The most important caution is to intervene immediately and get help such as therapy and counseling for your son and your family before he commits more serious offenses. See Chapter 10 if you are concerned that he is abusing drugs or alcohol.

The first step in getting help for your son and your family is to challenge the myths we discussed in the beginning of this chapter. As African Americans we must develop a "help-seeking attitude." This is one that is open to pursuing possible solutions that may be new for us. It means resolving the false idea that therapy is just for sick or crazy people. It means being willing to do whatever can really help your son—and quickly.

Many parents put off seeking help in the hope that their son will outgrow the problem. But the truth is that kids often don't outgrow serious issues without help.

Are there any African American therapists?

Yes, thankfully, as we enter the twenty-first century, there are many more African American psychologists, social workers, psychiatrists, marriage and family therapists, drug and alcohol counselors, and pastoral counselors. However, there is still a shortage for the number who need help and the needs of the community.

If I want a therapist, how do I find one?

See the Resources section at the end of this chapter. Associations such as the American Psychological Association (APA), National Association of Social Workers (NASW), American Association of Marriage and Family Therapy (AAMFT), and the National

Association of Pastoral Counselors can help you find reputable therapists in your area.

How do I find a black therapist?

In the Resources section are numbers and addresses for organizations such as the Association of Black Psychologists and the Association of Black Social Workers. If you call or write their national offices or look them up in a local phone book, they can help you find someone in your area.

How do I know who the good therapists are?

The best way to locate a good therapist is by word of mouth. Ask your family members, friends, work associates, ministers, church members. Ask your pediatrician or family doctor. Try to get referrals from individuals who have had a good experience with a particular therapist. You can also call the local mental health association and describe the problem and ask for a referral. Be sure to use your school as a resource. Discuss the question of a referral with your son's school guidance counselor and ask them who they would recommend. Also, ask them to consult other guidance counselors for suggestions of good therapists. Don't forget to check with your medical insurance provider about your coverage for therapy. Many insurance companies have limitations as to what kinds of counseling and the number of sessions they cover.

Suppose my son refuses to go to therapy?

The strategy that we have found most useful is to get a list of referrals and call and interview them yourself. When you have found two to three therapists whom you feel would be good to work with you and your son, sit down and discuss this with him. Most kids refuse initially. Be firm. Tell your son (in a calm, unaggressive manner) that he has no choice about going for therapy but he can choose the counselor he feels most comfortable with (from the two to three you have screened).

Who Are These People?

If you are going to get the best help for your son, it's important to know the difference between a counselor and a therapist, a psychiatrist and a psychologist.

Therapist: This is a global term that might include a social worker, psychologist, psychiatrist, or a marriage and family therapist who is licensed to provide therapy (also called psychotherapy).

Counselor: Sometimes the word *counselor* is used synonymously with *therapist.* In other cases it refers to pastoral counselors who provide spiritual guidance or school counselors who provide guidance on academic issues, or a drug and alcohol counselor.

Psychologists have doctoral degrees (Psy.D. and Ph.D.) in psychology and do psychotherapy, counseling, and psychological testing.

Psychiatrists attended medical school, have an M.D., and are licensed to prescribe medications. Many also do psychotherapy.

Marriage and Family Therapists have a degree in marriage and family therapy (usually a master's, sometimes a Ph.D.) and provide family therapy or counseling and marriage counseling or "couples therapy."

Clinical Social Workers (CSWs) have a master's degree in social work (MSW) and are licensed to provide therapy.

Drug and Alcohol Counselors are a special category of counselor with a specialty in the treatment of substance abuse. Many are taking training to become a certified addiction counselor (CAC).

Does my son have to believe in the process for it to work?

Absolutely not! It is very important, however, that you pre-screen therapists who have been trained to work with adolescents. Few adolescents come into therapy willingly. A good, skilled therapist who specializes in working with adolescents can engage them in the process.

Should I be involved in the therapy?

Absolutely. Interview therapists and search for one who will work with you as well as your son. Therapists work in different ways. There are three main approaches:

1. Adolescent individual therapy—usually the adolescent is seen alone. The parents meet regularly with the therapist also (sometimes together, sometimes separately).
2. Family therapy—the whole family is seen together.
3. A combination of numbers one and two. This allows the therapist to work with you and your son and your other family members in different combinations or all together.

Any of the above approaches can be effective when conducted by a competent therapist. If you are a parent and have had a hunch that your son needs help, don't wait. Get help for him now. The Resources section below will assist you in finding the help you need.

RESOURCES

Books

Boyd-Franklin, Nancy. *Black Families in Therapy: A Multisystems Approach.* New York: Guilford Press, 1989.

Grier, William, and Price Cobbs. *Black Rage.* New York: Basic Books, 1992.

Siegler, Ava. *The Essential Guide to the New Adolescence: How to Raise an Emotionally Healthy Teenager.* New York: Dutton, 1997.

Organizations

American Association of Marriage and Family Therapy (AAMFT); (202) 452-0109

American Association of Pastoral Counselors; (703) 385-6967 (Christian counselors).

American Psychological Association (APA); (202) 336-5500

Association of Black Psychologists; (202) 722-0808

Association of Black Social Workers; (202) 529-6127

National Association of Social Workers (NASW); (202) 408-8600

14

❖

KEEP YOUR EYES ON THE PRIZE.
HOLD ON . . .

—CIVIL RIGHTS MOVEMENT SONG

A Parent's Survival Guide

Raising children, particularly a black teenage son, is one of the most difficult jobs in the universe. We have likened this process to helping our sons to navigate a minefield without having one blow up in their faces. Throughout this book we have given you a number of ideas as to how your son, with your guidance, can emerge victorious in life. But you are of no use to your son or the rest of your family if you become overwhelmed or burned out. In this chapter we want to remind you of the importance of giving to yourself and treating yourself with care. This chapter is therefore dedicated to you—just you.

Be Good to Yourself

It is so hard to take the time for yourself when you are trying to raise children, have a relationship with a partner, and work a full-time job. Many parents, especially mothers, feel that they must focus all of their attention on their children, particularly when they are having problems. It may surprise you to learn that this approach usually results in overkill, burnout, and exhaustion and depletes us of the energy we need to help our kids. No matter how much we may feel that our children deserve most of our attention, set a little time aside *regularly* so that we can regroup, renew, and reenergize. As role models for our children, we need to show them how to achieve balance in their lives as adults. This includes lessons on how to treat yourself well, and how to be a good parent, a good partner, a good friend, and a good person.

We do not want to come across as flippant when we recommend that you be good to yourself. You need to understand how significant this message is for good parenting as well as good health. The truth is that parenting can be very stressful! Being home with the children, constantly surrounded by their demands and needs, can be chaotic and overwhelming—even while you love it. Those who also have a full-time job outside the home can be "running on empty" most of the time. It is difficult to take ourselves out of those circumstances when we are in the middle of them. What we are suggesting is that you plan time away from your daily routine to do something for *you*, no matter how small.

Treating ourselves well can sometimes just mean simply ducking into an ice cream store, sitting down alone, and savoring the moment of peace. (If calories are a concern, you can have delicious fat-free frozen yogurt.) At other times we try to plan something more special, such as a night out at a movie or dinner. Some friends of ours in New York City purchased a hotel weekend package, left the kids with grandparents, and treated themselves to the culture and entertainment of the Big City, just like any tourists.

Here are some things you can do to be good to yourself:

- Give yourself "quiet time." A little solitude or alone time, even if it is late at night after everyone has settled down, or a quiet cup of coffee early in the morning before your family awakens, can be a gift to yourself.
- Exercise. What a helpful way to manage stress, get a little alone time, and do something positive for your body all at once! You might find it helpful to take brisk walks or jog. Do this three times a week for a half hour each, and you will see health benefits and be able to clear your head so that you can think things through without being overcome by stress. A regular game of basketball, tennis, etc., with your friends can recharge your emotional, physical, and social batteries.
- Pamper yourself. Sometimes getting a haircut, having a mas-

sage, getting your nails done, or going shopping (even window-shopping) can help you to feel nurtured and taken care of. Try a new nail polish or hair color, get a pedicure, or buy a new accessory. Do something that reminds you that you are special.

- Read a good book, rent a video you've been wanting to see, or watch television in the quiet of your room.
- Talk to a friend. Sometimes getting together with close friends for some adult time (even on the phone) can take your mind off your troubles or provide you with sources of support.

Nourish Your Spiritual Side

Many of us take care of our bodies but forget that parenting takes a large spiritual toll. It can drain us. You will need to find and develop ways to nourish your spiritual self if you are to maintain your optimism throughout raising your children. By spiritual we do not necessarily mean religious. Many African Americans (in fact, many people of African descent) have a deep cultural sense of spirituality that sustains us. We know about hard times, but we remind ourselves that some good will come from our efforts in the future. We know that "this too shall pass."

There are many ways to nourish your spiritual side. One way to do this is to take the time to go inside yourself—or go within. By that we mean finding a little quiet time, even late at night or early in the morning, to meditate on something positive. This could be a special prayer time when you talk to God openly and honestly about your worries, or when you thank God for your blessings. Remember to pray with a positive intent. You can say, "Thank you, dear God, for bringing my son safely through the teenage years. He is successful and happy in his life. He is involved in giving something back to his community." As you talk to God, try to visualize your son doing and fulfilling the goals you want him to aspire toward and achieve.

If you find yourself frantic about your son, frustrated with his behavior, worried sick about his safety, just stop and take a moment to pray. Listen to your heart. Find a place of solitude, peace and quiet, and reflect. Center yourself. Seek guidance from friends, family, your spiritual leader. Sometimes we get so caught up in the treadmill of daily life that we forget we need to take a "spiritual break."

We often get so caught up in doing everything ourselves, particularly if we are raising children alone, that we forget to remind ourselves that we are never alone. (Neither are our children.) When you send them off to a new school, or a party with a group of friends, or just out to hang out with their boys, and you have done all that a responsible parent can do, the rest must be guided by faith. Faith that the spiritual beliefs and values you have instilled in them will aid their judgments and safely guide them until they return home. Faith that your teachings about life will serve them well on *their* journey in life.

One of the greatest challenges for African American parents is acting on faith, that is, believing everything will turn out all right when our son's behavior indicates only trouble down the road. Generations of African American parents have survived their worries for their children by turning to God as our source of strength to persevere. No matter how much we may want to hold our son's hand through life experiences, we must let him go to learn some things on his own.

When things get difficult in raising your son pray for positive outcomes. Remember that you are one of the primary persons who he must know believes in him. It is equally important that you believe in yourself and what you are doing as a parent. (See Chapter 3 for more ways to nourish your spiritual side.)

Positive Images and Affirmations

It is very important to hold on to a picture in your mind of the kind of positive outcome that you want for your son. This "creative visualization" (see Shakti Gawain's book in our Resources section at the end of this chapter) will enable you to stay focused on the positive aspects of your son. Visualize your son achieving, surviving, and thriving in his life. Also say or write "positive affirmations" every day. For example:

- Carl is a terrific kid and I love him so much.
- Joe is doing great in school.

- Kalim has gotten all A's on his tests.
- I have gotten help for Yusef.

There are wonderful books of positive affirmations available today, including Iyanla Vanzant's books *Acts of Faith* and *Faith in the Valley*, that can help you in this process.

As you visualize or imagine a positive outcome for your son, avoid allowing negative images to form in your head. If we don't do this, we run the risk of developing or actualizing those negative pictures. We often *act* the way we think and feel. Here are some "pictures" that can be helpful:

- Picture your son walking proudly at his high school and college graduations.
- Picture your son happy and involved with the family at a holiday dinner or family reunion.
- Picture your son as a young boy sitting next to you. Now picture him as a young man sitting in the same place.
- Picture your son as a positive African American man with strong morals, secure self-image, excellent self-esteem, and positive racial identity.
- Picture your son leading others and giving something back to our people and our community.
- If your son is involved in drugs or alcohol addiction, picture him free from drugs, healthy, and actively working on his recovery.

Even if your son is driving you crazy, high on drugs, suspended or expelled from school, in trouble with the police, or failing a grade, hold on to the image of him succeeding as a man and put the power of your spiritual beliefs behind that vision. (See also Chapter 3 for more positive spiritual messages and affirmations.)

Take Time for Yourself and Your Partner

From the time our children are born, they are all-consuming. Our love for them leads us to be involved in their lives and to want what is best for them. This is so real for many of us that we lose sight of our own needs and our partner's needs. In our professional practices, we often have the experience of meeting with a family and asking the parents, "When is the last time you had an evening alone together?" They often look at us as if we have just asked them a very bizarre question.

If you have a spouse or a special person in your life, take time to nurture that relationship. Whether you are married to your "significant other" or not, your "couple time" is important to your mental health (and theirs) and can help to sustain you through the difficult times. Try to take one evening a week when you go out together and do something relaxing. If you are not in a relationship now, go out to a movie or dinner with a good friend or friends. (Try not to spend the whole evening discussing your children.)

Try spending an evening together in light conversation and fun activities, not solving problems. Fill the night with laughter. Recapture the spirit and magic that brought the two of you together. To get time together, ask your mother or sister if your kids can stay with them for the night and plan a special evening at home for you and your loved one. Some couples or friends plan mutual child-care arrangements when once a month—or at some other regular interval—each takes on both sets of children so that the other couple can be alone, and vice versa. Here are some suggestions for your special evening.

- Rent a video you both want to see.
- Put on soft music.
- Light candles.
- Create a romantic atmosphere.
- Put flowers in your home.
- Try some delicious scents or scented candles to give your home an especially sweet-smelling aroma.
- Make a special meal for your partner.
- Cook a special meal together.
- Go out to dinner and come home and relax together.
- Order your favorite takeout food.
- Relax.
- Give your loved one a massage.
- Take a Jacuzzi or a warm, scented bath together.

Any of these ideas can create a relaxed, easy evening that will help you and your loved one recharge your batteries and renew yourselves. They can help you to find the energy and willpower to continue to give as a parent, particularly during the difficult time of adolescence. Find your own ways to relax and reduce the stress from the demands of parenting.

Learn Stress-Management Techniques

We are consistently surprised at the number of parents who don't know the extent of their stress. They know they are under pressure trying to meet their children's needs, but what they fail to recognize is the degree to which it is doing personal harm to their physical and mental well being. We suggest learning stress-management skills such as:

- Make a list of specific things that stress you. Think about how those things or situations come about.
- Learn to anticipate the things that stress you and devise a strategy to defuse them. Maybe it's taking a time-out right then and there, taking a few deep breaths, and reciting your affirmations. If you have a few minutes, utilize "progressive relaxation." For example, rest in a comfortable chair, close your eyes, and focus your attention, beginning with your head. Tense your forehead first and then think, and feel it relax. Continue through each part of your body (e.g., shoulders, arms, stomach, legs, thighs, etc.), making yourself tense and then relaxing the part you are focusing upon.
- Come up with different ways to reduce your stress; include a regular exercise routine.
- Evaluate your stress reduction strategies periodically; alter them as you get to know yourself better.

Don't Be Alone. Isolation Is Deadly

Isolation is the most difficult challenge that a parent can face. Even if you are a single parent, you do not have to be alone. Seek help. Look for support. If you are open to it, it is closer than you think.

- Reach out to others. If you are a single parent or find yourself alone with the responsibility for your kids, surround yourself with other people. For some parents, reaching out to wise elders in your family or your community can ease the loneliness and the burden. It also allows you to see that others have challenges too.

- Write a letter, place a phone call, or E-mail loved ones who live far away and ask for help or advice. Don't feel that you must limit yourself to people who live close by. Many parents are embarrassed when their children are having trouble, especially if it's trouble with the law or suspension from school. Remember that other parents, especially older ones or older relatives, have already "been there, done that" in their lives. Is there someone special in your family or "play" family from years ago whom you have not talked to in a long time? Someone who has been helpful in the past, but time and circumstances have put distance between the two of you? Reach out! Often, these are the folks who can show empathy, concern, and offer helpful suggestions.

- Reach out to other *parents* in your community. This might mean calling parents whom you know casually and admire, and let them know your concerns. If they have children around the same age, they are likely to have dealt with similar issues. These may be people who have successfully raised their kids. Ask their help, advice, and prayers for your son (and family).

- Search for and find a supportive "church family." (See Chapter 3.)

- Look for parent support groups in your community. Check first with your son's school; the local mental health center or services; the Department of Social Services, or for drug- and alcohol-related concerns, AA and Al-Anon (see Chapter 10). Ask in your community about churches, organizations, special programs, or any other groups offering activities that support the way you want to raise your son. If you have access to a computer, go on-line and search for Internet resources, Web sites, or chat rooms where you can "talk" to other parents and professionals.

- Why not start an informal support group of other parents with teenagers? You don't have to have answers for one another—just the sharing of experiences can be very helpful and therapeutic. There are often people in African American communities who would love to start or operate support programs but have never been asked.

- In addition to whatever help you get for your son or the rest of your family, seek counseling for yourself. Sometimes this can be for a short duration, sometimes it can be for more sessions. Don't wait until you convince your son, your other children, your partner or spouse, or your whole family to get help. Go now for yourself!! Believe it or not, this can often be the best way to take care of and "give to" yourself. If you have no one with whom to discuss your concerns, or everyone seems to be making judgments about your son or you that you do not agree with, seek the help of an experienced therapist or counselor. Do not be alone!

Believe in Miracles

Every day in all of our lives, small miracles occur. They may be concrete, e.g., money comes from an unlikely source when we desperately need it and have been praying for it. Or they may be more intangible, e.g., a difficult situation unravels itself unexpectedly. As we watch our kids get taller and "grow into themselves," we are witnessing daily changes that are miraculous. Often, we are so close to the issue or problem that we don't see the positives. One Sunday one of our favorite preachers reminded parents that sometimes we "see every mess" and "miss the miracles." Malcolm's family is an example of this:

Malcolm was in what the old folks used to call "deep trouble." He had gotten all F's on his report card and was failing all of his classes in school. He had been hiding out in the hallways and cutting class. His mother and father were at their wit's end. They had threatened, bribed, cajoled, and punished—nothing seemed to work. Finally, Malcolm's mother began praying in earnest for him. She prayed positively, believing God

could turn him around. Malcolm's parents met with his guidance coun-
selor, who recommended that he attend a school-based counseling pro-
gram. This counseling program worked for Malcolm. Slowly, he began to
turn around. He started attending class more regularly. His parents
began to hope.

When the next report card came out, Malcolm had gotten mostly C's
and one D. His parents were devastated. They were hoping for A's and
B's. In despair, they again met with his guidance counselor. Much to their
shock and surprise, the counselor challenged them. She said, "Wait a
minute, I know you are upset because you hoped for A's and B's, but you
have missed the miracle here. Malcolm is going to class every day; he is
keeping regular appointments with his counselor; he is going for tutoring
and extra help; and, most important, he has brought up all of his grades
and is passing all of his subjects!"

She pointed out to them that even though he wasn't yet where they
wanted him to be, he was going in the right direction. If all they noticed
was what he had not accomplished, they would miss his progress and he
would give up and go back to failing. On the other hand, if they empha-
sized even the small steps toward those A's and B's, he would be motivated
to try harder and work toward an even bigger "miracle."

Malcolm's story is a wake-up call for all parents. We worry
about our kids, but as African American parents, sometimes it
feels like "all we do is worry." We cannot let our worries blind us
to the small positive changes our children make. Sometimes we
are so focused upon wanting our children to take giant steps that
we overlook the little steps needed to achieve most goals.
Miracles are made up of a lot of little things often overshadowed
by the big event.

Count Your Blessings

We all remember that when we complained about one or
another aspect of our lives, our grandparents or other family
elders would say "count your blessings." They could always put life
in perspective by bringing up examples of people who had troubles far worse than what we were complaining about at the time.
The lesson would be: don't forget to focus on your blessings and

those of your children and be thankful even when hardships come, for this is when character is shaped and strong faith is built.

Make a list of your son's positive points and "blessings" when he is in trouble or has done something that has really upset you. (During those times you may actually have to *write down* his positive points to believe they are real!)

The Miracle of a Mother's Faith

Dr. Ben Carson was brought up by a single mother who had to work as many as three jobs to keep her family together. She told her sons that they could do anything they set their minds to. Ben did so well in his predominantly white junior high school that he won a prize as the best student.

During his teens, Ben went to an inner-city high school, and all the negative messages he was getting from society and his peers—that there was no way a black man could succeed—began to influence him. He was drawn to the streets, where his crowd was into drugs and alcohol. His grades fell. He had just about given up.

But his mother hadn't given up on him. This deeply spiritual woman finally got through to him that he was going nowhere fast. Ben started to study again and won a scholarship to Yale. He went on to medical school at the University of Michigan and is now the director of pediatric neurosurgery at Johns Hopkins Hospital in Baltimore and one of the top practitioners in his field.

His religious faith is as strong as his mother's. It is God who has given him the gift of his hands that he uses to save children's lives. He has written two books, *Gifted Hands* and *Think Big*, which have provided inspiration for many parents. (Story from Michael Ryan, *Seattle Times/Seattle Post*, 1988)

Keep Hope Alive

So often when we are worried about our kids, we tend to go immediately to the worst case scenario. He fails one course and we see him as a "bag man" living on the streets with no job and no future. On paper, this may sound ridiculous, but we do not live our lives on paper. There is not a parent alive who has not had at least one moment of "extreme thinking."

During these times we need to force ourselves to focus on the positive. Our minds can either help us achieve our dreams or bind us in fear. If we dwell on the negative, negative things are more likely to happen. If we dwell on a positive outcome, it is more likely to occur.

We often believe that our son's problems and our problems are unique. No one has quite been through this before. With this attitude and belief we overlook the wisdom and lessons of African American elders. They parented with many fewer resources and opportunities than we have now. Many have vital lessons to convey to us from their life stories. Most know a lot about prayer and patience.

Sometimes we pray and are not willing to wait. We expect positive results by tomorrow afternoon. When the "miracles" do not occur right away, we become discouraged. Sometimes our hope and faith begin to fade. It is so important in all aspects of our lives, but particularly as parents, that we "keep the faith." As older black folks used to say, "God may not come when we want him to, but he always comes on time."

Often, we do not even recognize the blessings when they start to come. After a period of drought in our lives, we may want the blessings so much that we sometimes forget that the blessing may be preceded or accompanied by unanticipated difficulties. Remember that all things happen for a reason. Stay focused on a positive outcome. You can make a difference in your son's life if you follow many of the ideas that we have presented in this book and keep your hope alive.

RESOURCES

Carson, Ben. *Gifted Hands*. Grand Rapids, MI: Zondervan, 1992.

Carson, Ben, and Cecil Murphey. *Think Big: Unleashing Your Potential for Excellence*. Grand Rapids, MI: Zondervan, 1996.

Gawain, Shakti. *Creative Visualization*. New York: Bantam, 1982.

Vanzant, Iyanla. *Acts of Faith: Daily Meditations for People of Color*. New York: Fireside, 1993.

————. *Faith in the Valley*. New York: Fireside, 1996.

Quotations and African Proverbs

Bell, Janet Cheatham. *Famous Black Quotations*. New York: Warner, 1995.

Copage, Eric. *Black Pearls for Parents: Meditations, Affirmations and Inspirations for African-American Parents*. New York: William Morrow, 1995.

Haley, Alex. *The Autobiography of Malcolm X*. New York: Dell, 1980.

Mays, Benjamin. *Quotable Quotes of Benjamin Mays*. New York: Vantage, 1983.

Stewart, Julia. *African Proverbs and Wisdom*. Secaucus, NJ: Citadel Press, 1997.

Vanzant, Iyanla. *Acts of Faith: Daily Meditations for People of Color*. New York: Fireside, 1993.

INDEX